CELILO TALES
WASCO MYTHS, LEGENDS,
TALES OF MAGIC AND THE MARVELOUS

Indians Spearing Fish at Celilo Falls (c.1905).
Special Collections Division, University of Washington
Libraries, Gifford photo #714

TO THE MEMORY OF
Richard M. Dorson
Who Showed Us the Way

CELILO TALES
WASCO MYTHS, LEGENDS,
TALES OF MAGIC AND THE MARVELOUS

by
Donald M. Hines

Great Eagle Publishing®

CELILO TALES: WASCO MYTHS, LEGENDS, TALES OF MAGIC AND THE MARVELOUS

by Donald M. Hines

Published by:

Ɖｍ꓿

Great Eagle Publishing, Inc.
3020 Issaquah-Pine Lake Rd SE
Suite 481
Issaquah WA 98029-7255 U.S.A.

PUBLISHER'S CATALOGING IN PUBLICATION
(Prepared by Quality Books, Inc.)

Hines, Donald Merrill, 1931-
Celilo tales : Wasco myths, legends, tales of magic and the marvelous / by Donald M. Hines
p. cm
ISBN 0-9629539-5-4

1. Wasco Indians--Mythology. 2. Wasco Indians--Legends. I Title.
E99.W37H56 1996   398.2'089'97
          QBI96-20118.

Library of Congress Catalog Card Number: 96-094025

CONTENTS

PART ONE
INTRODUCTION

PART TWO
CELILO TALES: WASCO MYTHS, LEGENDS, TALES OF MAGIC AND THE MARVELOUS

I. TALES OF THE ORIGINS OF MAN, ANIMALS AND PLANTS, PHENOMENA

ILLUSTRATIONS

Frontispiece
1. Indians Spearing Fish at Celilo Falls (c. 1905)

Facing Page One
2. Indian Woman Drying Fish at Celilo

Between Pages 18 and 19
3. Wasco-Warm Springs: Ida Palmer Walultuna and Baby
4. Warm Springs "Wich-i-up"[Tipi]

Between Pages 57 and 59
5. Eda Holloquila, Warm Springs Indian
6. Warm Springs Sweat House
7. *Tots-homi*, Warm Springs Indian

Between Pages 90 and 91
8. Burial Site on Memaloose Island, Columbia River,
15 miles West of The Dalles (1890)
9. Indian Burial Grounds, Memaloose

Facing Page 111
10. Celilo Area Indian Woman (c.1910-1912)

Facing Page 153
11. Native and Dugout Canoe, Celilo,
Columbia River (c. 1897)

Facing Page 175
12. Indians Fishing at Celilo Falls

Indian woman drying fish at Celilo. Special Collections Division, University of Washington Libraries, NA 745.

PART ONE
INTRODUCTION

I. A CULTURAL OVERVIEW
OF THE WASCO INDIAN NATION

A. Geographic Locale

Formerly the Wasco Indians dwelt in three villages located along the Columbia River's southern shore--from about the modern town of The Dalles, Oregon, eastward to within about eight miles of the mouth of the Deschutes River.[1] Their inhospitable terrain alternated between bare sheets of basaltic rock, to areas whose thin soils were held in place by sparse grasses, to still other areas of sandy silt containing willow thickets and a few clusters of cottonwoods. Indeed, the river banks were generally narrow, and extended back and upward in several steep steps to almost perpendicular basaltic cliffs about 300-450 meters high from which an open plain stretches southward for hundreds of square miles.

The Wascos were often plagued by high winds which blew sand about and made life unpleasant. Even today the Columbia River gorge, extending westward through the Cascades Range, remains a natural funnel-like passage to adverse weather systems-- hot summer winds, or else fearsome wintry blasts with sub-zero, wind-chilled temperatures. As a result, Wasco habitat could be subject to summer temperatures exceeding 100° F, while winter temperatures might exceed -25° F., with precipitation perhaps 6-8" per year. Trees [for firewood] and game animals were remarkably scarce. The dominant geographic feature near the Wascos was the great falls of the Columbia River at Celilo, which was first written of by the Lewis and Clark Expedition in October 1805. Indeed, several systems of violent rapids extended from about the John Day River westward past Celilo perhaps 160 kilometers to present day Bonneville Dam. So great was the force of water, so great were the underwater obstructions that the river appeared literally to turn on its side in its torturous progress through the rapids toward the sea.

B. Location of the Wascos

The Wascos' tribal name--*Galasq'o*--means "those who have the cup." And the "cup" referred to was a cup-shaped rock and outlet of a renowned spring of clear cold water or *wa'cq!o*, from which came the name of their chief village nearby--*wa'sq!o*. Unfortunately, the Wascos' spring was obliterated by construction of the railroad along the southern shores of the Columbia River as recounted in tale 14 "Wasco" hereafter . Still, the name "Wasco" is preserved in names on the land: Wasco County, Oregon; and the town of Wasco, Sherman County, Oregon, and more. By the Indian treaty of 1855, signed near Walla Walla, Washington Territory, with the *Teninos*, *Paiutes*, and *Wat'lalas*, the Wascos were removed to the Warm Springs Reservation on the easterly slopes of Mount Hood where they reside today. No large tribe, according to a 1910 census the Wascos numbered 242; in 1937 the U.S. Office of Indian Affairs counted 227.

C. Subsistence and Fishing
Techniques

A sedentary people and a "salmon culture," the

Wascos fished for their subsistence, especially for salmon whose teeming spring and fall runs were taken from about Celilo and the systems of rapids. No famine here, the Wascos took not only varieties of salmon, but suckers and eels and the mammoth sturgeon. To a lesser extent the Wascos harvested edible roots and berries which were dried for winter use. Least important was the hunt for game animals. During low water times, the Wascos selected likely fishing sites on the river banks and built rickety fishing platforms or fishing stations. Later, from these platforms Wasco fishermen netted or gaffed salmon. At other times, small fish were caught with hook and line or by basket traps. Wasco women split open the fish and laid them out so that the flesh might air dry. Then, the flesh was pulverized and stored in baskets for winter-time use or trade. Indeed, Wasco and also Wishram villages were important rendezvous points for neighboring tribes who sought dried salmon.[2] Not least, with the landing of the first salmon of the season, the Wascos celebrated a religious ritual--intended to assure a good season's catch.

D. Linguistic Boundaries and Culture Forms

With their cross-river neighbors, the Wishrams, the Wascos belonged to the eastern most or upstream branch of Chinookan linguistic stock. Wasco society consisted of three main levels: 1) chiefs [chieftainship was hereditary]; 2) the common folk; 3) slaves (obtained by capture). The Wasco village served as the main social unit. No clan or totem organization was apparent, and "Guardian Spirits" were strictly personal in character.

Wasco housing consisted of two types of dwellings. As protection against the fierce and frigid gales blowing off the Columbia River the Wascos resorted to winter houses: built partly underground and roofed with cedar bark. A number of families lived within, their bed platforms set around the walls. The Wascos' summer house consisted of tipis, of a framework of poles plus a covering of tule mats, or cedar bark. Sweat houses were frequently built and used for purification or for curing ailments; they also had a quasi-supernatural significance.

The Wascos possessed neither metal nor ceramic arts. But they worked in wood or animal horn to make bowls and spoons, and did twined basketry, including bags and various forms of stiff baskets. The Wascos' dress in winter likely consisted of blanket robes made of the pelts of bear, deer, or coyote. In summer, they wore breechcloths, moccasins of deerskins and perhaps sleeve-less shirts of raccoon or coyote. Examples of Wasco body decoration included flattened heads, done in childhood when pressure was applied to an infant's forehead, and pierced ears, with perhaps <u>five</u> holes in each ear.

E. Rites of Passage, Tribal Arts

The Wascos observed puberty ceremonies for both boys and girls. Girls were subject to the usual menses taboos, including isolation, after the fulfillment of which a menstrual dance was held. Boys "trained" for acquisition of strength--and, likely, both boys and girls sought to obtain one or more guardian or *tahmahnawis* spirits. At death the Wascos interred or else placed a corpse on a board in a "dead people's house." Later, the dead were located and rehabilimented by family mem-bers. Slaves were sometimes buried alive to accompany a wealthy chief to the next world.

Wasco art forms included an oral literature which makes much of the character of Coyote who plays a great role as a culture-hero, but also as a fool and buf-

foon. Few graphic forms such as petroglyphs or pictographs occur in the vicinity of the Wascos, in contrast to
these artforms which remain from around Spedis, the
chief Wishram village.[3] Finally, Wasco religious ideas
centered on the acquisition and manifestation of supernatural power obtained from one or more guardian
spirits, as well as the magic-centered machinations of the
shaman.

F. Modern History of the Wascos, the Region

The Wascos are gone--and the Oregon shores of
the Columbia River, the third mightiest river in the U.S.,
are deserted now, the fish runs sorely depleted. No
longer fishers of salmon, the Wasco Indian tribe resides
now on the Warm Springs Indian Reservation many
kilometers south of the river. Extraordinary change has
occurred: now, along the Washington shores of the
Columbia River runs Washington State Highway 14, and
next to it the Burlington Northern Railroad track. And
along the Oregon shores courses the route of Interstate
highway 84, and beside it the mainline tracks of the
Union Pacific Railroad running eastward from Portland,
Oregon, toward Boise. With the close of construction in
1953 of the great hydroelectric dam at The Dalles,
Oregon, last in a series of Columbia River dams, came
final change--with the river barricaded, the water level
was raised 110 feet thereby submerging the falls and the
systems of rapids. Now commercial and recreational
boats traffic where formerly fishing platforms leaned
over the raging waters, and a hapless Indian canoer,
caught in the river's maelstrom, would have been swept
over the falls to a sure death. Although the river banks
are silent now, perhaps some nights beneath a wan moon
the river shores are again peopled by tribal ghosts from

the past.

II. THREE PIONEERING ETHNOGRAPHERS

A. Jeremiah Curtin

At least three early investigators preserved for us details of the life, culture and customs of the Wasco and Wishram Indians. First was Jeremiah Curtin, helped by his wife, Alma Cardell Curtin. Jeremiah Curtin was born 6 September 1835 in Detroit, Michigan, the son of Irish-immigrant parents. Possessing a natural linguistic genius, he entered Harvard, albeit at the advanced age of twenty-four. There he knew with some degree of intimacy Lowell, Longfellow, Child and others. No isolate academic, he sought out diverse peoples among whom he was able to make himself agreeable, and his linguistic genius enabled him to achieve friendly relations with people across boundaries of race and social levels. He delighted in swapping yarns and hearing ancient story-tellers of many cultures and languages; he was indeed a good mixer. At age twenty-nine he went to Russia and served as a diplomat to the Russian Imperial Court at St. Petersburg. When nearly thirty-seven he married. He spent the major portion of his life studying first hand the languages and the culture of Indian tribes of the New World.

In his *Memoirs of Jeremiah Curtin. . .*;[4] Curtin reveals for us his intellectual strength, along with his plan of study of the Indian cultures of the Americas, p. 501 ff. "For fifteen years, or more, I had studied the primitive people of America, my object being to go as far back as possible in investigating the history of human thought. When the western hemisphere was discovered, North and South America contained the most varied and

most extensive museum of the mind in its earlier conditions that the world has ever seen. Over an area about
3,000 miles in width, at its widest, and more than 9,000
long, there were primitive peoples, kindred to each other,
but speaking more than 800 languages which though
kindred, were not intertribally intelligible. Those languages contained an amount of material for the elucida-
tion of the history of speech development which had a
unique value. Those various tribes had philosophies of
life, accounts of the origin of things, and systems of
religion which resembled one another closely, but which
were still greatly varied in detail; that is, the underlying
ideas were mainly the same, but the working out and
treatment varied from tribe to tribe.

"The same view of the origin of things prevailed
everywhere, and that view, judging from what we have
obtained so far of Indian ideas, was substantially the
same as that which the earliest aggregations of men held
on the eastern hemisphere, whether they were of Aryan
or other stocks. This being the case, it is evident that
what the Indians held in their heads and what they had
to show to the investigator of their social and political
institutions were of vastly more value to mankind than
anything else connected with them, or even than they
themselves were if considered apart from what they
knew."[5]

During the winter of 1884-85 Jeremiah Curtin and
his wife travelled by stagecoach and train from California
north to Portland, Oregon. They arrived during January
on the heels of an immense snowstorm which had left
seven foot high piles of snow. Two days of fog plus the
possibility of another snowstorm led an impatient Curtin
to depart Portland for The Dalles, Oregon. Unwittingly
travelling in the teeth of several regional weather systems, the Curtins arrived only to find The Dalles battered
by a fierce snowstorm, and its hostelries filled with

snow-bound guests. Only by crowding guests together was a small room finally found for the Curtins at the Umatilla Hotel.

At last on 22 January, riding berobed in an open horsesleigh, Curtin and his wife set out for the Warm Springs Indian Agency. The road was <u>not</u> thickly obscured by fog all the way, for in places the sleigh passed upon a narrow cut on a high bluff, the frightening abyss only too visible. Upon reaching what is likely the modern village of Oak Springs, a thoroughly chilled Curtin and his wife obtained a sleeping place on the floor of the unfinished living room in the dwelling of a storekeeper. The harsh weather prevented their travelling for several days more. At last they hired a youth as guide, obtained two horses, and set out for the Warm Springs Agency. But within a mile the fiercely blowing winds, and snow which covered the trail two to three feet deep with only a thin crust cruelly cut and tired the horses. The travellers were forced to walk much of the way, falling often, through snow that reached to their knees. At last, their strength ebbing they reached Simnasho on the Agency, and the house of the doctor of the Simnasho division of the Agency. Here also resided many Indian children. Curtin and his wife were given sleeping quarters at the house of a Mr. McCoy nearby.

The house, unfinished, was not ". . suitable to live in during cold weather," Curtin notes. Still it was the most comfortable place in Simnasho. Curtin and his wife were given the best room which was up a flight of stairs. " Overhead were beams covered with boards. Our writing table was an old barrel, our chairs a couple of boxes and a chair with the back off. There was one small window; fortunately, it was on the south side, and the sun came in nearly all day. The McCoys had seven irrepressible children, and there was always a fight going on. Mrs. McCoy was a frail woman, who in earlier life had had a terrible experience. After an almost fatal illness, she became insane, and was taken to the Portland asylum where she spent eighteen awful months."[6]

And so about February 1 Curtin took up study of the "Warm Spring language" with an Indian named McKay whose wife was matron of the Simnasho school. On Sundays Curtin (and wife?) attended worship services at the schoolhouse, but Curtin's description of the scene is neither one of spiritual promise nor of missionary effectiveness. The winter of 1884-1885 was severe enough, but in early February 1885 a heavy rainstorm or "chinook" came, and Curtin had much to complain of from the roof leaking into the familial bed. But Curtin persevered, studying tribal language with MacKay during the day, listening and noting the myths and traditions of McKay's people. On February 9 snow began to fall again, heavy, driven by a fierce, cold north wind. Food for the many Mccoys plus the Curtins gave out. At last about mid-February the Curtins set out for the Warm Springs Agency.

Perils confronting the Curtins included flooded streams to be forded, and deep snows to be crossed. At last, after beholding the frozen corpses of numerous horses, dead of cold or starvation, they reached the main Agency, and were welcomed by the agent, Mr. Gesner. Curtin notes his pleasure: "Once more we sat at a comfortable table and saw clean faces around us, a pleasure which only a person who has spent weeks in a family where there are many unkempt children can appreciate. That evening, for the first time since leaving The Dalles, I had my shoes polished."

Under the tutelage of another Indian, Charley Pitt, Curtin resumed study of the Wasco language. But not long thereafter, Pitt departed to retrieve an errant, runaway wife. Curtin discovered his former tutor, the Indian McKay, had come to the Agency, and so resumed his language studies with him. Curtin and wife observed some of the Indians' tribal customs such as "the raising of the dead" when bodies of the deceased were taken up, wrapped in new blankets, and then buried once more.

On April 20, 1885, Jeremiah Curtin and his wife[7] left the Warm Springs Agency. Curtin notes, "I had obtained a good working knowledge of the Wasco language; I had taken down a vocabulary and all the myths the old men of the tribe could remember."[8] Fortunately, in 1909 Sapir published for posterity the twenty-five Wasco narratives which Curtin had collected.[9].

Setting out from the Agency Curtin and his wife retraced their original route: to Simnasho, to Oak Grove [now Wapinitia?], to Tygh, and The Dalles. Curtin hired a boat and was rowed to the Washington side of the river for a brief viewing of the rocky, barren countryside. Departing The Dalles for Portland by steamer, Curtin and his wife entrained southward toward Ashland, Oregon. There they boarded a stagecoach to California and further adventures.

B. Edward Sapir

Born in 1884 in Germany, Edward Sapir was five years old when his family emigrated to the United States and New York City. Early recognized for his intellectual promise, he received a Pulitzer fellowship to Columbia College, from which he was graduated in 1904. While doing graduate study in Germanics at Columbia, his interest in language studies brought him into company with Franz Boas, pioneering teacher-field worker in the anthropological study of language. During July and August of 1905, Sapir journeyed to the Yakima Reservation in southcentral Washington. There, led by his linguistic interests, he sought out and copied down in the

Wishram tongue numerous tribal narratives of the
Wishram peoples. The majority of Sapir's language and
narrative notations were taken mainly from three informants, plus four others who gave up perhaps one version
each. Sapir's work was published in 1909 as *Wishram
Texts, Together with Wasco Tales and myths, Collected
by Jeremiah Curtin.*[9] Although Jeremiah Curtin's
twenty-five collected Wasco narratives are included,
details of Wasco culture or language [10] are lacking. Still,
the wealth of data about Wishram Indian life and culture
which Sapir had also collected led University of Washington Anthropology Professor Leslie Spier in 1924 and
in 1925 to very briefly visit the reservation, to search out
and interview more Wishram informants. As an off-
shoot, he collected five Wasco narratives from Frank
Gunyer, a middle-aged Wasco who also acted as his
interpreter. Alas, no further information is given about
the informant.

Sapir's notes concerning both the Wishram, and
the Wasco lore are frustrating to the modern researcher.
Sapir's comments predate the great works of collecting
and scholarship directed to American Indian oral literature. More, Sapir's views derive from a very small ac-
quaintance with American Indian traditions. As a result,
his pronouncements are not always reliable.

C. Lucullus Virgil McWhorter

Lucullus Virgil McWhorter was born in Harrison
County, West Virginia, on January 29, 1860. Disliking
formal study and confining classsrooms, he preferred to
study nature firsthand, to be out-of-doors. Greatly
interested in the historical past, he had read in archeolo-
gy and closely examined Indian remains in his native
West Virginia. McWhorter was concerned with accurate
observation and with careful and accurate notations about

his findings. In l903 he moved from Ohio to the vicinity of the Yakama Indian Reservation to take up cattle ranching. In his new locale, McWhorter began studies of Plateau archaeology, of Indian culture and life, and especially of oral lore. His scientific interests led him to warm and active friendships with many Yakamas with whom he hunted and camped, welcomed in his home and shared food. He participated in many tribal ceremonials, was adopted into the Yakama tribe, and was given the name *He-mene Ka-wan* or "Old Wolf," which, along with "Big Foot", were names McWhorter frequently used in his voluminous correspondence.

Over the years McWhorter continued to collect and to preserve a record of traditional Indian culture found on the Yakama Reservation, culture which he perceived was already fading from tribal memories. Then, at his death in 1944, his papers were placed in the library-archives of Washington State University, Pullman, Washington. Included are thousands of items: books, photographs, manuscripts, journals, manuscript fragments, letters, and mementos.[11] Of particular interest are McWhorter's efforts to collect the oral myths, legends, tales and other narratives of other Indian groups -- including the Wasco tribe. McWhorter's collecting techniques, by today's standards, were less than satisfactory. Self-taught, he patterned his collecting methods after the bare outlines of collecting particulars obtained from the Bureau of American Ethnology, found subsequently in his papers. Commonly he collected narratives heard around a campfire, after a hunt, or narratives recited during a longhouse ceremony--in proper context. McWhorter would listen, and then as soon after as possible would write or typewrite from memory the narratives which he had heard. Or, his Indian friends wrote down and translated into English for him numerous tribal narratives. Having considerable facility with the Yakama language, McWhorter sought to be accurate, detailed and thorough. He did not rewrite tales into literary forms like the short story. Instead, he often appended to tales his questions and an informant's answers which explained numerous cultural details of the stories, or he cited story details shared by other narratives. What is of critical importance--McWhorter collected and added to his files all sorts of Indian narratives--from a myth to a legend to a magical belief-- and more. No practiced folklorist, he knew little of the conventional genres and when to stop collecting; so he collected all that he heard. And he collected in depth as best he knew how--his labors comprise a priceless legacy of traditional oral lore and life for the Wasco Indians and numerous other contiguous tribes.

III. INTENT OF THIS WORK

This work seeks to provide a comprehensive edition and collection of traditional narratives of the Wasco tribe. We have searched out and compiled what we believe is the largest, the most complete body of traditional narratives for the Wasco people. What bibliographical search plus luck has discovered is all here.[12] Included here are primary sources, narratives taken directly from the lips of Wasco narrators, texts of inestimable value. More remarkable for this late date, the texts found herein derive from memories of tribal informants who were alive at the time of the tribe's assignment to the Warm Springs Reservation, and whose cultural knowledge and language skills were absolute. These tale texts, then, are as complete and as authentic as possible. They have not been rewritten. The likelihood of discovery of more traditional and authentic told Wasco narratives is, we believe, remote. Second, bibliographic annotation from without the Wasco and the Wishram tribes emphasizes the traditionality, the authenticity of the tales: as deriving out of an oral milieu, as vital narrative forms, as an inimical part of the tribal culture. Finally, we would plead that the modern reader of these tales should "listen with his eyes.' By this we mean that while reading the reader should imagine a narrator's voice, hear vocal devices which create characters, and sense the varied pace of a narration which finally brings the tale to its conclusion.

The narrative texts in this volumes derive from three sources:

1. Twenty-five Wasco tales collected by Jeremiah Curtin which appeared first in Edward Sapir's *Wishram Texts, Together with Wasco Tales and Myths. . ..*

2. Five Wasco texts which first appeared in Leslie Spier & Edward Sapir's *Wishram Ethnography.* [13]

3. Seventeen texts collected by L.V. McWhorter which were extracted from Folders 1511, 1512, 1513, 1515, 1516, 1522, and 1523 of the McWhorter Papers, Washington State University Library, as cited in Nelson A. Ault, *The Papers of Lucullus Virgil McWhorter.*[14] These narratives have not appeared previously in print, and are used here with permission.

With the kind permission of Dr. Earle Connette and his staff, and his successor Prof. John Guido, Head, Manuscripts, Archives and Special Collections, Holland Library, Washington State University, I turned over the fading, penciled pages of the McWhorter Collection. Using photocopies of McWhorter's original texts supplied me by the WSU library staff, I have made only those minimal changes of spelling or direct discourse to maximize reader understanding. The tales have not been rewritten, but preserve the oral sense of their original narration.

This work constitutes the definitive canon of known traditional narratives and genres for the Wasco Indians. In order to demonstrate the traditional nature of the varieties of narratives here, I have grouped the tales into categories (e.g. myths, legends, tales) which may or may not have been evident to the original tribal raconteurs, but which the modern reader and scholar require for a more complete understanding now of the tribal lore.[15]

In creating this work I have especially relied on Laurits Bødker's *Folk Literature (Germanic)*.[16] And we have freely consulted Stith Thompson's *The Folktale*[17]; also his *Tales of the North American Indians*.[18] Here are primary texts told or translated by tribal members plus their interpretation of the lore. I believe the authenticity of the tales is high, even though they were taken down during the early twentieth century, at least 50 years or more following the culturally destructive move of many tribes and many bands onto the same reservation. Here is an extensive record of the mental life of the Wasco tribe to inform the modern reader who is now far removed from the past. These collected tales enable study of Wasco narrative stylistics, even the belief systems of the tribe. Particularly possible now is comparative study with neighboring tribes, and neighboring culture areas, something previously impossible.

IV. ENGLISH LANGUAGE AND TRADITIONAL WASCO NARRATIVES

The English language versions of the Wasco narratives have posed no small amount of anguish for me.[19] To be like the original--attempting to reproduce pristine, pre-1855 Wasco language forms--or to be readable to moderns? We have opted for wide readability. Curtin's texts present less of a burden for their reproduction here. Still, some of his sentences, overlong, have been reformed into two for ease of reading. And new paragraphs have been ordered with each change of speaker, with each change of topic.

V. ORGANIZATION AND SUBSTANCE OF THE WORK

The traditional narratives in this work have been grouped into categories after the scholarly example and folkloric scholarship in Stith Thompson's *Tales of the North American Indians*. Within each category each of the tales bears a descriptive title, given by the Indian raconteur or by the original editors. Then, each narrative is given a number which marks its assigned place in the canon of Wasco traditional narratives, along with variants. And narrative variants are listed from complex to simple. Details describing the informant from whom the tale was obtained, along with the time of the original narration plus other details about the tale, are given in List of Informants at the end of this volume. Finally, the tale itself appears in the form of its first telling.

A. Tales of the Origin of Man, Animals and Plants, Phenomena. These traditional oral narratives comprise myths of the Wascos. The narratives relate of the origination of the region's Indians and their characteristics, of the origins of the sun and the moon. Some tell of the coming of death to man, and relate of the origin of the salmon runs. Also told are the sources of some animal characteristics and appearances.

B. Tales of Legendary Beings and Places. These narratives explain the origins of particular landforms, of the nature of present climatic conditions, of a race of people who lacked mouths, of volcanic eruptions on nearby mountains, of river monsters, and of monstrous serpents able to swallow people.

C. Tales of Magic and the Marvelous. These traditional tales relate of marvels and magic powers possible among the Indians, imagination being the only limiting factor: of an arrow chain or a sky rope enabling movement of people back and forth between the sky-world and the earthworld; of contests in magic among shamans where their powers are displayed; of magical plant-men created; of humans fleeing this world to live amongst the world of water animals; and of a person who becomes a cannibal, devours himself.

D. Tales of Conflicts and Adventures. These Wasco narratives relate of marital or parental conflicts: of neglected wives who cohabit with an animal; of social isolation of incorrigibles; of an owl-ogress who preys on bad children. Also recounted is a grizzly bear who transforms himself into an old man and lures hunters to their deaths; of a gambler-adventurer whose luck leaves him when he wagers, and who then loses his life; but his sons bring him back to life.

At the back of this volume are appendices of explanatory matter which can be useful to the reader. First, **NOTES TO THE NARRATIVES** are included. Given by the original informant or supplied by the collector, these notes provide important background details and explanations. Second, an **INDEX OF MOTIFS** lists the motifs extant in each narrative. I have employed Stith Thompson's *Motif-Index of Folk-Litera-*

ture;[20] also Thompson's *Tales of North American Indians*. In this manner, I have sought to note details of character, plot, or background which exist in the oral literature of the Wascos. The motifs have been helpful in assigning a text to a particular category. More, the motifs have also underscored the presence of magic which pervades the oral literature, even the Indian cultures. Third, **COMPARATIVE NOTES TO OTHER PLATEAU INDIAN TALES** are included which cite comparable versions of each Wasco narrative from among Plateau Indian tribes found northward from the Columbia River to Central British Columbia. A listing of the tribes, the collections of tribal tales, and short titles used in making the Comparative Notes appear in Appendix Three. The traditionality and authenticity of the Wasco oral narratives found herein are assured by the number of comparable versions which are told among the other tribes over the Plateau Region. Fourth, a **LIST OF INFORMANTS** contains biographical data, if available, on taletellers, details of their tribal life, the authenticity of their narrated tales. Fifth, a **SELECTED LIST OF READINGS** is included which provides the inquiring reader with a list of useful works on the tribal life and lore of the Wascos and their immediate neighbors. Finally, **ACKNOWLEDGEMENTS** of sources and of individuals for whose help I am indebted concludes this work.

Donald M. Hines

Wasco-Warm Springs: Ida Palmer Walultuna and Baby.
Neg. #317179, Dixon photo 1913, Wanamaker Collection,
Department of Library Services, American Museum of
Natural History.

Warm Springs "Wich-i-up" [Tipi]. Oregon Historical Society, Neg. OrHi 36823.

PART TWO

CELILO TALES: WASCO MYTHS, LEGENDS, TALES OF MAGIC AND THE MARVELOUS

I. TALES OF THE ORIGINS OF MAN, ANIMALS AND PLANTS, PHENOMENA

1. COYOTE IS SWALLOWED BY *ITC!I'XYAN*[21]

Over at *Nixlu'idix*, where the *Wi'cxam* village now stands, Coyote was going east up the river. He looked north at the hills, and saw five men running down towards him. They said, "Old man, don't you go up along the river. Go by the hills. If you go along the river, you will be swallowed."

"Who will swallow me?"

"*Itc!i'xyan.*"

"Oh, I'll run away. He can't swallow me. I run like the wind."

Coyote went on. Finally he thought, "Perhaps there is such a thing that can swallow me." Then, thinking awhile, he said, "I'll go up on the hill and get a long log and put it across my shoulders. Then, *Itc!i'-xyan* won't be able to swallow me."

He got the log, came down, and travelled up the river. As he went, he called out, "*Itc!i'xyan*, swallow me!" He plagued *Itc!i'xyan*. At last Coyote lost consciousness; he did not know anything.

When he revived, he found himself in a dark place. He wondered where he was. Could it be that *Itc!i'xyan* had swallowed him?

He heard a sound as of a bell a little way off, and the voices of people whispering. He sat with the log on his back, and said, "People, make a fire, and I'll stay all night." He felt around, and found, as he thought, grass and pieces of wood, and said again, "Why don't you make a fire?" No one answered. What he took for grass was people's hair, the large pieces of wood their bodies, the smaller pieces of wood their bones, which had been there for years.

Coyote didn't yet know where he was. So he sat down, brought out his two sisters, the two Cayuse girls, as he called them, two pieces of his own excrement,[22] and said, "My sisters, what is the matter? Where am I?"

"Oh, we won't tell you. You are such a man that if we tell you, you will say, 'Oh, yes! I knew that before, but forgot it for a moment.'"

Coyote began to throw up spittle with his hand, and said, "Here, let rain come."

"Oh, don't, don't do that; we will tell you. You were warned by the five men not to go up along the river, but you would go. You wouldn't listen to advice. Now you are in the belly of *Itc!i'xyan*."

"That's just what I thought," said Coyote. He put away his sisters where they were before. Then he took his fire drill and made a fire, taking pitch from the log on his back. When there was light, he saw the remains of all the people, some with canoes, others without. He called to the fire all that were able to come to warm themselves. Eagle came, also Weasel, his younger brother.[23]

Itc!i'xyan now said, "Come out, Coyote, I didn't want to swallow you."

"How can I come out? There is no door," said

Coyote. He looked up and saw something moving above his head, breathing, growing larger and smaller. This was *Itc!i'xyan's* heart. "It is too high to reach," thought Coyote. He made a ladder of two canoes, went up, and with his flint knife cut at the root of the heart.

Itc!i'xyan said, "Get out of me, Coyote! I didn't try to swallow you. I don't want you."

Coyote said, "I don't know how to get out." Then he told all the people to lock arms. When *Itc!i'-xyan's*[24] heart was cut and dropped, he blew a tremendous breath, and threw all the people out near Celilo, but Coyote about six miles further south over the Celilo hills.

Eagle went west, and Coyote east.

2A. THE ASCENT TO THE SKY AND RETURN TO EARTH[25]

There was once a boy who was told by his mother never to shoot high up in the air. But this made him wish to shoot up, and at last he did shoot. His arrow stuck in the sky; then, in trying to shoot it down, he hit that arrow in the end, shot again and hit the second in the end, and so he kept shooting till his last arrow was near the ground.[26] He stood and thought a while, then climbed up on the arrows, and went to the other side of the sky. He looked around and saw tracks everywhere and a nice road. "I'll follow this road," thought he, and went on.

At last he saw a crowd of persons rolling along. He called out to them and asked, "What are you doing there, where are you going?"

"We are going into the heads of Indians down below." These people were Nits, all old white-headed people.

He went farther, saw a great crowd of people coming, and asked, "Where are you going?"

"Oh, we are going below to eat the blood of people." These were Body-Lice.

Soon after he met a crowd of red people, and asked, "Where are you going?"

"Below to eat the blood of people." These were Flea people.

"What are you carrying on your backs?"

"Oh, those are our humps."

Soon another crowd appeared, each with a pack. He asked, "Where are you going?"

"Down below."

"What have you got in your bundles? I am hungry."

"We have nothing to eat."

"Well, open your bundles; let me see." One put down his bundle; the boy opened it. That moment everything was filled with darkness. The boy begged them to tie up the bundle. They did so, and there was light again. These were Ground-Squirrel people, and there was a vast number of them.

They said to the boy, "The people below have nothing but light now. When we get there, one of us will open his bundle, and while it lasts it will be dark. Then light will come. And when we are tired of light, another of us will open his bundle, and there will be darkness." They passed on.

Soon he saw a man coming with an arrow through his body. As he passed the boy, he fell dead. Straightway another man came along with his hair tied up on his head; he had a bow and arrows in a quiver on his back. "Have you passed a man," asked he, "with an arrow through his body?"

"Yes," answered the boy, "and he fell a short

distance behind you."

"You are my son-in-law," said the man. "Go on! You will come to my house. When you do, go in."

The boy went on his way, saw a mountain-sheep with an arrow through it. It just passed and fell dead. Soon a man came up with an arrow and asked, "Did you see a sheep?"

"Yes, it fell a little way from here."

The man said, "You are my son-in-law." The boy did not answer; he did not know what to say. The man said, "As you travel this road, you will see a great many feathers and much paint. Keep on, you'll come to my house."

After a time the boy came to a house. It shone very brightly, but near by was a black house, black smoke coming out of it. He opened the door of the bright house and went in. Everything shone in the house. They cooked huckleberry-roots and other food for him. He saw a young woman sitting there, and his heart failed him--she was so beautiful.

Now the people from the black house came over and tried to steal him. They surrounded the place, but they could not get in, and he would not go outside. At last the people hid him in the house. This was Sun's house. The girl was the First-Blush-of-Morning, and she was bright and beautiful. The boy had her for his wife. The man who was following the mountain-sheep was old Sun himself; he was on a journey. The first person, who was after the man who was shot through, was Death. His people lived in the black house and tried to get the boy.

After a time First-Blush-of-Morning bore two children which were fastened together, boys. The young man said to his wife, "We will go to the river and wash our heads." After they had washed their heads, she sat down, and he put his head in her lap. As he lay there, he scratched on the ground and made a little hole. Through this hole he looked down to the world below, and saw his sister mourning, going from the spring to the house.

Blue Jay ran up to her and said, "I am your brother, I've come to life." He would run against her and almost push her over, for she was nearly blind from mourning. All the people of the place were mourning. The men were coming home with bundles of bones. They had been everywhere hunting for his bones, and had collected many of all kinds. The young man cried at what he saw. Then he rose up and went home with his wife. He lay on the bed five days and nights. They did not know what the trouble was.

Old Sun asked his daughter if she had abused him. She said, "No."

Then he said, "He must have seen his old home below. Let us take him back."

Sun's wife told her daughter to get some of old woman Spider's cords to make a basket.[27] She got the rope and a basket. They told him they were getting ready to send him home. His boys were already well grown. They brought him food of all kinds, all kinds of berries that are picked on trees above, all kinds of vegetables that the ground above produced. At that time there was no fruit or vegetables here below.

When all was ready, they went to the hole that the young man had made by pulling up grass by the roots and scratching the ground. They lowered the basket through the hole with the father, boys, and mother in it. Old woman Spider came, and they spliced the rope whenever it was giving out. They lowered it gradually till it came to the ground on a hill half a mile above the Wasco spring. (To this day the place can be seen where the basket came down. There is a hollow or basin in the hill.)

The man got out of the basket and ran to the house just as his sister started for the spring. Blue Jay came up, snatched her bucket, and said, "I'm your brother."

The man now came to her. He took hold of her hand and said, "I have come. Tell our father and mother to clean out the house five times and burn sweet stuff five times. Then we shall come."

His sister said, "Our mother is blind." He went to the house, drew one of his own hairs across her eyes, and immediately she could see as well as ever. They cleaned the house five times, and the fifth day the brother came with his wife and two boys. They had a feast and gave many presents.

The boys were running around. Now Blue Jay had his tomahawk ready to cut the boys in two, for he knew they were the grandchildren of Sun. He thought that it would be well to spread them out, not to have both in one place. All were astonished to see two children, so fastened together, run and step as one and shoot as one. Crowds of people came from every place to see them.

The fifth day the boys ran outside. Blue Jay was ready. He hit the boys and made two of them; this killed both of the boys. The woman saw this, ran, caught her boys, and said, "I'll go back to my father Sun and take both of my boys with me, one on each side. Every time there is war in any place, I'll show myself with my sons on each side of me. When there is no war, I'll appear without my sons."

The woman had given the relatives of her husband, who were Ants and Yellow-Jackets, many gifts- -robes, skins and ornaments, fruit and vegetables. All these disappeared when the woman went away. The people tied them around their waists with strong strings; but they pulled away, almost cut the people in two. This

is why those people have such small waists now. The
woman became the sun in heaven, and her sons are the
shadows sometimes seen. There was no sun on earth
before this.

2B. SKY ROPE[28]

A little boy was taken to the sky, where he grew
up.[29] A woman forbade him to go to a certain place.
There were a people who ate nothing but human eyes.
These people wanted him to marry their daughters, of
which there were five. His own people found him and
cleaned his stomach of eyes, bones, etc.

He married the youngest daughter of the Sun.
They liked him because he was a good hunter. He went
to the forbidden spot [another?] where he found a hole.
He looked down to the earth. He saw his brother, who
had no eyes, crying for him. He felt sorry for his
brother.

He went back and lay down, for he did not know
how to descend. His wife asked him what was wrong.
He told her. She said she would get two old people,
Spiders, to make a rope for him. They let him down.[30]

She said, "Tell your people to clean their house
five times [or for five days] before you enter."

He met his brother there, crying, and asked,
"Why do you cry?"

His brother said, "Because I lost my brother."
This younger brother said, "I do not believe you are the
lost one. I think you are the trickster Blue Jay." But he
found it was his brother.

The older brother told him to instruct the people
to clean house: then he would join them with his family.

So the younger brother told them.

The sky family brought all sorts of things from the sky. Now the family had plenty to eat; before this they had been starving. The sky couple had twin boys who were fastened together. The Sun's daughter told her brother-in-law not to take the twins anywhere for fear something might happen to them.

Blue Jay thought, "Perhaps I can split them apart." He took his axe and cut them apart. But when they parted, their entrails were dragged out.

The woman was sewing when her thread broke. She knew that something had happened. Her brother-in-law told her. She found them split in two. She was so sad that she wanted to go home. She said, "Now I will take my sons back home. The only time you will see them is on those occasions when you see a bright light on each side of the sun when it is shining." This is a sign that some one is going to be very sick or die. (A star near the moon has the same significance.)[31]

3. TWO BROTHERS BECOME SUN AND MOON[32]

A woman and her two children lived below The Dalles.[33] An old man lived some distance from them. One night the elder boy, who was about four years old, began to cry. The mother brought him everything there was in the house, but still he cried. At last she concluded to send him to the old man, whom she called grandfather. She said to the boy, "He will tell you stories. Go to him."

The boy jumped up and ran off to the old man's house. The old man asked, "What do you want?"

"I want you to tell me stories."

The boy lay down by the old man, and he said, "Once there was a spring, and water flowed from it, and grass grew around it,'*tawna, tawna.*'"[34]

"Oh," said the child, "that is very short."

"No, that's a good story. It's long enough." The boy was angry and ran home.

His mother said, "He must have told you a short story."

He only said there was a spring, and water ran from it, and grass grew around it; then he said '*tawna, tawna,*' right away." The woman was provoked because the old man did not tell the boy a long story and keep him quiet. She went over and scolded him.

He said. "I thought that was enough to quiet him, and that that was all that was wanted."

The boy cried again. She sent him again, and the old man told the same kind of a story. The woman scolded him for not telling longer stories. This happened five times. Then the woman was very angry with the old man, and determined to move away, and she moved off to some distance.

The woman's younger boy talked like an old man when not more than a year old. He would tell about things which had been and would be. He had a very large stomach. When the elder boy punched it with his hand, it sounded strangely, something like a bell. The elder boy was stupid, did nothing but cry and laugh.

One morning the mother told him to take the little boy out and play with him on the sand. He snatched the child by the hair and dragged him out and around on the ground. The child could not walk yet.

The father of the younger boy was Spider. The woman had left the father before the child was born, but the boy was constantly talking about his father. He would say, "My father is following us. He has gone up

on a rock, and is looking for our fire. He has crossed
the river." This made the woman very angry. She
would shake the child, but right away again he would be
talking about his father. He seemed to see him and to
know all he was doing.

The elder boy dragged his little brother around
all day in the sand and dirt, nearly killed him. Next
morning when the child woke up, he said, "My father is
going to kill himself because he cannot find us. He will
heat rocks under a tree, then he will climb the tree and
fall on to the rocks." "*Oali, oali*," the child would sing,
and so he went on day and night.

He would rouse his mother in the night and say,
"People over there are doing so and so," and he would
sing, "*Oali, oali*." He would roll over against his brother,
and the brother would kick him back, but the child did
not cry; he seldom cried.

Again he would say, "I see a man hugging a
woman over there." He looked everywhere, and saw
everything that was going on in the world, and kept
telling what he saw night and day. His mother and brother did not like him.

One day the mother told the elder brother to take
the younger one out doors and step on his stomach,
saying, "Then all of that big stomach will go off, and he
will be like you." The boy took the child out, put him
on his back, and stamped on his stomach. Immediately
snakes, frogs, lizards, and everything of the reptile kind,
came out of the boy and ran off. Then the child got up
and went into the house with his brother, and stopped
singing, "*Oali, oali*." He never sang it again.

The mother told the boys to make bows and
arrows, saying, "I'll give you five quivers, and you can
fill them. I'll trim robes for you with shells, then I'll tell
you what to do." The boys made the arrows.

She trimmed them beautiful robes, then said, "I

want to send you to kill Sun." In those days Sun never moved out of his tracks, always stood directly overhead, and no living being could go far and live -- so great was the heat.

The mother said, "When you kill Sun, you can stay up there. One of you can be Sun, the other Moon." The boys were delighted. They started off and travelled south. When they got a little east of where Primeville[35] now is, they wrestled with each other. Spider boy got thrown, and at that spot a great many camas-roots came up. At every village to which they came, they told the people where they were going; and all were glad, for all were tired of Sun and his terrible heat. Finally the boys turned and travelled east, till they were nearly overcome by the heat.

At last they came to a place from which, looking to the left, they could see a great ball of shining fire. They looked to the right, and there was a second ball of shining fire. They had gone up in the air, and had come to Moon's house. It was on the left side of Sun's house, not far away. Old Moon and his daughter lived there. Moon's daughter was very lame. She waited on the boys, brought them fruit of all kinds, huckleberries, and other things. The boys were amused as they saw her walk.

Moon's house was full of light, bright and dazzling. The boys ate, and then went out and came as near Sun's house as they could. It was so bright and hot that they couldn't get very near. They took their arrows and began to shoot at old Sun, who sat in his house. With their last arrow they killed the old man. Immediately there was no more strong light.

They pulled out their arrows and said, "We cannot both be Sun, we must kill Moon." They killed Moon. Then they argued as to which should be Sun.

The elder said, "I will. I am older than you are.

You can be Moon and take his daughter." The younger
brother agreed to this.

Now the people below were very anxious to
know where the two boys were who had travelled to the
east. As the heat grew less and less, they said, "It must
be that the boys have done as they said." The mother
knew that they had been able to accomplish all they
wished for. Now they went through the sky, and Moon
followed Sun.

4. THE SUN-LODGE[36]

There were five children; the mother was old.
Four of the children died. The one child, a son, found
Meadowlark and [who?] told him what had killed the
four children. This son found a strong *tahmahnawis*
spirit.[37]

The old mother cried all day, all night; all day,
all night. For many days she cried for her children. She
spit on a rock while crying. All day, all night she spit
on that rock. That rock turned to a person. That rock
then had two children.

Coyote [*E-tal-i pus*] changed that Rock-person
into the sun. Coyote made a big lodge around the sun,
a sun-lodge. You can see it, a big circle like a tepee.
Sometimes you see two little suns inside this circle, this
lodge. They are the two children of the Rock-person,
now the sun. Coyote did that work. When you see the
sun, when you see the sun-lodge with the little suns
inside, you can know that Coyote did all that work.

5. LEGEND OF THE GREAT DIPPER[38]

There were five persons, five brothers. They were the Wolves. They ran all over the country every day, hunting. Coyote watched them all the time. He ate with them, ate what they brought from their hunting: deer meat, elk, all kinds of meat. Every evening the Wolves talked about seeing something in the sky. One evening Coyote asked the oldest Wolf brother, "What do you talk about? What is it you see in the sky?"

The Wolf would not tell. The old Wolf was sly, always afraid. Wise with years, the old wolf of today is hard to trap.

The next evening Coyote asked the next oldest Wolf brother the same question. The Wolf would not answer him.

The next evening Coyote asked the third oldest Wolf what it was that they talked about, what it was they saw in the sky. The Wolf would not tell him.

The next evening the Coyote asked the fourth Wolf brother the same question. The fourth Wolf said to Coyote, "Maybe if I tell you, you would tell my brothers. They would be mad at me."

One morning the five brothers all got together. The fourth Wolf spoke, "Coyote asked me what we are talking about, what it is that we see in the sky. I said to Coyote, 'Maybe if I tell you, you will tell my brothers. They would be mad at me.' What do you think? Are we going to tell him what we see in the sky?"

The Wolves had one little Dog. The youngest Wolf said, "We will go tell Coyote what he asks about. We can do nothing with them. They are way up in the sky, those two things. What do you think, my brothers? Will we tell Coyote?"

The brothers answered, "Yes! We will tell

Coyote all about it." The Wolves were all satisfied to
tell Coyote. One day Coyote came in and they said, "We
saw two animals in the sky. We do not know how we
can get at them. They are away up high."

Coyote said, "All right! We will go see! We will
go up and see."

The youngest Wolf asked, "How will we go up?"

Coyote answered him, "It is well. I will show
you how we can go up without trouble."

It was the middle of wintertime. Coyote got five
quivers filled with arrows. He shot one arrow towards
the sky. The arrow struck the sky, stuck there. Coyote
shot a second arrow. It stuck the end of the first arrow,
struck the end and held fast. Coyote shot all of his
arrows. They reached the ground, a shaft from the sky
to the earth.[39] Coyote had cut rings [spirals] around the
arrow shafts so he and the Wolves could hold tightly
with their hands. The oldest Wolf always carried the
Dog. There were no stars in the sky at that time.

The next sun all went up the arrow-way. Coyote
went first, followed by the five brother Wolves. Many
suns, many nights they climbed. They all arrived at the
sky, reached there safely. They saw these two animals
plainly. They were Grizzly Bears! Coyote said to the
Wolves, "No one go near them! They will tear you to
pieces."

The two youngest Wolves went up close. They
were not afraid. The two next youngest Wolves followed. Oldest Wolf stayed behind with the Dog. He
was always behind, always careful, always afraid. The
youngest went up closer. The Grizzlies did not get mad
at them. They all stood there just like a good show.

Coyote stood back. He looked at them. All was
a picture to him. Coyote smiled. He walked about
looking. He was thinking about it, thinking what he
would do. He thought, "I am going to picture this for

the different people who are to come. They will look at
it. They will think, 'There is a story about it.'" Coyote
pictured them there. He made them stay there in the sky,
five Wolves and a Dog. The two Grizzly Bears had
always been there.[40]

When Coyote came down, he took the arrow
from the sky, took it away. When he had passed the
second arrow, he took it off and so on till he came to the
ground. The Wolves could not come down. When
nighttime came, Coyote went out and looked at the nice
picture in the sky. There they were: two Grizzlies, five
Wolves and a little Dog.[41]

Coyote said to the bird *Whoch-whoch*,[42] "Maybe
I will die! You tell the new people what I have done.
Pretty soon there will be many stars growing in the sky.
It is my work."

Whoch-whoch got the story from Coyote to tell
to us. From this sun, now we know. You see this bird,
Whoch-whoch, when he flies up singing. He is telling
you this story, how Coyote pictured the sky. It is good
to know the *Whoch-whoch*. From them, the Grizzlies
and the Wolves, came the stars, as Coyote pictured them.

Coyote came this way from the sunrise. He
traveled a long distance to this country. One night he
looked up and saw many young stars. They were pretty
thick, all growing rapidly. In the meantime he had made
Whoch-whoch to tell it all everywhere, scatter all around
the news of what he had done. He asked *Whoch-whoch*,
"What is wrong with those stars up there? Too many of
them."

Whoch-whoch answered, "Oh! Those are stars
growing full in the sky. They are growing fast. If they
grow pretty full in the sky, they may fall down. This
earth will become all frost."

Coyote got scared about his work! Coyote took
[made up] his mind, "I will go up again! That is my

work! I will go up again."

Coyote took his five quivers of arrows. He shot them upwards, making a trail as before. He climbed again to the sky. He rounded up the stars, like war parties in camp, all different places. You see sometimes stars pointed together, maybe squares. That was Coyote's work. He placed them that way.

The big white road across the sky,[43] Coyote made that trail. Coyote said to the stars, "You must not grow too fast. You must keep together! If you want to go somewhere, fly as the lightening, speed like the light! You do that! Never grow too fast!"

Coyote put up a knife of stars. Watch that! Coyote put up a bunch of stars. Watch them![44] Sometimes this bunch comes up in the evening over the mountain as trails the sun. These stars give luck when the bow-and-arrow-woods are in bloom. This luck is for gambling, horse racing, or anything you may gain.

6. BRIDGE OF THE GODS[45]

When this earth was first made, the Animal and the Bird People were living all over the land. They were the only tribes at that time and that day. Some animals were great and could kill people, could do mighty wonders. I will tell you of one, and how the Bridge was made.

From the sundown in the West was a great bird. It lived there, and all the people were afraid of it. This animal was Thunderbird (*Noh-we-nah klah*). A law was made by this bird, made in five high mountains. The bird made five high mountains and said, "I make this law, the law that if people pass over the five high mountains, I will kill them. They must not come where I live."

Wolf (*Hal-ish*) was one of the greatest of animals. He did not believe the law. He said, "I will go! I will be the first to see what Thunderbird will do to me."

The Wolves were five brothers. They said, "I will go!" The Wolves went to the first mountain. The brothers stood in a row; all stepped the right foot at the same time. Nothing hurt the Wolves. Then, the left foot was stepped, all at the same time. The five brothers were dead.

When the people learned that the five brothers were dead, Grizzly Bear (*Twee-ti-yah*) said, "I will go! I will take a chance! I do not think that I will die like the five Wolves."

There were five brothers of Grizzly Bear. They went to the first mountain. They stood in a row, stepped the right foot, all at the same time. But when the left foot was stepped, the Grizzly Bears fell dead, as did the Wolves.

The Cougars (*Wy-you-wee*) five brothers, said, "I will go try! I will take a long step. I will leap over the mountains." The Cougars went, and at the first leap all were dead.

Then the Beavers (*Yeh-kah*), five brothers, said, "I will try. I will go under the mountains. I will not get killed like the Wolves, Grizzly Bears, and Cougars. I will go see about this law." The Beavers tried, and all five brothers were killed.

Coyote's oldest son was a great man, greater than all others. He said, "I will go talk to the mountains. I will go talk to this great law, the mountains. I will break the law down, or see if it will not break down, that the people may live and pass to the sunset."

Coyote's sons were five brothers. They went,

and two of the sons talked to the five mountains, the law.
The mountains were made to move up and down, dance
and shake, but nothing more. The five brothers were
killed the same as the others. The five laws in the five
mountains still stood. None could pass them to the
sunset.

Coyote's sons, the five brothers, had not told
their father what they were going to do. Coyote had
instructed them never to go away from home to stay
overnight, and when they did not return, he knew that
they were dead, killed by Thunderbird. The old man
knew all. He was wiser than his sons, wiser than all
others. He had been told from *Wha-me-pom-mete* [land
above]. The Great Man above had instructed him in
wisdom. After his sons, the five brothers, had been gone
five nights, Coyote said, "I know that my sons are all
dead. The Animal has killed them. Thunderbird has
killed them with his five laws, the five mountains."[46]

After five days and five nights had passed,
Coyote cried. He cried long, wailing among the mountains and caverned rocks. He went to a lonely place and
cried. He rolled on the ground lamenting, for he was sad
and miserable. His heart was poor, heavy and lonely.
He prayed to the Great Man for strength to save his five
sons, strength to bring them back to life. Coyote cried
and prayed. After he had cried and prayed for a time,
the answer came, "You cannot break this great law of the
Animal. You cannot go over the five mountains, the five
laws. The law stands there as made by the Animal, by
Thunderbird."

But Coyote continued praying, rolling on the
ground in a lonely place in the mountains. He was far
away from everyone. Then he was told, "The only way
you can do is to go up to *Wha-me-pom-mete*. It will
take you five days and five nights to go. There you will
be instructed how you may get your five sons back to

life."

Coyote heard and went up, went up for five days and five nights into *Wha-me-pom-mete*. There he told about his troubles. He said to the Great Man, "You are wise. You know of the great Animal who has made the five mountains, the five laws. None can pass over them; none can go to the sunset. My five sons are killed. I wish you to give me a law, the strongest kind of law, so I can whip [best?] the Animal that the people may live."

The Great Man answered Coyote, "Yes! I know the five mountains. I know the mountains, the five laws. I know that people coming from the sunrise are not to pass over the five mountains. They must not see the Animal, Thunderbird, who lives at the sunset. He must not be seen by anybody." This was told Coyote by the Great Man who lives in the land above.

The Great Man said, "Yes! You know yourself. You are a strong man. You are almost as strong as I am. You ask how to kill Thunderbird. I will tell you. We will kill him; I will help you. I made the earth; I made all the Animals. Some I made greater than others. Thunderbird is the strongest, was made the strongest. I will help you. I will blind the eyes of Thunderbird. Then you can go over the five mountains, the five laws, and kill him."

Coyote answered, "*Ay-ow* [All right!] I wish you would help me."

The Great Man said to Coyote, "Do you know on earth a great bird called Eagle (*Why-am-mah*)? Do you know his sons and daughters, his children? When you go back to earth, find Eagle. He has law, has powerful strength. Find his son, his youngest son. Pull a feather from under his wing, a small feather and downy. This feather has strength, has power running out from the heart. It is strong of the heart, because it grows near the heart."

Coyote heard, and he turned back toward the earth. For five days and five nights he came and landed on earth. He knew where Eagle lived, where his five children lived. The Great Man said, "You go to Eagle. Tell him about me, how I have given you strength to come to him. Ask for his youngest son's feather. Ask for the feather light and downy, the feather growing next to his youngest son's heart."

Coyote went to Eagle, told him all that the Great Man had said. Then he asked, "Can you give me the feather from your youngest son? Can you give me the feather growing next to his heart? All the people are being killed by Thunderbird."

Eagle made answer, "If the Great Man sent you to me, I will help you. If he told you to come to me, then I will give you my strength, my power to fight Thunderbird."

So Eagle picked this feather[47] from his youngest son, where it grew under the wing next to his heart. Coyote was to be turned to a feather, small and so fine that it could not be seen going through the air. Such a feather goes too fast. The Great Man (had) said, "Ask Eagle for his strength, for great power to help you. I will help you. If you go ten days and ten nights without drink, without food, you will be changed to a feather. You can then go anywhere."

So Coyote went hungry for ten days and ten nights, no food, no water. He was then turned to a feather like the one given him by Eagle. He flew through the air towards the five mountains, but he remained a great distance away. Coyote was instructed to create a noise like Thunder (*Enum-klah*), rolling far away, as he passed through the air. This he did for the first time, rumbling and low, off towards the sunrise. The second and third time, he made a slow, deep noise in the distance. Thunderbird heard and said, "How is this? I alone was given the power to make that noise from sun to sun. This noise I now hear must be given from *Wha-me-pom-mete*. I am dead! I am dead! I am dead!"

The fourth time, Coyote made the noise louder and closer to Thunderbird. Thunderbird became angry. He said, "I will kill whatever this is that is coming close to me." Thunderbird then made a mighty noise, a greater thunder in answer to Coyote. Coyote went into the air, higher and higher, darting and whirling so rapidly as not to be seen. Then Thunderbird was afraid! Scared! He felt sure of death. He sought the deep water, to hide there. He heard Coyote far above him. He knew that if one more noise, the fifth thunder came, he would be dead. Coyote prayed again to the powers of *Wha-me-pom-mete* to help him one more time, to help him kill Thunderbird that the people might live, that his five sons might come back to life. The Great Man of *Wha-me-pom-mete* heard Coyote and helped him.

Thunderbird shrank deeper in the water, scared! Coyote, above him and invisible, now brought a greater noise than ever, a crash like the bursting of this world. The five laws, the five mountains, crumbled and fell. The fragments, floating down the *n-Che-wana*, created the many islands along its course. The giant body of Thunderbird formed the great Bridge across the *wana* at the Cascades. This Bridge was of the first mountain and was mostly stone. It stood for many hundreds of snows, no one knows how long, and then it fell. The Indians said that in time it would fall, and it did. Some of my ancestors, old people, saw and passed under that Bridge. I do not know the number of snows since that time, but they are many. It was the law, the rule, that when the canoes journeyed through that water-way, no Indian was to look up. None must see the Bridge, must not look up at the rocks of the bridge.[48] After killing the law made by Thunderbird, after breaking down the five mountains, Coyote said to Thunderbird, "The people are coming, lots of people. A second people, the Indians are coming. You shall not kill them as you have killed the present people. Once in a while you may produce a great noise, make the earth tremble, and the people will be afraid. You can strike the trees and high places, but you can never be great as you were." The five sons of Coyote and all the people killed by Thunderbird came back to life.

When I was a little girl, this story was told me by my father, who heard it from his father, who heard it from his father, and perhaps still farther back. I do not know, but some of them saw the Bridge, passed under it in canoes. I was not to tell all the story, not even to my own children. But I have told it to you, and it is true. There is no more to tell.[49]

7. THE STAR ROCK OF THE TUMWATER[50],[51]

Schoc-o-les tom (supreme power--deity) sent Coyote to the sundown to see about the fish, to see why fish did not come up the *Che-wana* [river/Columbia River]. He sent his son, *Schoc-o-les tom-e-yah-kon*, to see about the buffalo at the sunrise. All buffalo were in one tepee at the sunrise; they could not get out. No people were there, but buffalo were there. When the big time came, when the people got life, they would fill that tepee. They would eat there. They would keep the buffalo there for themselves. Nobody else could get in that tepee. Every snow it would be that way. *Schoc-o-les tom-e-yah-kon* tore down that tepee, let the buffalo go free for all the people.

Coyote came this way towards the sunrise. He found the Wascos and Wishoms having trouble. The Wascos had a rock, all diamonds and silver, big! A great rock was lying there on the shore-rocks of the *Chewana*. The Wishom Indians went in at night and tore that rock away. They brought it to the Wishom side of *wana* (river). When they tore that rock away, silver and diamonds were all over their hands. They rubbed their hands on a dog. That is how the silver fox came.

The Wasco Indians talked every night about that rock, about the trouble. They said, "What has become of that rock?" The Wascos said "Who has done this? We do not know! That rock was ours! Have the Wishoms torn it away? Have they taken it from us in the night?" The Wascos talked, made laws every night. Every night they made laws about that rock, how to get it back.

One Wasco married a Wishom girl.[52] He stayed with the Wishoms a long time. He found they had that rock. The Wishoms told him about it. The Wasco went back to his father, to his mother. He said, "The Wishoms have that nice thing. I saw it myself, that stone of light and fire. It is there. The Wishoms are hiding it from us."

The Wascos talked and talked! Finally they said, "We are going to fight for that stone, for that light!"

But another Wasco said, "No! Make the Wishoms pay! Make them give us slaves or something for that stone of light. If they do not pay, then we will fight afterwards."

The *Chi-nach* (married) man said, "I saw the Wishoms have a nice thing, too. It is a star of the water. In the night they have a star. It shines all over, everywhere. It makes light overhead and in the water. That star makes light the light, breaks the darkness. We will go tear it away, as the Wishoms tore away our stone."

The chief said, "All right! We will go!"

In the middle of the night the Wascos went. A thousand men went to the Wishom side of the *Che-wana*. They found the star-rock, a big rock in the water. All nice and shiny, it was there. They took it, that rock, across the *wana* (river) to the Wasco side. They took it to the Wasco place. The Wishoms and Wascos fought about it. Many suns they fought. It was bad fighting on both sides.

Then came Coyote. He made them stop fighting. That was silver and gold for which they were fighting. The Wascos had silver; the Wishoms had gold. That was why they fought. They did not know that it was money, did not know that it was same as money. Coyote stopped that fight. He stopped the fighting of the Wascos and the Wishoms.

Then, after this time *Schoc-o-les tom* made his son, *Schoc-o-les tom-e-yah-kon*, to come to the Wasco-Wishom place. He said to Coyote, "Where are you from?"

Coyote answered, "*Schoc-o-les tom* sent me where the fish were held at the sundown, all shut up! They could not get away. I found it, the trouble. I tore out the dam. Fish will now be for all the Indians, for all people. It will be free food for everyone."

Coyote then said, "Where are you from?" *Schoc-o-les tom-e-yah-kon* made answer, "*Schoc-o-les tom* sent me to the sunrise where the buffalos were shut up in a great tepee. They could not get out. I found it! I tore that tepee away. Buffalo are now everywhere, for everybody, food and skins. That was my work."

Schoc-o-les tom-e-yah-kon then said to Coyote, "Who is the first man? You or me?"

He said that. Coyote answered, "I am the first man!"

Schoc-o-les tom-e-yah-kon again spoke, "What

is your name?"

Coyote told him, "I have no name." Coyote made a mistake when he said, "I have no name!"

Coyote said, "What is your name?"

The man answered, "*Schoc-o-les tom-e-yah-kon!* What do you think! Who is the first man? You or me?"

Coyote again answered, "I am the first man."

They talked a long time about who was the first man. *Schoc-o-les tom-e-yah-kon* finally said, "Well, my friend! We are pretty closely tied about the first man. You'd like to be the first man; I'd like to be the first man. You see two mountains, *She-ko-un* (Mount Hood) and *Pot-to* (Mount Adams). You see these mountains standing where the sun rises. I will give you my shovel. If you move those mountains to the sundown, then I am satisfied. You will be the first man, if you move them to the sundown. If you cannot do this, then I am the first man."

Coyote heard these words of his friend. He said, "If I cannot move these two mountains to the sundown, then you are the first man. All right! Where is your shovel?"

Schoc-o-les tom-e-yah-kon took one eagle feather, one feather from his wing, and said, "Here is the shovel!"

Coyote took the feather. He stood up, commenced talking about spirit-power. He talked, sang a spirit song. Then Coyote shot that feather off towards the mountain. Mount Hood shook, trembled, but did not move. Five times Coyote shot the feather! Five times the mountain shook but did not move. Mount Hood still stood there where the sun comes up. Then Coyote shot the feather at Mount Adams. Mount Adams shook, trembled as did Mount Hood, but did not move. Five times Coyote shot the eagle feather! Five times the mountain shook but did not move. Mount Adams still stood where the sun comes up. Coyote now said, "I give up! You try! If you move the mountains, then you are the first man!"

Coyote's friend made answer. "All right!" *Schoc-o-les tom-e-yah-kon* now took the one eagle feather. He prayed to *Schoc-o-les tom* to help him move the mountains. Then he pointed the feather at Mount Hood. Pointing the feather, he turned slowly round to the sunset. That mountain moved with the feather. Mount Hood moved to where he now stands, in the sunset. Then he did the same to Mount Adams, which moved to where he stands today, far from the sunrise. *Schoc-o-les tom-e-yah-kon* then said, "I am the first man!"

Coyote made answer, "Yes, you are the first man!"

Schoc-o-les tom-e-yah-kon said to Coyote, "My friend, this we have done with the buffalo, with the fish. These are now free. None are to sell; none need to pay. You go eat fish without paying, the same way with buffalo. Any man can kill buffalo; all can eat without paying, make tepees, rawhides, robes, clothing from the skins; all is free! All can eat fish of all kinds, salmon and eels; all free. All can sleep there on buffalo robes. None are to pay."

Coyote said, "All right! We have done this work for the people who are to come. The laws are good."

This was the law made long ago, made for all Indians - Wasco, Wishom, Klickitat, Yakima. All tribes obey that law. But other people came to where the sun comes up! They have made different laws. Everything now is to pay. White man's law, Indian law are different. One is pay! Pay! Pay all the time; pay for everything. The other law says there is nothing to pay for what *Schoc-o-les tom* created for all.

I have told you how the Wascos and Wishoms

fought. It was silver and gold, but they did not know. They did not know that it was money, but they fought for it. This is Indian history. Old folks tell about this, told from long ago. I did not see this myself, those nice things. I did not see the stone rubbed on the dog-fox, the star rock in the water. If it is there today, I could show it to you. I do not know if it is there somewhere.

Coyote brought the fish and stopped the Wasco-Wishom fight.[53] They jumped Chinook salmon. They jumped dog-salmon. They jumped! They jumped! They jumped! I can show you there, their tracks.[54]

8A. COYOTE'S BIG MISTAKE[55]

It was nearer the beginning, before man came to this earth, that there lived a great Coyote Chief. He was ruler of all the land, ruler of everything that lived. He thought himself the bravest, the wisest of all, and that everything was afraid of him. This big Coyote Chief had one daughter whom he loved above everything. It made no difference that the young men were in love with her. Coyote would not let her marry, would not let her leave him. One sun, this daughter grew sick and died. It was the custom of that time that when anyone died to let them lie for five suns, then step over the body five times, when they would return to life. So when his daughter died, Coyote thought to wait five suns when life would be restored, and she would be with him as before.

Now this old Coyote Chief used to fall asleep, at which time he would die and sleep for five suns, talking with his spirit-powers, communicating with his secret *tah*. This he did when his daughter died, awaking on the fifth sun. While thus sleeping, he saw that which was in the future snows, events to come with the dawning suns. He called the people together, telling them of his message. He said, "A new people are coming. Strange and different from us, they will be a higher race. The earth is to be changed and made better."

But on this fifth day, Coyote's daughter did not get up. The old chief then knew that something was wrong, that his daughter was dead beyond life. He went to the mountains, crying, calling to his daughter. He sought lonely places, rolling on the ground in grief. Among the cliffs and dark woods, he wailed in agony. For five suns Coyote did nothing but cry and call to his daughter. Then on this fifth sun, he heard her voice calling him, telling him to come up to the highest mountain, to the top where she would talk with him.

Coyote was now glad. He climbed to where his daughter had directed, high and solitary. There she met him and told him not to cry for her. She said, "I am in a good place; I am not dead. There is no trouble where I am, no distress of any kind. It is a fine country, always light with no darkness. The spirit life is best. Do not cry. It hurts me."

But Coyote was lonely. He asked his daughter to return to earth and be with him again. He had been sad since she left him. Finally she told him that if he would do as directed, she would come back and be with him always. Coyote promised, for he was glad that his daughter would never again leave him.

She then gave him a pack, telling him that it contained Life. She said, "You must carry this on your back to the valley where you live. There you can untie it, and all those who have died will return to life and live forever. You must not look back on the trail. No difference what you may hear, what sounds come to you, you must keep going and not turn or look back." Coyote took the bundle and promised his daughter that he would not look back nor stop until he reached home. If he heard anything, if strange and mysterious sounds or any kind of noise followed him, he would pay no attention but keep going. Nothing could stop him or make him look back over the trail.

With the pack, Coyote started for the valley where he lived. His heart was light, for now his daughter would be with him always. But as he walked, the pack grew heavier and ever more heavy. He drew near his home, traveling down into the valley. He heard strange murmurings back of him, coming with the air. He did not stop, did not look around. He hurried for he was nearly home. Only a short distance more, when he would be at the doorway of his lodge.

Back on the trail, Coyote now heard the musical murmur growing. Louder, still louder it came. Voices were in that pack, now laughing, talking, singing. Heavier grew the pack, and Coyote was becoming very tired. But he did not stop; he did not look backwards over the trail. The strange noise-sounds were taking form. *Eh*! That was his daughter's voice! She was singing as in other suns. Staggering under his load, Coyote stopped, listening. He turned and looked around everywhere. He could see nothing, could only hear his daughter's song among the many other voices.

Lonely to see his daughter, Coyote stood considering what to do. Why should he continue any farther? Why not see what was in the pack. Why was it becoming so heavy? He thought to let everything out of the bundle. He was so near home. Tired and not wanting to wait longer to see his daughter, the old Coyote Chief untied the pack. Loosening it, he beheld the people long dead. He saw grass growing from cadaverous eyes, ears, nostrils and mouth. The dead were all about him! He saw his daughter who looked at him pityingly.

She said, "Oh, you made a big mistake. I told

you not to stop, not to look back, but carry the pack home. You made a big mistake! These people will now go back to their graves. Had you not opened the pack, had you done as I told you, they would all have come back to life. They would have lived forever. This earth would have seen no more dying. But now, the new people who are coming, as you saw in a sleep-vision, will die as have the first, the older kinds of people. You made a big mistake! I am going now. Good-bye!"

With this, the dead people all vanished, returning to their graves. Saddened by what he had done, poor Coyote cried, cried, cried! He would see his daughter no more in life.

8B. ORIGIN OF DEATH[56]

Eagle helped Coyote get his wife in this way. Eagle knew where the dead stay. They went down the Columbia River to find this place. Coyote saw a boat. He called very loud to the man, "Bring your boat here."

Eagle knew that the man was a shade who took the drowned in his boat. The man would not come to shore. Eagle did not like the way Coyote called. He took him under his wing and jumped over to the boat. Then they were ferried across. They saw a smoke on this island.

Eagle said, "Let us go to that house." They saw two old people living there.

Eagle asked, "Why do you live here?"
"Our children all died, so we live here. At night they come here."

"Where are the dead?"
"Way over there where a big frog looks after

them. He lives in a big house. He swallows the moon. The souls lie there and only rise when it is pitch dark."

They told them [Coyote and Eagle] to kill the big frog. "People tell the frog when it is time to swallow the moon. She makes five leaps to reach the moon. She puts the moon in her stomach. Then the dead wake and have a good time."

Coyote saw this; he stayed in the corner of the house during the day. He heard his wife having a good time. He was jealous and wanted to jump out to catch the man with his wife. But Eagle held him. In the morning the frog spat the moon out; it was daylight.

The old folks said, "The only way is to kill the frog and use his body to act as he does. That is the only way to get the soul."

"All right," Eagle said. "We will have to make a box." Eagle made the box. They killed the frog and skinned her. Coyote put on the skin. They told him to make five jumps. He practiced.

At night he slept there in his disguise. Two men said, "Frog, make your jump." He jumped, but not quite far enough.

Some of the dead suspected. They disputed among themselves whether it was Frog. Again he jumped, but not far enough. By the fifth jump most of them were sure it was not Frog. Coyote caught the moon and tried to swallow it, but it stuck out of his mouth a little. They thought it was Coyote. He put his hand over his mouth to cover the moon.

The dead came into the house until it was completely filled. Coyote heard his wife. Eagle called, "Let the moon go." He was at the door holding his box over the opening. Coyote spat the moon out. Then, when it was light they all left the house but they [the dead] were caught in the box.

These two told the old people that they had all

the souls. They shouted to the man in the boat, but again he would not come ashore. Eagle took Coyote under his wing and jumped to the boat. They went across.

Eagle carried the box. They travelled up the river. When nearly home, Coyote heard the people talking in the box. He asked Eagle to let him carry it. He said, "You are a great man and yet you carry it. I am only common; let me take it." Eagle resisted, but finally gave it to him.

Coyote was curious to look into the box. He told Eagle to go ahead of him. Eagle said he would wait, but Coyote insisted. Eagle suspected that Coyote would destroy the people in there. He went on. Coyote opened the box, slowly, but the powerful spirits came right out, and went back where they had been brought from. Coyote tried to close the box, but he could keep only one crippled man in it.

Eagle knew at once what the other had done. Coyote carried the box on and gave it to Eagle. Eagle said, "I do not want it now." He let the cripple go.

He said, "If I had brought it here and opened it properly, people would live again in the spring just as the trees do."

9A. COYOTE AND THE TWO SISTERS
OF THE *N-CHE-WANA*[57]

Salmon and all fish were held from the people. Two Sisters had a big dam at the mouth of the *n-Che-wana*. Coyote made his body into a nice piece of *op-cod-id* (alder wood), which is fine wood for fire. It burns good, makes no sparks. This *op-cod-id* was all carved, looking good. The youngest of the two Sisters found the *op-cod-id* floating on the *n-Che-wana* when they were out in a canoe catching wood. She said, "Look! See the nice wood! We will take it to burn."

But the older Sister said, "No! Leave it alone! It is bad wood. Do not take it!"

The Sisters let the wood go. Coyote then went back up the river. He changed his body into a small baby laced on the *skein* (cradleboard). He floated down the *n-Che-wana*, crying. The two Sisters heard him. The youngest Sister said, "Look! There is a nice baby. Maybe its people all drowned. Maybe it is left alone. We will take it, raise it for ourselves." The older sister said nothing. They took the baby, took it to their lodge. They cooked a big salmon for it. The baby ate; it grew fast.

The Sisters went out to dig roots. Coyote took five arrow-wood sticks. For five days he worked hard to tear out the dam, to let fish go up the river. Every night he was a baby, a growing baby on a cradleboard. But in daytime, he was a strong, big man, digging fast with his five arrow-wood sticks at the dam. On the fifth day he finished; the big dam went down. All the fish came up the *n-Che-wana*, Coyote driving them. He changed the two sisters into Chi-col-lah, a small bird.[58] That bird comes up the river ahead of the salmon. Coyote made that rule, that law.

Driving his salmon before him, Coyote came up the *n-Che-wana*, building fish traps as he came. He also did many other things. At [what is now] Vancouver, he found a people without mouths. They took food by smell only -- cooked salmon, deer, bear or anything. They smelled it, then threw it away. Then they took another piece and did it the same way.

Coyote watched these people for a time, watched them eat by smell. Then he took a sharp flint arrowhead from his pack. He stepped up to one of the men sitting, smelling food. He said to him, "What are you doing? What is wrong with you?"

Then Coyote jerked back the man's head. He slashed him across the face with the sharp flint, made a mouth for him.

The man went, "*Wa-a-au-au-u-a!*" Then he found he had a mouth. He jumped! He called, "I got mouth! I got mouth!" Then that man ate salmon, did not throw it away.

Other people wanted mouths. Coyote cut mouths for them. After that the people knew how to cut mouths, knew how to make them good. They did it for each other until all had mouths.

The Chief of these Vancouver people asked Coyote, "What is your name?"

Coyote told him, "I have got no name." The Chief offered Coyote his daughter for a wife. Coyote said, "No, I do not want any wife. I get women when I want. I will go on now. I want to be free."

9B. COYOTE DECEIVES EAGLE, AND STOCKS THE COLUMBIA WITH FISH[60],[61]

Eagle's grandfather was Coyote. Eagle was hunting most of the time in the mountains, and when he came home one day, Coyote said to him, "I have found something for you--a nest of eagles on a rock. They have nice feathers for arrows."

Next day they went out to a rock, and Coyote said, "Take off your clothes." Eagle was handsomely dressed in beads, had long shells all over his leggings and robe. He took off his clothes and went up the rock.

He pulled the feathers out, tied them in a bundle, put the bundle on his back, then looked down and saw that he was very high up; the rock had gone up nearly to the sky. Then he looked at the feathers on his back. They were not eagle feathers at all, but coyote entrails.

Coyote had already put on Eagle's clothes, made himself look like Eagle, and gone home. He had Eagle's flute, and played on it. When he entered the house, he said, "I wonder why my grandfather does not come. I told him to come quickly." At bedtime Coyote lay between two of Eagle's wives, Mouse and Woodpecker. Next morning Coyote moved away to another place, said nothing more about his grandfather. Every day he moved his camp.

Eagle spent many days on the high rock, and grew thin. At last old Thunder came and split the rock; along the split came brush and sticks. By means of these Eagle came to the ground. Then he followed his grandfather [sic].

Two of the wives had not gone with Coyote. They knew he was not Eagle, but they followed on behind. One of these two wives cried all the time, "My husband, my husband!"

Every day Eagle found the ashes of a camp. One day he found the ashes warm, and said "Tomorrow I'll catch up with them."

Next day he overtook the two wives, and they told him everything. He said, "Go tonight and camp with Coyote. I shall be there." He came. Old Coyote saw him, and began to cry, took off his clothes.

Eagle said, "I don't want them now."

Coyote said, "I have been crying all the time. I thought you were dead."

Eagle said, "All right! Keep my clothes and keep my two wives." The old man was very glad. They lived together many days, and Eagle hunted.

One day he said to Coyote, "I killed two nice bucks. Tomorrow I'll show you where they are." Next day they started, went down five gulches, and saw the bucks.

The old man said, "I'll stay here tonight; tomorrow I'll cut up the meat." He made a fire and lay down to sleep. It began to rain, rained all night.

Next morning the old man woke up and found that his bucks were nothing but hanging bushes. He said, "I see! I did this. This is my fault. My grandson has paid me back." He did not feel badly, and started home. He passed the first gulch, full of deep roaring water. He swam way down to the next one--the water was still higher there; came to the third, the fourth; there always more water. The fifth he could not cross.

He was carried down to the great ocean. There he saw two women with a large canoe. They were very bright, shone more brightly than the sun. Their paddles were of white wood, very beautiful. The women stayed there, and kept the fish from leaving the sea and going into the river. They worked there every day.

Coyote thought to himself, "How can I manage so that these women will take me into their canoe?" He turned himself into a piece of wood and floated down.

The elder woman said, "Oh, that is very nice wood; catch it, catch it!"

But the younger one said, "Don't touch it, don't touch it!" and they let it pass.

Now he turned himself into beautiful white wood, and floated along. The elder sister said, "Oh, catch that!"

The younger one said, "No, no! Let it pass." It passed. He turned into a different kind of wood.

Every time the elder one wanted to catch it; but the younger one said, "No, let it pass."

After the fourth time he turned himself into a little baby on a cradle-board. As it floated down, crying and rolling on the water, the elder sister said, "See that little boy! Catch it, catch it! Its father and mother must be dead. We must save the baby."

The younger sister had grown tired of talking. The elder sister took the baby and carried it to their house. They had all kinds of fish. The elder sister put an eel's tail in the baby's mouth for it to suck. They went for wood, and left the baby. While they were gone, Coyote cooked himself all kinds of fish, ate a great deal. When they came home, he was a baby again, sucking the eel's tail.

Next day, while the sisters were gone, he made a long stick to dig roots. When they got home, he was a baby sucking the eel's tail.

Next day, when they went off, he went out to dig roots. He told his stick to be strong; but when he dug into the ground, it broke. The next day he made another stick, dug deeper. With the last stick he broke down the dam the sisters had made to keep the fish, and all the salmon crowded up the Columbia River. Then Coyote took ashes and blew on the sisters, saying, "Hereafter you will be birds. People will soon come who will want these salmon. You will be birds henceforth."[62]

10. CHIPMUNK'S STRIPES[63]

A cannibal woman grabbed at Chipmunk. Her fingers scratched the marks on his back.

11. RACCOON[64]

Raccoon and his grandmother had five potholes filled with acorns in the rocks near the Columbia. She gave him only one and a half acorns to eat. He stole the contents of all five holes, defecating in them instead. He hid under the ashes. She took a stick and struck him across the back and tail, making the marks that raccoons have today.

He made five big balls of berries with thorns sticking out all over. He fed them to his grandmother. He brought water to her, using her basket hat. But he first punched a hole in the bottom, so that she got very little. She began to sprout wings and finally flew off to perch as a rock that is there now. Raccoon, grieving, sat down and rubbed his buttocks along the rocks. These marks can still be seen.

Warm Springs sweat house. Oregon Historical Society, Neg. OrHi 36815.

Tots-Homi, Warm Springs Indian. Oregon
Historical Society, Neg. OrHi 36844.

II. TALES OF THE LEGENDARY

12. PANTHER AND WILDCAT FIGHT
WITH THE GRIZZLIES[65]

Panther and Wildcat lived together about two miles and a half below The Dalles, in Oregon. Wildcat stayed at home, kept house all the time. When Wildcat grew large enough to hunt, he killed rabbits with bow and arrow not far from home.

One summer Panther brought in a buck shin-bone, hung it up, and said to Wildcat, "No matter how hungry you may be, don't eat that shin-bone."

"All right," said Wildcat.

Panther was out late one day hunting. Wildcat was lying down hungry at home, looked, and saw the shin-bone. He took it down, and, placing it across one stave, struck it with another. The bone broke, the marrow flew out and quenched the fire, and there was no more fire near.

Wildcat looked, and saw a fire on the other side of the Columbia River, but could not find a boat. Then he swam across and found a house, went in, and found two old blind sisters, who had each five large fire-brands which they kept counting over and over.[66]

Wildcat took one of them. The first sister found only four, and accused her sister of stealing.

"Oh, no!" said the other.

Wildcat put back the brand. She counted again, found the number to be right, and said, "O sister! I was mistaken. All is right."

Wildcat laughed. Then he tried the sister on the left hand in the same way, with the same result. Wildcat laughed to himself.

He went out and got some cedar, and tied it up in bundles the same size as the fire-brands, set them afire, and substituted them. He took two fire-brands, and, going up the river to a large stone at the bank, tied them upright to his ears, so that they stood up like asses' ears, swam across, and took them home.

When two-thirds of the way across, the ears got hot; when almost there, he could hardly stand it; and when he had reached the bank, he hurled the brands away and washed his ears. Then he picked up the fire again, and went home and made a new fire.

On the instant that he was starting the fire, Panther was drawing his arrow on a deer; the bow broke, and blood streamed. Panther knew at once that something was wrong at home. He thought Wildcat had been at work. He returned home and asked, "What have you been doing?"

"The fire went out."

"Where did you get it?"

"From the old women across the river."

"They will attack us now," said Panther. "Get our *aksku'tcian*."[67]

Wildcat got it, and they sharpened it very sharp. They cut a tree with four blows, then three, then two, then one. Then, by showing it, a great cottonwood-tree fell.

Panther now stripped, painted himself yellow, red, and black. Wildcat had the *aksku'tcian*. Panther had only his breech-clout, and was going to fight with his hands.

Presently they heard the cry, "*Hoig, hoig, hoig!*" The ground trembled, a great storm was rising, hail and rain then followed. This was old Grizzly, who said, "Who has stolen our fire?" He called out five times, "Who is it that has stolen our fire?" And every time he cried out, the storm would come heavier and heavier.

Now old Grizzly came to the house, smashed one end of it in, and Panther and Grizzly clinched.

Panther said to Wildcat, "Brother, hit him with your weapon."

Bear would say, "Here, what are you doing?" and Wildcat would get afraid and run up the smoke-hole.

But Panther would say, "Come and strike him with your weapon;" and Wildcat would come down again and be about to strike, when the Bear would call out to him gruffly, and he would run away again frightened.

At last Panther said, "Strike, my strength is giving out." Then Wildcat struck and cut off the hind legs of the Bear. He died, and they threw him out and covered him up.

Now the second Grizzly came with a greater noise and a heavier storm. And wherever the hail would hit Wildcat when he came to the door to look out, it would cut right into him. That is the reason his head is all covered with black spots. The second came striking the ground, and pushed in the end of the house and roared the while.

Now Wildcat was not frightened so much this time. When the Bear came in and he was called on, he would come down. Panther and Bear began to fight. Then Panther called on Wildcat, and he came and cut off the Bear's hind legs and threw him out.

Now the third [Grizzly] came with rain, hail, and wind. (The three Bears were as white as snow.) The earth shook with the storm he brought. They had just got their house up again. When the third Bear came and nearly threw it over, only the part was left where Wildcat was. Panther wrestled with the third Bear, and was thrown and nearly killed. Then he called on Wildcat, "Come, brother, I'm nearly gone." Wildcat cut off the Bear's hind legs and killed him.

The fourth Bear came with the noise of thunder and with lightning, and the wind blew so that it carried great rocks with it. Panther was thrown four times now, and Wildcat waited and watched to be called on. At last Panther screamed out, "Come down, I'm nearly killed."

Wildcat jumped down quickly, but the Bear roared out so terribly that it scared him, and he went back again. He came down three times. Each time the Bear would turn on him and throw up dust and roar so, that he ran back. At last he got down and cut off Bear's hind legs, and the Bear died.

Now the fifth Bear came. The earth trembled as he came with thunder, lightning, hail and rain; and he threw the house to the ground. Now the Bear began to fight with Panther, fought terribly. At last they went up into the air, fighting out of sight, and great pieces of flesh would fall, piece after piece. Panther was white, Bear rather dark.

Now Wildcat built a fire and burned the flesh of Bear, but saved that of Panther. About sundown Wildcat saw them coming down little by little, still clinched in a death struggle, nothing but bones with the heart of each one hanging on to him. All the flesh and intestines were gone. Now as they came to the ground, Bear was at the bottom. Wildcat burned Bear's body and heart, and put Panther in the water.[68]

Now five days and nights passed, and Wildcat was very lonesome. On the sixth morning Panther called out, "Brother, are you awake?"

Wildcat sprang up quickly -- he was so glad that Panther was alive again. He built a fire without delay, and cooked for Panther.

When he had eaten, Panther moved the house and took the dead bodies of the five Bears, threw them across the river, and turned them into great rocks. These rocks are there to this day. The fifth was burned.

(These rocks are called the great bears and the wolves. On each of these four rocks there is a hollow top. In early days the Indians would send their children to sleep on these, one night on each rock, till they had slept on all four, in order that they might receive strength from the spirit of the rocks.)

After Panther had done this, he said, "We must separate here and take our second form. What help will you be to people?"

Wildcat said, "I shall live near the river. And if any young man will obey me, I will make him a great hunter."

Panther said, "I'll go to the Cascade Range. And if any young man will obey my word, I shall make him a great warrior and a great hunter."

13. THE DEAD CANOEMAN OF
THE *N-CHE-WANA*[69]

It was in the early times, in the days of the Animal People, and near [what is now] Lyle [Washington]. A man and wife were in a canoe on the *n-Che-wana*. The man became sleepy. He said to his wife, "Let me sleep on your lap. Do not be afraid if you see anything."

The woman let her husband lie across her lap. He went to sleep; he was [appearing] dead. Soon worms began creeping from his shoulders, falling on her lap. Then the woman knew that her husband was dead. She pushed him from her lap. This brought the man from sleep [death]. He said, "Why did you do this? Why did you throw me from your lap?"

The woman made reply, "You were dead! I was afraid!"

Then the man placed his wife on an eagle feather and threw her to a cave in a smooth cliff along the *n-Che-wana*. The woman is still there, turned into stone.

14. WASCO[70]

Wasco was a spring about the size of a common drinking dipper.[71] A round hole was in the rock; cold water came for everybody. It was there at Wasco, Oregon, about twenty steps from the *n-Che-wana*; I saw that spring. Cold water was for everyone, fine water, good!

Near this Wasco, this spring,[72] about six feet away, was a small hole in the rock. A little water was there. Deep, that hole was deep! A rope let down sixty feet found no bottom. That hole was big *tahmahnawis* medicine. You went there with the sky all clear, sunshine everywhere, all nice and clear. If you put a stick in that hole, the clouds came. It rained, made rain on a hot day, made rain any time. If you took the stick out, the clouds quit. The sun shone, all clear. This was at Wasco.

About thirty steps, maybe forty steps below the spring, below the deep hole in the rock, you saw a boulder, a round rock. One time a mean boy, a mean, mean boy who fought, who did bad things, came one evening to this rock. He pressed his fingernail into it, kept pressing hard. That rock fastened to the nail, tore it off. That nail is seen there now, sticking in the rock. That boy was a mean fighting boy.

The old folks showed that fingernail to boys and girls, showed it to their own children. They told them not to be mean, not to be like that bad boy, but to mind what was told them. This is why Indians have good children. They make them mind instruction.

15A. BATTLE OF THE *AT-TE-YI-YI* AND *TO-QEE-NUT*[73]

In that day the Wolves (*Lal-a-wish*) were five brothers. They talked against *To-qee-nut*, Chief of the Salmon, Chief of all Fishes. The Chinook Salmon (*Qee-nut*) talked against the Wolves. The Wolves prepared to fight the Salmon. Coyote (*Speel-yi*) was a great Chief. He said, "I cannot stop the people from fighting, but I will be there too. I will fight for the Wolves." So the news went to all the people that the Wolves would fight against the Salmon people, fight the Chinook people.

There came the *At-te-yi-yi*, the five brothers, the icy, the strong cold Northeast Winds before whom none could stand.[74] These five brothers said, "All right! We will be there to fight for the Wolves."

So they got together, the five Wolves and the five Wind Brothers. They talked this way, "What will we do with the Salmon?"

The Wind Brothers said, "We think this way. We will wrestle with the Salmon. If we throw him down, ice will be all over the *n-Che-wana*. Ice and cold will be over all the water, cold everywhere."

The Wolves said, "All right! When you throw him down, we will fight and kill all his children. None will be left."

They sent word to the Salmon, "You come! Bring all your children and have a big time on the ice of the *n-Che-wana*. Bring all your people."

To-qee-nut, the Salmon Chief, said, "I cannot help this, my people. I cannot refuse this fight. We will all go, my people. We will all go to meet this boaster."

So all the people went, lined up on each side to fight or wrestle. The Wolves spoke, "All ready for the big trial of strength? *To-qee-nut*, you wrestle with oldest Wind Brother. Wrestle with him first."

To-qee-nut went to wrestle with the oldest Wind, who was not strong, *To-qee-nut* said to his wife and children, "I am afraid! I am afraid of the Winds. Be careful! If you see they are going to beat us, you run away. Run quick and hide."

Both sides were looking on, watching to see the great wrestling match. The Wolves called, "Now ready! Now go!"

The big man of the Salmon and the oldest brother of the Wind, both stripped for wrestling, walked out on the ice, out on the *n-Che-wana*, all covered with ice. The Wind could stand on the ice, but *To-qee-nut* could not stand. They went out a short distance, out on the ice. All the people were looking at the big men wrestling. *To-qee-nut* threw Wind down. Always the oldest brother was not strong. *To-qee-nut* threw Wind down, and from the Salmon side came the victory cry, "*Ow-ow-ow-ow-ow-ow-ow-ow-o-oo*!" The Wind Brothers said nothing. They could not say anything. They kept still.

Then the second Wind Brother stepped out on the ice to wrestle with *To-qee-nut*. He was a little stronger than his older brother, but *To-qee-nut* threw him. Then his people again set up the long shout of triumph. The Wind Brothers kept still. They could not say anything. But all the time *To-qee-nut* kept thinking,

"I will die! I will die! They are five against one. They are too many for me. I will die! The Wind Brothers are too strong for me."

Then the third Wind Brother stepped forth to wrestle with *To-qee-nut*. He was a little stronger than either of the older brothers. He stood strong on the ice and threw *To-qee-nut* down hard, threw him quickly. He was dragged and killed on the shore of the frozen *n-Che-wana*. The Wind Brothers yelled, "*Ow-ow-ow-ow-ow-ow-ow-ow-o-oo!*"

Then the five Wolves ran against all the young Salmon, all the young children. There were lots of Wolves, Coyotes and Foxes. All fought the Salmon people. They had first killed the Chief, *To-qee-nut*, then his wife. She had lots of Salmon eggs, eggs in her belly. They threw her down, burst her open. The eggs spilled out. It was on a flat rock; the eggs were scattered all about.

All the Salmon people were killed, children and all. The Wind Brothers and all the people on their side now set up [yelled], "*Ow-ow-ow-ow-ow-ow-ow-ow-o-oo!* The *Qee-nut* are no more! We will now all the time have it cold. Ice will be all over the *n-Che-wana*, cold all the time, ice."

All the Wind side yelled that it would be cold, not warm. Coyote thought, "I did wrong helping the Wolves. They killed a good man, a good people."

The Wolves called loudly to their people, to their side, "Come! Help kill the eggs on the rocks! We do not want one left to grow."

They came and scattered the eggs, destroyed them. That time Coyote stood away back, far back. Coyote did not help destroy the eggs. He said, "We killed a good man, a good Chief! I am sorry!" He talked that way. Coyote was sorry. He nearly cried.

The Wolves yelled loudly, "We have killed all, killed all the Salmon! We have done a great work! Now it will be cold all the time."

The rock where *To-qee-nut's* wife was killed was cracked deep. The eggs were there, lots of eggs. One egg was deep down. One Wolf called, "One egg, I cannot get it. It is too deep in the rock."

Other Wolves came and tried to lick the egg from the crevice. They licked once, twice, once, twice! They could not get it. They said, "If we don't get it, it will come to life. There will be other Salmon grow up."

The Wolves all tried to lick the egg from the rock, but they failed. All stood with their front feet in the same place, making but two tracks. These tracks can be seen to this day, there in the rock where they stood. It is near the Tumwater, on the Washington side of the *n-Che-wana*, at Wishom.[75] Finally they gave it up. They said, "Let it go. It is dry; it is dead now. It will not grow." They quit. All gave the long, "*Ow-ow-ow-ow-ow-ow-ow-ow-o-oo*!" They had killed all the Salmon, all fishes, and it would now be cold all the time. The five brothers, the Wolves, went to the mountains. They said, "We quit now."

The five Wind Brothers stayed on the *n-Che-wana*, had a cave where they stayed. It was a rock cave at *Wah-pe-us*[76] and was cold, cold and icy. They talked, talked together. "We killed him now! We killed the Salmon! We killed him! His wife and all his children are dead, killed by the Wolves. It will now be cold all the time. It was our work, our big work to do this."

All the Wind people went off the next day, left that place. Clouds came up, came up fast. The clouds grew darker and darker. It rained, rained, and the Spirit which rules helped the one Salmon egg. The egg began to swell. It rained; water went there where the egg was in the split rock. Clouds stayed, and it rained, rained more and more. The egg swelled bigger, still bigger.

The Spirit still helped, helped that egg to come to life. It rained five days and five nights, when a little fish came out from that egg. On the sixth day it went into the river, went with the water from the rock.

The little fish grew. It went down to the mouth of the *n-Che-wana*, near the ocean. At the mouth of the *n-Che-wana*, it found its grandmother, an old woman. From a little Salmon he grew and found his grandmother, found her far down where the *n-Che-wana* enters the ocean.

The grandmother knew from away off, knew from where she was, that her son had been killed by the Wind Brothers, thrown on the ice and killed by the Wolves. She told the little boy, "My son, your father was killed, killed by the Wind Brothers. His wife and all his children were killed, all but you. I knew it before you came. I am glad, glad that you have come, my little grandchild. I am glad you have come back."

The grandmother caressed her little grandchild, talking to him all the time, telling him how glad she was to see him. She knew, knew when the fight was going on, although she was far away and near the sea. The little Salmon boy said, "Tell me how my father was killed. Yes, tell me how I saved myself alone, how I am alive today."

She told him all, knew all and told it to him. Then she worked to make the boy grow, to make him grow fast and strong. She had Indian medicine to rub on him. She made him bathe every morning. It was to make him grow, to make him strong.

She said, "You prepare! Bathe in cold water all winter. Practice! Try your strength, grow strong, and in the spring go fight the Wind Brothers. I am going to fix it, fix five baskets of oil, Salmon oil for your feet to stand strong on the ice.[77] There are five brothers of the Wind against my grandchild. I will help you to stand strong before them."

All winter the boy bathed in cold water, bathed, took hard exercise all winter. When spring came, he was big! Tall! Strong! His grandmother said to him, told him often, "I am glad, my grandchild! I am glad! You will be strong, stronger than my son, your father. You will not fall before the Winds."

Early spring came. The boy went outside the tepee. He looked around, all around. He said to his grandmother, "Now look at me!"

She had a small mat lodge, lived there. She went out to look at him. She watched him to see what he would do. He was big, tall, strong. He went a short distance to a thicket and pulled up small trees, pulled them easily and threw them on the ground. His grandmother was glad, glad that he was so strong. She said, "That is right, my grandchild! You will be strong enough in two moons more."

That is the way the Indians used to be. They did those things to make them strong in the hunt, strong in the battle. The boy twisted trees the size of his arm, twisted them to their roots. He would say, "Look at me! See how strong I am, how I can twist and pull up trees."

The grandmother was pleased. She would watch her grandchild and say, "Yes! You are strong my grandchild. You are now stronger than was your father. You will not fall before the Winds."

These things he did for five days; then he pulled up trees that fifty men could not shake. The grandmother said, "That is right! You will beat those people, the boastful Winds. You will not be thrown, will not be killed by them like your father."

The boy was now stronger than ever. He went outside and said, "Look at me! See what I will now do, my grandmother."

There were big rocks lying around. One was bigger than the others, a great rock like a tepee, like the mat lodges of the people who are gone. He walked to that rock, picked it up. He threw it to the middle of the *n-Che-wana*. He threw it easily; it was not hard for him to throw it.

The old grandmother was glad, glad that her grandchild was so strong. She said, "Oh, my grandchild! You are strong! You are brave! The Winds, the cold, bad people cannot stand before you. You will beat them. You will not fall before them. I will help you; I will give you the five baskets of oil for your feet."

In this way *We-now-y-yi*, the son of *To-qee-nut*, grew up; this way he prepared himself to fight the cold Winds.[78] He said, "I will fix it; I will fix it about this boastful Wind."

The old woman was sorry because her first son had been killed. She cried, but she was now glad that her grandchild was so strong. He would stand and fight the Wind Brothers, stand on the ice at *Weh-pe-us*, on the *n-Che-wana*.

For six moons did *We-now-y-yi* prepare for the battle, for six moons, until salmon would run in the spring. Everyday he practiced at everything: lifting to get strong feet; throwing to get strong arms; running, jumping, to get strong legs; pulling up trees, to get a strong back, strong shoulders. He thought to get a strong mind, strong head. He said to his grandmother, "They cannot beat me! The Winds cannot stand before me. Five days more and I will go fight the five brothers, the Winds. Get ready the five baskets of oil."

The grandmother answered, "Yes, my grandchild, I will fix the five baskets of oil for you, for your feet to stand strong on the ice. You will not fall."

The Winds had a slave woman, a sister to the old grandmother.[79] They watched her closely, would not let her go anywhere. They treated her badly. The Winds had a sister, *Ats-te-yi-yi*, a cripple, a sister to the Chief Wind. Every morning this *Ats-te-yi-yi* would go out, then come and befoul the old slave woman's hair. It was all bad. The grandmother told *We-now-y-yi* all about this, how her sister was nearly starved with no food, no robes. Cold all the time with icicles hanging to her hair, she was nearly dead.

We-now-y-yi finished the five days. He finished practicing, finished preparing for the battle. "Good-bye, my grandmother. I am now going to meet the Wind Brothers on the ice of the *n-Che-wana*. I will kill the Winds, the five brothers who killed my father. Good-bye! I will go now."

The grandmother put her arms around him, caressed him. She said, "All right! Go! Be strong before the Winds. Take these five baskets of oil. When you get to my sister, she will tell you all about this oil, how to use it. She knows and will fix it for you. Go! Good-bye, my grandchild. You will not fall before the Winds. You will beat them on the ice, beat them in the wrestling match."

We-now-y-yi answered, "All right!"

We-now-y-yi came on foot. He came to the Cascades. There he threw trees, threw rocks far out into the river. He pulled up big trees, threw them into the *n-Che-wana*. He tore big rocks from the ground, hurled them far out into the water. He felt strong. He practiced his strength on everything, in every way as he came. He kept saying, "Nothing can beat me! Nothing can stand before me. I am *We-now-y-yi*, the *To-qee-nut's* son. I

am stronger than was my father. The Winds, the five
brothers, the cold Winds cannot stand before my breath.
I will beat them! I will throw them on the ice of the *n-
Che-wana*. I will kill this cold. It cannot stay everywhere all the time."

Thus *We-now-y-yi* traveled up the *n-Che-wana*.
He came close to Celilo, where the Winds lived in the
rock cave. The *n-Che-wana* was covered with ice, cold
all the time. Salmon was the warm wind, the Chinook
wind. *We-now-y-yi* was his son. He got close to the
Winds. He thought, "These people will know that I am
coming."

Thoughts, like breath, go ahead. The old aunt,
covered with ice, cold, starving, sat in her little mat
lodge. The breath of *We-now-y-yi* broke the icicles in
her hair. They fell to the ground. She groaned, "*Ah-h-
n-nn*! He is coming back." She knew all. Then *We-
now-y-yi* walked slowly. He saw the little mat hut, this
side of the Winds' cave-house. He went in.

She could only whisper, "I am poorly! They are
treating me badly! Every morning the sister of the
Winds comes and filths my hair. Every morning you
will hear a noise at the door. It is her. She comes but
does not look at me."

We-now-y-yi answered, "All right! I will fix her!
I feel sorry they make a slave of you. Go out and cut a
rosebush with thorns. Tomorrow I will fix this girl, this
lame sister of the Winds."

The old aunt went out and brought back the
rosebush with all its thorns. Then they slept a little. In
the morning they got up. The aunt said, "Sit near the
door; hide your rosebush near the door. She will come.
She will not look around; she will not see you."

We-now-y-yi sat by the door. Soon he heard a
noise coming. Yes! It was *Ats-te-yi-yi*! She came in!
She did not look around, did not look at the old woman.

When she backed near the old aunt, *We-now-y-yi* struck her on the naked [buttocks?] with the thorny rosebush, struck her hard. *Ats-te-yi-yi* cried, "*Owo!*"

Ats-te-yi-yi ran out of the house, blood running down her legs. She hurried back to her brothers, the Winds, and said, "Our enemy has come to life! I do not know how he is alive, but he is there in the mat-lodge with the old woman. I do not think that the old woman did this to me! I do not think that she struck me with the rosebush thorns."

Ats-te-yi-yi told her brothers this, how she had been struck. They answered, "Yes! Last night we were a little afraid. Last night the warm wind came a little, and we were afraid. It is he! It is Salmon come to life again. He has come to meet us on the ice, to wrestle with us on the ice of the *n-Che-wana.*"

Then the Wind Brothers sent word to all the people, to everybody to come and see the great wrestling match, see it again that day. The five Wolves came from the mountains. The big chiefs came, all the chiefs of the Foxes, the Birds, all came bringing their people. Word was sent out, "Salmon has grown up! Salmon wants to wrestle, has come to wrestle with the Winds."

We-now-y-yi had his five baskets of oil. The old aunt fixed them, made everything ready. That meant five baskets of oil against the five Wind Brothers and against the five Wolves. The old woman put oil on his feet, on the feet of *We-now-y-yi*, the strong. The Winds saw him. They called to him friendly, "Is that you, our friend? Have you come to wrestle with us?"

We-now-y-yi made answer the same way, "Yes! I have come to do this thing. I have come to wrestle with you, my friends, wrestle on the ice of the *n-Che-wana.*

The Winds thought, "He is only one; he is not strong. We are five; we are strong. We will kill him, this boasting Salmon."

It was near mid-sun. All went to see the wrestling, went near the bank of the *n-Che-wana*, all covered with ice, ice made by the Winds. The five Wind Brothers laughed at *We-now-y-yi*, laughed long! *We-now-y-yi* answered, "I will be there! I will meet you on the ice of the *n-Che-wana*."

Ats-te-yi-yi, the lame sister, was there. The people all wanted to see. Coyote, the big Chief said, "I am glad that my grandson is here to fight the Winds. I will help him."

Both *We-now-y-yi* and the old woman went out. She had the five baskets of oil. All the people looked at him. See! He was a big man--strong, strong arms! Strong legs! Strong all over! Strong head and strong heart. Coyote looked at him, sized him up. Coyote said, "Yes! We will win! We will beat the Wind Brothers. *We-now-y-yi* is stronger than was his father. He will stand strong to wrestle."

All five of the Wind Brothers were to wrestle against *We-now-y-yi*, the Salmon. He said to his aunt, the old woman, "Soon as I get to the place on the ice, pour one basket of oil at my feet. Pour it on the ice at my feet."

She answered him, "All right! I will pour the oil. It will make you stand strong."

We-now-y-yi stood in his place. The old aunt poured the oil at his feet, poured it on his feet, on the ice. All the people were looking at him. All the people were anxious to see him. He looked big, looked strong, all stripped on the ice for wrestling. The Wolves were a little afraid. The oldest brother, the oldest Wind, stepped out to wrestle with *We-now-y-yi*. He was not so strong looking. They tried strength four times, when

Wind was thrown on the ice, killed. His head was cut, burst on the ice. Coyote gave a long, "*Ow-ow-ow-ow-ow-ow-ow-ow-o-oo!*" It was the cry of the victor. The Wind and their people could not say anything. They had to keep still.

The second brother of the Wind stepped out to wrestle with the Salmon. He was a little stronger. They stood to wrestle, stripped naked on the ice. The old aunt poured oil at the feet of *We-now-y-yi*. All was ready! Right away they wrestled. It was the same way as with the first brother, only a little longer, a little harder struggling. Three times *We-now-y-yi* swung the Wind. Three times they swung and bent hard. Then the fourth time the Wind was whirled, thrown on the ice; his head burst, killed. Coyote again called the long yell of the victor, called it long and loud. The five Wolves stood mad. They said to each other, "They will beat us! Coyote! Coyote, the big Chief is against us."

The third Wind came out to match his skill and strength with that of the mighty *We-now-y-yi*. They stood. The old woman poured the third basket of oil at the feet of Salmon. *We-now-y-yi*, the Salmon, stood strong on the ice. They wrestled. *We-now-y-yi* turned the Wind three times, turned him slowly. Then he whirled him fast, threw him on the ice, bursting his head. The other two Wind brothers were scared. Coyote gave louder the cry of victory. His side called to the Wind Brothers, "Hurry up! Hurry up and wrestle! We cannot stand here so long!"

The fourth brother walked out on the ice. The old aunt came and poured the fourth basket of oil at the feet of *We-now-y-yi*, poured it on the ice at his feet. He stood strong, a big man. They began to wrestle. The Wind was stronger than were any of his three brothers who had been killed. He stood and wrestled strong. Four times he was swung by *We-now-y-yi*, four times slowly swung. Then *We-now-y-yi* whirled him quickly, threw him and his head burst on the ice.

Coyote cried the long call of the victor, of the best man. The last Wind Brother stood afraid. He said to himself over and over, "He will kill me, kill me sure. All my brothers are dead, killed by this strong Salmon. He will kill me, but I cannot run. It is the law that I must fight, must wrestle and die."

Coyote's side called, "Hurry up! Hurry up! Wrestle with Salmon. Do not be afraid!"

Slowly he came, came slowly out on the ice. He stood where his brothers stood, where all four of his brothers were killed. The last basket of oil was poured by the old aunt at the feet of *We-now-y-yi*. *We-now-y-yi* placed his feet. He said to himself, "I am going to stand strong, this, the last time."

Then they wrestled, wrestled harder, faster. The match was closer than the last two. The last and youngest Wind was strong, struggled hard. Six times did *We-now-y-yi* turn him, six times slowly. Six times he had turned him, then the seventh whirled him fast, threw him on the ice. His head burst like those of his four older brothers. The last of the Wind Brothers lay dead at the feet of *We-now-y-yi*, the son of *To-qee-nut*, Chief of the Chinooks. It was then that *Ats-te-yi-yi*, the lame sister of the Wind, ran crying to the *n-Che-wana*. All were after her to kill her. She went into the water through a hole in the ice. She escaped.[80]

Coyote yelled louder, louder the cry of the strongest side. All the people shouted, were glad. Coyote called, "We beat them! We beat them, those bad people. Now it will be warm. We will have nice, rich food. The salmon will come, all the salmon we want to eat. Now we will all stand, all run against the five Wolves."

Coyote said this. He ran against the Wolves, heading all the people fighting against them. The Wolves fled to the Cascade Mountains, are there yet. The Wolves said, "Coyote is Chief! We cannot beat him! We cannot stand before him."

Coyote was then the big Chief; he commanded. He said, "*Ats-te-yi-yi* has escaped into the water. For this reason it will be a little cold, but not as cold as it has been. It cannot remain cold all the time."

The ice at that moment melted in the *n-Che-wana*, ran down to the ocean. There is now only a little ice in the winter, a little ice during a few moons only. This was many thousand snows ago. There is no record, but that is the talk. That time Coyote said to *We-now-y-yi*, the big Salmon Chief, "I am going to foretell. From here, from *Wah-pe-us*, from *Skein*, people will live to the mouth of the *n-Che-wana*, to the ocean. They will be different people, different from all kinds of bird and animal people, and all will eat freely by and by. Nothing will be paid. Food is for all kinds of people, free."

The Salmon Chief said to Coyote, said when they were together, "Yes! You put it down that way, put the law that way. All will be friendly and good. We killed the Wind Brothers. They were strong, but we killed them. These bad people are now dead. We will have no more war at this time."

It was that way. And now from that time, Coyote said, "Other people will come; and when they meet and have a big time, when they play games of any kind, the Coyote call by the victors will be given, '*Ow-ow-ow-ow-ow-ow-ow-ow-o-oo*!' The beaten party must keep still, cannot say anything."

That is the law, given by Coyote at that time. It stands today, in games and in war. That cry is the cry of the victor only.[81]

15B. BATTLE OF COLD-WIND
AND CHINOOK-WIND[82]

At one time there were five [Cold Wind] bro-
thers[83] and one little sister, *Tah-mat-tox-lee*. They lived
at *Ta-mant-towla* on the *n-Che-wana*. Their father and
mother lived not far from there in a cave. From that
cave the five sons came to stay at *Ta-mant-towla*, to
wrestle with anyone who would meet them. Cold-wind
(*Thirn-nah*) called to anybody, called from sunrise to
sundown to anyone to come and wrestle with him. *Tah-
mat-tox-lee* was lame. When her brothers were wrestling, she would throw water from five baskets, one at a
time, on the ground. This formed ice so the one wrestling with her brothers could not stand.[84] The wrestling
rule was that the one thrown down must have his head
cut off by Coyote. Coyote always came with his flint
knife ready. Piles, great piles of dead lay where Cold-
wind had conquered. None could stand before him.[85]

Eagle and his wife lived at a spring, *Ta-man-
towl-lat*[86] across the *n-Che-wana* opposite *Ta-mant-towla*,
where Cold-wind stayed. Eagle's son had married the
daughter of *Nihs-lah*. He had brought her from *Sko-
lus*.[87] Chinook-wind was five brothers who lived with
Eagle. Nine were in that lodge of Eagle. Although
Eagle's son lived so near Cold-wind, he never answered
when called to wrestle. He stayed away. But at last he
went to wrestle and was killed. *Tah-mat-tox-lee* poured
water on the ground, making ice. Eagle's son could not
stand. He fell, and Coyote cut off his head. Cold-wind
now boasted the more.

Chinook-wind, the five brothers, now went out
to wrestle. Cold-wind killed them all. *Tah-mat-tox-lee*
was there with her five baskets of water. She poured
them, one at a time, over the wrestling ground. The ice

threw Chinook-wind brothers down. Coyote cut off their heads with his flint knife. Cold-wind was more boastful then ever.

The wife of Eagle's son was with child. She went back to *Sko-lus*. She said to her father-in-law and mother-in-law, "I will leave two feathers, one red, one white. I will leave them standing here over my bed. Watch them. If the red feather falls down, the child is a girl. If the white feather falls, the child is a boy. Then you can rejoice, for he will come and wrestle with Cold-wind."

The girl went back to *Sko-lus*, leaving the two old people alone in the lodge. She left them alone near the boastful Cold-wind, just across the *n-Che-wana*. Finally the feather fell. The old man said to his wife, "You threw the feather down?"

His wife answered, "No! It is a son born. In five days he will come to see us."

The old man cried. He did not believe her. He cried, for his heart was lonely. Cold-wind was growing more cruel each day. Eagle's wife said, "If it is a boy, we will live. If it is a girl, Cold-wind will kill us. But it is a boy! We will live." The old man stopped crying.

Every day *Tah-mat-tox-lee*, the lame girl, would come. She would pour cold water on them to make fun of them. All but the two old people were dead at the lodge. She laughed at them. There were none to answer to the call of Cold-wind to come and wrestle.

When the son was born [at *Sko-lus*], his mother told him how his father and the five Chinook brothers were killed by Cold-wind, how the two old grandparents were still living lonely in their lodge at *Ta-man-towl-lat*, how *Tah-mat-tox-lee* came and poured cold water on them every day. They would soon be killed. His mother said, "You stay here at *Sko-lus* five days, then go see the old people. It will take you five days to go. You will

grow to be a young man as you travel. You must practice your strength while going. Pull up pine trees; throw
them about. Pick up big rocks; cast them from you.
Leap! Build the Sweathouse (*whe-acht*); take sweats.
Go in the cold water. If you do not do this, if you do
not practice, you will be killed as was your father. You
will fall before Cold-wind as did the five Chinook
brothers."

The boy stayed five days at *Sko-lus*. Then he
started to go see his grandparents at *Ta-man-towl-lat*.
His mother said to him, "When you come to your
grandmother, catch the biggest salmon. Have her get all
the oil out of it, roasted at the fire. Get all the oil. Save
it in five baskets."

As the boy traveled, he practiced his strength,
doing as his mother had told him. He tore up pine trees
and threw them about. Some he pitched across the *n-
Che-wana*. He picked up big stones, hurling them far
from him. Before he arrived at *Ta-man-towl-lat*, he
could pitch great rocks to a long distance. He grew big
and strong. He was a man.

When the boy reached the old people, they were
in their earth-lodge hovering over their little fire. He
stood outside the doorway. He heard them crying, shiv-
ering with cold. He stepped inside the lodge. The dim
light revealed his form, a strong man. The old people
were glad, glad to see their grandson. The grandmother
said to the boy, "One more night and we would be dead,
killed by *Tah-man-tox-lee* pouring water on us. We are
glad you have come."

Early next morning, the boy stripped. He dived
into the *n-Che-wana* where the water was deep. He
caught the biggest sturgeon,[88] as his mother had told him.
He brought it to the shore, laid it on the rocks by his
robe, where Cold-wind could see it. Cold-wind looked
across the *n-Che-wana*, saw the big fish lying there. He

saw the boy putting on his robe. He knew that a strange
man had come to wrestle with him. The boy caught up
the great sturgeon by the head with one hand. He held
it out at arm's length so Cold-wind brothers could see
how strong he was. He carried it to the lodge. The
sturgeon's tail dragging the ground cut a deep line in the
earth. You can see that mark today. It is called *Ta-man-
towl-lat* (place cut in the ground).[89]   Soon as the boy
reached the lodge, the grandmother took the sturgeon and
cut it into small pieces. She took the oil out of it by the
fire. Cold-wind was all the time calling, "Hurry up!
Come out and wrestle now! Do not stay in the lodge
like an old woman."

The next morning the old man, his wife, and the
boy went out from the lodge. They had the oil in five
baskets. They got in their canoe, covered the baskets so
Cold-wind could not see them. They crossed the *n-Che-
wana*, to wrestle. While crossing, they saw the oldest
Cold-wind brother standing stripped for wrestling. *Tah-
mat-tox-lee* had poured water on the ground to form ice.
It was already ice. The boy said to his grandmother,
"Let them pour water first. Then you pour oil over the
water [ice] quickly. They cannot stand. I will throw
them sure."

He told her over many times how to do it. They
reached the other side of the *n-Che-wana*. The boy and
the grandmother with the five baskets hid under her robe
got out from the canoe. The boy went up to Cold-wind,
all stripped for wrestling. They began wrestling hard.
Coyote was there with his flint knife. He said to them,
"I will be on the side of the one who whips [the other].
I will cut off the head of the one who is thrown down."

The boy was matched. The lame girl had made
ice. He called to his grandmother, "Now! Throw the oil
quickly!" The old grandmother threw the oil from one
basket. Cold-wind could not stand. He was thrown

down. Coyote cut off his head and carried it to the old man in the canoe.

Second Cold-wind brother came to join in the wrestling. The lame girl made ice, but the grandmother poured a basket of oil. Second Cold-wind could not stand; he was thrown, as was his brother. Coyote cut off his head, gave it to the old man in the canoe. The third brother came; then the fourth brother came. They were both thrown by the boy, their heads cut off by Coyote. They stood strong, *Tah-mat-tox-lee* pouring water, bringing ice. But the boy would call to his grandmother, "Pour the sturgeon oil quickly!"

Then the fifth, the youngest Cold-wind brother wrestled. *Tah-mat-tox-lee* poured water, forming new ice. The grandmother threw the fifth basket of oil, making the ice slick. This youngest Cold-wind brother asked Chinook-wind[90] if he could not live. He did not want to die. Chinook-wind did not answer. Three times Cold-wind asked if he could not live. Chinook-wind kept silent. He asked the fourth time, the fifth time, if he could not live. Then Chinook-wind answered, "No! You killed all my people. You cannot live."

He then threw Cold-wind to the ground. Coyote cut off his head, as he had the four brothers. Coyote carried it to the canoe, to be taken across the *n-Che-wana* with the other heads.

Tah-mat-tox-lee ran away crying. Coyote ran after her, laughing at her. He said to the lame girl, "Are you sure Chinook-wind whipped them?"

Five times Coyote asked this; then the lame girl answered, "Yes! I will be cold only a few days. Then Chinook-wind can come. I will have to stop."

Coyote said, "All right! You stay there where you now are. I will stay here and watch you."

They are there yet. You can see *Tah-mat-tox-lee*, the lame sister of Cold-wind brothers, where Coyote placed her. You can see Coyote nearby watching her, laughing at her. They are both rocks, big rocks. The place is where lots of *his-to mah* are to be found.[91]

16. FOOD SMELLERS[92]

A people on the Columbia had no eyes or mouths. They ate by smelling the sturgeon. Coyote opened their eyes and mouths.

17. *AH-TON-O-KAH* OF *SHE-KO-UN*, A WASCO LEGEND OF MOUNT HOOD[93]

There were five small people, old, short [dwarf] people called *Es-cho-o-likes*. They lived on Mount Hood [*She-ko-un*]. There was also a big woman, large, big with long breasts, living on that mountain. This woman was *Ah-ton-o-kah*. If that woman liked you, she would take care of you.

You went to the berry patch near Mount Hood, good berries. There you found out about this big woman. If you had lots of folks with you, if you got separated from your folks, you called! Your people maybe had gone to camp. They did not hear you. You called again! Nobody answered you. You called again, called loudly! Maybe you called five times; then *Ah-ton-o-kah* answered you. She called the same way. You called; she called. By and by you followed her. She grabbed you! *Ah-ton-o-kah* took you to her lodge on

Mount Hood. She kept you a long time, then turned you loose.

Then you went back home. You told all about *Ah-ton-o-kah*. You told all about her big lodge up there, all about the big room. *Ah-ton-o-kah* had plenty in her lodge, had plenty of deer, plenty of elk, lots of birds, all kinds of food. Everything was nice, was clean in that big lodge of *Ah-ton-o-kah*. Bones were all piled separate and nice, deer bones, elk bones, bird bones. All were kept separate, all kept clean. *Ah-ton-o-kah* had plenty. She made good friends with you. When *Ah-ton-o-kah* called, all the leaves, all the pine needles fell to the ground.

Three white men first came to the Mount Hood country. They found out about that mountain, wanted to go to the top of Mount Hood. They had nails in the bottom of their shoes for walking on snow, on ice. It was in spring, maybe early summer. Three Indians, *Sketush*, *Isaac* and *Yes-sum-you*, went with the white men. They went half way up the mountain. Fire commenced on top of Mount Hood. That mountain shook, trembled big. It threw fire on the men. The white men were crazy, crazy like whiskey drinkers. They did not talk! They only cried! cried! cried! They rolled down Mount Hood, all badly scared. The Indians said, "We go back now! We cannot see people on Mount Hood."

They all came back, white men, Indians, all. The nails in the white men's shoes were all worn off. The rocks were too sharp, too rough. The *Es-cho-o-likes* made that fire to come, made Mount Hood shake. They did not want people to come up there where they lived.[94]

18. *NIHS-LAH,*[95] A WASCO LEGEND
OF MULTNOMAH FALLS

I will tell the whole story. A Chief's son from the ocean came up the *n-Che-wana* looking for a girl [wife]. He found a young woman at Multnomah Falls.[96] He had come without letting his parents know. The girl went with him without letting her parents know. The boy took her to his people at the big water, unknown to her people. Coyote claimed the girl as his granddaughter; so he went with her. She took all kinds of berries found in the country about the Falls as gifts to the boy's people. Coyote came along, following behind. When they arrived at the home of the boy, his parents told him, "You cannot keep her. She must go back home."

They would not keep her; so Coyote and the grandchild sat down for five nights, waiting for the boy to come out of the lodge. He did not come, did not return to the girl. Coyote then went alone to consult his five sisters. When he asked his sisters, they answered him, "We will not tell you. You always say, 'That is what I thought.'"

Coyote must know; so he said, "If you do not tell, I will make the rain and hail come down and kill you."

The sisters were scared. They said, "We will tell you. For five days the boy has not come. It is no use. His parents will not have the girl. She must go back home."

Coyote was great, was brave. He could change anything as he chose. He said to the granddaughter, "Never mind! We will go back."

Coyote and his granddaughter then came back to Multnomah Falls and said, "Here we will stay."

The girl brought with her all the roots and berries that she had taken to the big water, and today they are found about the Falls. Coyote said, "From the ocean the boy came out. We will never be friends, but enemies always. He had no respect for you, my granddaughter."

Coyote then called the boy from his distant home and made him half fish and half human. The tail part was salmon; the upper portion was man, with long flowing hair. This being was as large as the largest sturgeon. Coyote placed the transformed boy in the *n-Che-wana*, near the Falls. He named him *Nihs-lah*. Coyote announced to the boy, "When the people pass by the Falls, you will come out and be seen about every two moons. You will become mad. The wind will blow hard; the waters rising high will kill the people. This will be well, for we are enemies."

Coyote placed the girl on the opposite side of the *n-Che-wana* and called her *Sko-lus*. She is there to this day, the tall cliff, the rimrock above the river. This story my parents told me when I was a little girl, nearly one hundred snows ago.

When the fish-and-man image would rear itself from the water near the Falls, immediately the wind would sweep up the *n-Che-wana*, a mad gale. The water would rise high up the rocky cliffs, and all the people in boats in midstream would be killed. When a girl, I saw the *Nihs-lah* rise from the river, and several people were killed out in the middle of the stream. The monster appear to stand half as high as the mountains. It was visible for only a moment.

It was learned that by keeping the canoes near the girl's side of the river, the people in them would be saved. In an earlier day, some white people were drowned when *Nihs-lah* suddenly stood high above the water. It was bad.

When Coyote transformed the boy into *Nihs-lah*, he became mad and caused the Bridge of the Gods to fall.[97]

19. STORIES OF THE *GY-U-BOO-KUM*[98]

It was near Grand Dalles, on the *n-Che-wana*. A young woman went some distance from the village to dig camas. She carried her sister, a little baby, with her. She came to the camas patch. The little child wanted to sleep. The girl placed a large basket on the ground. She laid the papoose down by the big basket to sleep. She went two bow-shots away to dig camas. She filled a small basket and went to empty it in the large one. The big basket was there, but no baby. The baby was gone. The girl stood looking around. She saw nothing of the baby. But on the ground was the print like a log had been dragged. All around where the basket sat was the smooth trace in the dust.

The girl ran to her tepee as fast as she could. The people saw her running, crying, crying when she got there. She told them the baby was gone. All the people went to look for the baby. The men had bows and arrows; some had spears. They saw the print in the dust. They saw where something had crawled like a big snake. They followed the trail where it went into the stones. At the foot of the bluff was a big hole where it had gone. The people thought it must be a big snake. It grew dark and all went home.

Next morning the people returned with *goom-stick* [pitchwood]. They brought a Snake Indian slave boy with them. They built a fire in the hole in the rock-bluff. They kept the fire burning for one day. Next morning they tied a rope about the slave boy. They gave him another rope and made him crawl in the cave. They told him that if he found the snake dead, to tie a rope to it. The slave boy went in that hole. He went far back under the rocks. After a time he twitched the rope, and they pulled him out. He told the people, "The *puch* is dead! The rope is tied to it!"

The Indians pulled the snake from the cave. It had a big mouth. It was half as long as a tepee pole with a very big belly. It had rattles like the rattlesnake, only bigger. They cut the papoose out of its belly. My grandfather saw this. None of the people have seen anything like it since. Nobody knows what it was.[99]

20. THE *GY-U-BOO-KUM*[100]

The *Gy-u-boo-kum* has short legs in front like a lizard. One pretty girl, about twenty snows, never married, was sent into the mountains to *Cino-wot* Creek. She went to look all night for *Tahmahnawis* spirit. She was awake all night, along there where spirits stay. It is a lonesome place.

In the morning the girl was sleepy. She lay down on a broad rock and slept. The *Gy-u-boo-kum* smelled her. He came to her; he swallowed her, swallowed her head first. Two men saw her swallowed to her knees. The *Gy-u-boo-kum* smelled the men. He was not hungry, so he ran in the cave. It was a rocky cavern, deep.

The next day people went to the cave, bringing plenty of pitchwood. They built a fire in the mouth of the cave, made the rocks hot. The *Gy-u-boo-kum* came out; the men killed it. The girl had already melted in its belly.

I saw one of these big snakes just before my father died. It was in the mountains, about twenty miles from *Win-quat.* I was hunting. I saw him maybe one hundred feet away. He was all wrapped together on the ground. He was as big [around] as you. He was ugly! When he smelled me, he made a noise with the bell on his tail, "*Gr-r-r-rr-r-r-rrr-rr-rrrrr!*"

I went numb! I could not run! I stepped and I fell down, all numb. I rolled down the mountain, rolled myself down just like crazy. I rolled down! down! down! down! down! away from that place. I had a gun, but I did not want to shoot that Thing. He was too big, too ugly. I only wanted to get away. He rattled a bell on the end of his tail hard. I heard it good. For one moon afterwards I heard that bell in my ear. It was bad! I never went back to that place. I never hunted there again.

Burial site on Memaloose Island, Columbia River,
15 miles west of The Dalles, 1890. Oregon

Indian burial grounds, Memaloose Island. Oregon Historical Society, Neg. OrHi 9536.

III. TALES OF MAGIC AND
THE MARVELOUS

21. FIVE STARS VISIT THE EARTH[101]

One night, after going to bed, five girls were looking up at five stars.[102] The eldest said, "I should like to have that star for a husband," picking out the largest.

"I should like to have that one," said the second, pointing out a smaller one.

"And I that one," said a third, till the youngest said, "I should like to have that one,' pointing to the smallest star. It was so small as to be scarcely visible. These same stars had visited the girls the night before, but they did not know it.

As they talked, the youngest said, "Mine is the prettiest, it is so dim and small." The girls fell asleep, talking of the stars.

That night all five stars came down. This was when the stars were people and could go anywhere.

In the morning the stars arose and left the girls. The one who looked smallest was in reality the largest and heaviest of them all. When his brothers arose and left, he could not go--he had become so weary with coming and going night after night. In the morning, when the girls woke up, they found the old gray-headed man lying by the youngest girl. When she saw the old man by her side, she jumped up and ran away. She did not want such an old man for a husband.

When the people found out, because of the old man's being left behind, that the stars were coming down and staying nights with the girls, the stars said, "We shall never go to the earth anymore."

And the old man said, "It shall be this way with the people to come. Whenever an old man marries a young girl, she will not like him, and will run away." And so it has been ever since.

Now the old star man turned himself into a bright, white, flint rock, very large, thick, and round. And the place where he lay was by the river, a great gathering-place for all tribes who lived near.[103] Every one knew this star.

Once, when the tribe that lived around the place of the star were camping away in the summer, their enemies came and threw the stone into the river. The people who lived around the star were on the right bank of the Columbia River. When they returned and found the star rock destroyed, they crossed the river and almost destroyed the Wasco cup. It was once very deep and large; now the cup is small.[104] After this star was lost, the tribe that possessed it lost the name of Star tribe, and became very common people.[105]

22A. COYOTE IMITATES FISH HAWK AND MOUNTAIN SHEEP, AND MEETS WITH VARIOUS ADVENTURES[106]

Coyote was hungry. He ran down the river where Fish Hawk and his wife lived, and asked for something to eat. They gave him a good deal of food. He was not satisfied. They gave him food five times, and at last asked, "When are you going home?"

"Oh, soon."

Fish Hawk said, "Come down to the creek with me." There was a tall stump by the water, and a hole in the ice. Fish Hawk jumped onto the stump, and from that into the water.

Coyote was terribly frightened, and ran around crying, "My grandson is drowned!"

But soon Fish Hawk came out with five different kinds of fish, and gave them to Coyote. He told him to carry them home. Coyote took them, and said to Fish Hawk, "Come and visit me."

"Very well! I'll come some time."[107]

One day Fish Hawk remembered Coyote's invitation, and went to his house. Coyote was glad to see him, and said, "When you are ready to go home, let me know."

Soon Fish Hawk said, "Now I am going home."

Coyote said, "Come down to the creek with me." Coyote climbed up on a stump near the place where he used to get water from under the ice. Fish Hawk smiled and wondered. Coyote began to shout as Fish Hawk had. Then he jumped, hit his head on the ice, and was stunned.

Fish Hawk was sorry for him, and called his [Coyote's] wife. She came, and said, "He will do anything that he sees others do. He told me that you jumped in and got fish for him." Now Fish Hawk sprang onto the stump, dived down, and brought out fish. He gave them to the woman and went home. Coyote had not come to his senses yet. About evening he recovered; she helped him up. He was as angry as he could be.[108]

A few days later Coyote got hungry, and went to visit Mountain Sheep and his wife, who lived by the bluff. He met Mountain Sheep, who said, "My wife is at home. I'll come soon." Coyote went into the house.

The man soon came, and said, "I'll get you something to eat." He took his wife by the nose and stuck a straw into it; blood, fat, and meat streamed out. They cooked all that came out of her nose. Coyote ate it, and thought it very nice.

When he had finished eating, Coyote said, "I'm ready to go home. I want you to come and visit me."

"All right! I'll come."

As Coyote started, Mountain Sheep took his knife, cut pieces of meat off his wife's sides, and gave them to Coyote, who was very glad, and said, "Be sure and come to my house."

One day Mountain-Sheep went to visit Coyote. They had a good talk. Then Coyote thought he would cook something for Mountain Sheep. He got his bucket, made a fire, and then took hold of his wife and ran a straw up her nose. She sneezed, struggled, and ran away. Coyote went outside, as angry as he could be.

Mountain Sheep said, "I'm not hungry. I only came to visit." He took a knife and cut off meat from his own two sides, put it down by Coyote's wife, and went home. Coyote had gone off angry. When Coyote came home, he saw the meat and was glad.[109]

Some time after this, Coyote got hungry, and determined to move out near the Deer people. The Deer people were glad to have him come. He got there in the evening, and they brought him food. He began to tell his adventures to them, and said, "Friends, I am alarmed. You and I are in danger. I see the tracks of the *Wala'-lap* out here. These people always feather their arrows with the tail feather of an eagle. We must be on the watch. I'm afraid they will kill some of us."[110]

Next morning Coyote slipped out, and lay hidden by the path where the deer went to hunt. When the largest one came along, he shot, killed him, and took his carcass home. In this way, as he needed meat, he killed the five brothers. The whole family consisted of five Deer.

He now decided to visit the Wolves. When he got to the Wolf house, they made him a servant to carry wood and water. He got very angry at this. A race was arranged. Coyote decided to go, so he made a couple of running dogs with horns on them. The Wolves ran on one side, and the dogs were with the party coming back. The dogs beat, won the race, and after that Coyote ran away from the Wolves.

After a time he came to an empty house. He went on. As he travelled, he heard a noise, looked back, and saw a rock as large as a house rolling after him. He wondered what this could mean. Soon the rock was almost on him. He ran with all his might, the rock came on all the faster. It hit Coyote and knocked him sense-less.[111]

Towards daybreak of the next morning he came to his senses, and remembered that the rock had struck him. "I'll run away from it," said Coyote. He jumped up, stole off, and ran with all his might. But about noon he heard a great noise, and again the rock was pursuing him. Wherever he ran, the rock followed, gained on him continually. He did not know where to go. At last he came to a soft muddy bottom between hills, and thought, "I'll go there. Let it follow if it can." The rock rolled on, got stuck in the mud, and Coyote escaped.

He went on towards the east, and came to a great pile of buffalo bones. He thought, "Oh, I am so hungry! I'll take these bones and carry them till I camp, then gnaw them." But he decided not to take them. Soon he heard a noise, looked back, and saw a buffalo-cow behind him.

She came up and said, "I'll give you meat. Those bones back there were my bones. You did not take them. I'll give you meat now." She cut off flesh all around her body, and gave it to him. He ate, was satisfied, and remained some time.

At last he said, "I can't stay here. I must travel to the east." He started off, and still he travels.[112]

22B. EAGLE DEFEATS FISH HAWK, AND PITIES SKUNK[113]

Fish Hawk was a great hunter and fisherman. He used to make holes in the ice, dive down, and catch fish all winter.[114] He was married to Coyote's daughter. Now Eagle came to The Dalles and got married. Coyote was proud of his son-in-law, and arranged for a race. He invited Eagle.

Eagle said, "I don't know anything about running. But if Coyote wants me to run with his son-in-law, he must come to me." But Eagle began to practice. Every evening before daybreak [sic.] he would go up the mountain and drive down a whole band of deer, and kill them all.

Coyote and his party came to invite Eagle. It was now given out that a man would try before any one ran, just to show himself. A man came out with a quiver on his back and a spotted robe on. He danced around a while, and then, in the presence of all, he disappeared. Every one looked around for him.

Eagle said, "He is there outside." And Eagle increased the heat of the sun on the spot where the man was, so that he burst immediately. It was a body-louse that had put on the form of a man, danced, then taken its natural form, and disappeared nobody knew whither. And no man was able to find out who he was till Eagle killed him with the heat of the sun. He had often been to dances and shown himself in this way, for a living.

Now Eagle and Fish Hawk went out on the ground to run. The sun began to grow hot. They ran together to the place where they turned, and got halfway back. Then Eagle brought on a rainstorm. It grew too muddy for Fish Hawk. He got all wet, and Eagle ran away from him. Old Coyote had to bring his son-in-law home; he was almost dead.

About the middle of winter, Coyote wanted Eagle to dive with Fish Hawk. Eagle said, "I don't know anything about diving, but I'll try."[115] Coyote and his son-in-law came to the water. Coyote had five withes stuck under his belt, which he was going to give to Fish Hawk. Eagle came bringing five withes in his hand. Each had a place open in the ice. Both went far up in the air, then dived down. Eagle struck the hole and went under the ice. But he caused Fish Hawk's place to fill with ice, so that Fish Hawk struck his head and nearly killed himself. Coyote raised him up, and he was just coming to his senses when Eagle came from under the ice with five strings of salmon and other fish. Eagle went home and sang part of the night. The feathers he wore for ornament fell through the bed. He told his brothers to hunt for them, then he gave the feathers to them.

Skunk was living in Eagle's village. He heard Eagle singing, heard his words. Next night Skunk sang, then said, "Brother-in-law, look and see what has fallen."

The brother-in-law lighted a fire, found a bundle of fish-bones, and asked, "Are these your weapons?" and he threw them to his youngest brothers. Eagle had heard what Skunk sang. As he was sitting outside next day, Skunk came along.

Now Eagle was sorry for him, and, pulling out five of his tail-feathers, gave them to Skunk and said, "Tonight you can sing and drop these."

Skunk was happy. He went home, and at dark began to sing. Finally he said, "Brother-in-law, light the fire and look under the bed." One after another refused. At last they threw out the youngest brother. He lighted a fire and found the feathers. Then all began to fight for them; the eldest brother got them, and the youngest cried.

After this Eagle went hunting. He always brought the breast of the deer home, but threw the rest away. His wife rubbed his neck because the load was so heavy.

Now Skunk imitated Eagle. He killed a little fawn, ate the flesh, brought home the upper jaw, and made his wife rub his neck. He had heard that Eagle brought the breast, and he mistook the jaw for the breast.

His wife opened the bundle and was disappointed. She didn't give him anything to eat, and would not let him sleep with her.

Next day Eagle met him, and said, "Tomorrow go with me, and I'll drive deer to you." Eagle killed many deer, put the breasts aside, packed the carcasses up, and made the pack become small and very light; then he gave it to Skunk.

When Skunk got home, he threw his bundle down outside, and asked his wife to rub his neck. She was very angry, and pushed him off.

A voice from outside said, "The meat is being carried off." The old woman sent the boys out to see.

They said, "There is a great deal of fat meat here." Now she was very kind to her husband, but he drove her off. It took a long time to bring the meat in-- there was so much. His wife never refused again to rub his neck.

The next time he saw Eagle, Eagle said, "You can always go hunting with me." Skunk was now better liked, and his wife always had meat to give away.

23. A SINGING AND
DANCING FESTIVAL[116]

Five brothers lived at the foot of Mount Hood on its south side. The eldest said, "Let us sing, brothers, and enlarge our house.[117] They sang till they had a very large house with five fireplaces in it. Now they got Black Fox to carry the news of their singing festival[118] to different villages, far and near.

The eldest brother said, "Bring fir bark." (They used to burn bark. They put a large log of wood on the fire, and put bark on top, and the wood was called "husband of the bark.") Now five Panther brothers, five Wolf brothers, five Wildcat brothers, and five Fox brothers came. The Panther brothers were taken to where the eldest brother had his bed, the other people were at the different fireplaces. There was one Elk to each fireplace. The eldest Elk had the first fireplace, and the youngest the fifth.

At midnight the eldest Elk began to sing. Then he arose, came to the fire, and said to the eldest Panther, "Get on my back." Now all the people were singing. Panther got on his back. Elk stepped astride of the fire. It blazed up on each side of him. The fire burned terribly, but Panther thought he could endure it if Elk could.

Elk sang five songs and stopped five times before he stepped out of the fire. Then he said to Panther, "You have a strong heart. You are hereafter my brother, and are worthy to be a great hunter."

The second Elk sang, took one of the Wolf brothers, and stood over the fire. Both were burned, but he sang five songs and stopped five times. Then he said, "You are my brother, and worthy to be a warrior."

The third Elk sang and took the eldest Wolf on

his back. He endured the fire; and Elk said, "You are a brave man, and shall be a great hunter." Elk was trying them to let them know what hardships they had to go through to be great hunters.

The fourth Elk took Marten on his back, told him the same. The fifth Elk took Black Fox. Black Fox was burning, he twisted and squirmed, but he held on.

Morning came; they ate and then slept during the day. The second night they sang, and the eldest Elk put the second Panther on his back. Each Elk put the second brother on his back, but they said nothing to them about being great hunters, for the eldest brothers had stood the test. The third night they took the third brother, and the fourth night the fourth brother. The Elk was burned almost black now.[119]

The fifth night Coyote came in. He was dressed very nicely in buckskin trimmed with porcupine-quills, his hair was hanging down below his knees. He opened the door and entered. Black Fox took him by the hand and led him to the fire; he went up to the eldest brother's fire.

Fox whispered to him and said, "When they sing, don't you get on their backs. You see how we are burned. And don't you sing."

Along in the evening the eldest Elk said, "A stranger is in our house tonight, and we expect him to sing. That is the rule of old times."

Coyote was afraid, but he said, "All right."

Coyote went away from the fire, took a club, began to beat time and sing. And he used words, for he passed himself off for a Nez Perce. He sang, "I come, I come all the way."[120] He walked up and down the house several times, and at last said, "Whom shall I carry on my back?"

The eldest Elk said, "Well, brother, carry me," and he put his arms around Coyote's neck. Elk's legs hung down, and he tried to pull Coyote over the fire. But Coyote said, "I don't dance over the fire as you people do." Still Elk pulled him towards it. Coyote kept saying, "The custom of my country is not to dance over the fire."

At last he stopped singing and sat down, saying, "It is the custom of old for the one who is carried to sing after the carrier stops singing."

Elk began to sing and wanted to carry Coyote. He could not refuse. He threw off his robe and got on Elk's back. This was the fifth and last night. Elk sang three times away from the fire. It blazed high and burned Coyote, who said, "This is not the way our fathers danced." But Elk paid no heed, and Coyote was burned up.

Next morning the sun rose, and the eldest Elk talked a long time to the people, told them what they would do for the people to come. Coyote lay outside dead. After all had gone away, Coyote came to life and wondered how he came outside. He thought that perhaps they had made such a noise, that he came outside to sleep. Then he looked at the blisters on his hands, and remembered how he had died.

24. EAGLE HAS TOBACCO MAN AND WILLOW WRESTLE WITH *ABU'MAT*[121]

There was a young *Abu'mat*[122] girl at The Dalles who always carried rattles in her hands. She could throw everybody. It was agreed that whoever could throw her should have her. Coyote came and began to wrestle with her; she threw him in a flash. He tried time after time, and kept saying to her, "All the people say that Coyote ought to have you."

As they wrestled, he would whisper, "Let me try again. Do now fall down. I'll not throw you hard; do fall." The woman wouldn't listen, but continued to throw him on his back every time.

Coyote would jump up, run to the people, and say, "She says that after she has thrown you all, I shall be able to throw her. Make haste to wrestle with her."

The fifth day Eagle saw that the girl was throwing everybody. He didn't know what to do. He was afraid to wrestle with her himself. As he came down the creek, he saw a willow waving, swaying back and forth. He decided to pull up this willow, which had a long root. He pulled it out of the ground and caused it to be a man.

Then he [Eagle] said, "I have made you a man to wrestle with that girl. Now I'll put you in the water for five days and nights, and you will be a strong man."

The sixth day Eagle went for the young man, drew him out of the water. The willow said, "I'll go today and try."

Eagle said, "All right." They started off, and went along the side of a hill.

Eagle said, "We ought to have more company." Thereupon he pulled out his pipe, scraped the inside of the bowl, and held it in his hand. He worked it till it got to be quite a long piece, then he put it down on the ground. Soon it rose up a man, and stood at his side. He called him *Ika'inkainus*.[123]

The three walked along till they came to a nice sandy place, when Eagle said, "Let us see who is strongest." They wrestled a long time. At last Willow threw *Ika'inkainus*. He fell heavily to the ground and broke in pieces.

Eagle asked, "Why did you throw your brother so hard?" Then he gathered up the pieces and rolled them between his hands, and again *Ika'inkainus* was a living man. They came to the wrestling place, and found Coyote still wrestling with the girl, teasing her to fall.

Coyote saw Eagle and the two men coming, ran up to them, and said, "Come and wrestle."

"No," replied Eagle, "I have only come to look on."

At last he agreed to try his men. He told *Ika'inkainus* to try. He arose, took off his robe, stripped, and went on the ground. They locked arms and struggled.

After a while she said, "You are making me sway."

"No, you are swaying yourself."

At last the ground began to move, and the woman said, "I am afraid you will throw me." Then she hurled him in the air. He struck the ground, and broke in pieces. When the dust cleared up, nothing could be seen of him.

Eagle picked up the bits, dust and all, put them in a bundle, took them out of sight, worked them between his hands, and made them a living man again. He made this man to amuse the people.

Willow began to wrestle with the girl. He twisted her around, and at last broke some of the outside roots of her body. She said, "You will throw me, and then you will be my husband." The fifth time he twisted her, he broke every root that she had. Coyote was very angry at this, and wanted to make war.

The woman rose up, and went away with Willow. Eagle went home. He said to *Ika'inkainus*, "You will remain here and become a great spirit for future people. Those who seek you will become medicine men."

Eagle took Willow, put him where he had found him, and turned him back into his old form. Then Eagle and the girl went to the mountains, and Coyote was not able to follow.

25. A HARD WINTER NEAR THE DALLES[124]

During a hard winter among the people at Dog River [Hood River], twenty-five miles below The Dalles, a great snowstorm set in. It snowed for seven months without stopping. The storm had buried the tallest trees out of sight, and the people lived under the snow.[125]

At the Cascades people were catching salmon. There was no snow there or at The Dalles. It snowed in one place. The people under the snow did not know that it was summer everywhere else. The way they found it out was this:

A little bird came with a strawberry in its bill to an air-hole they had made up out of the snow. They asked what it was that had brought such a storm, and at last discovered that one of the girls in their village had struck a bird. It was proved against the girl, and they offered her parents a great price for her. The parents would not sell her for a long time.

At last the people bought her, and, putting her on the ice as it floated down the river, pushed the ice into the middle of the stream. In that way they got rid of the snow. A few days later a Chinook wind came bringing heat. The snow melted away at once, and things began to grow.

The girl floated on, day and night, down the river. Five years she floated. At the end of that time she came back to the place where she had been put on the ice. When she returned, there was but a small bit of ice under her, just enough to hold her bones up. For she was almost gone, only skin and bones remained. They took her into the village. She died. She was no longer accustomed to the smell of people, and died from the odor of them. After a time she came to life, but it was a year before she could eat much.

Every summer after that she was nearly frozen to death, and went all bundled up. But in winter she was too warm, would take off all her clothes, and go naked.

26. THE BOY WHO WENT TO LIVE WITH THE SEALS[126]

The Chinook people, who lived at the mouth of the Columbia River, moved some distance to the east. At the end of the first day's journey they camped on the shore. One of the men had a little boy. After they had fixed the camp, he went with the boy to mend his canoe. After a while the boy disappeared.

The father thought he had gone back to the camp. When he had finished the canoe, he went to the camp and asked his wife where the boy was. She had not seen him.

They went to the river, tracked him to the water, and all said that he was drowned. Next morning the people moved on still farther up the river. The parents hunted everywhere for the child, but at last they too went. They could not find the child.

Two or three years after this another party went up the river. On an island in the river there were a great many seals, and among them a boy. Word was sent to the parents of the boy. People went out and watched for the seals to come to land, so that they might see the boy. They watched till the seals came up on the island, one by one, and soon the island was covered. At last the boy came up out of the water and lay down by the seals. The people crept up, caught the boy, and took him to shore by force. He struggled to get away from them, and tried to return to the water. At first he refused to eat anything but raw salmon and other fish, and he would not talk; but by degrees he came to act like other human beings. Finally his parents got him back to his right mind, and he became very industrious. He carved bows and arrows and worked all the time.

As he grew up, he used to tell many stories of how he had lived down with the seals.[127] He said that seals were just like people. They moved from place to place, camped at night, and would go as far as The Dalles. They moved around as the Indians did on land. The people had to watch him when he was in a canoe, for fear that he would go back to the seals. The seals were always floating around when he was near. He always called them by name. His parents always covered his head when he was in a canoe.

One day he threw the cover off, saw the seals, called them by name, said, "I am going," and jumped into the water. He came to the surface far out, and said to his father and mother, who were in the canoe, "I have a home down in the water. I will remain there hereafter."[128]

27. AN ARROWPOINT-MAKER BECOMES A CANNIBAL[129]

There was an arrowpoint-maker on the right side of the Columbia River, three miles below The Dalles. One day this man cut his finger with flint so that it bled.

He put his finger in his mouth, liked the taste of the blood, ate his finger off, then his hand, pulled the flesh from his arms, legs, and body, and ate it.[130] At last he had only a little bit of flesh left that was below his shoulders on his back, where he could not reach it. He was a skeleton now. Nothing but the bones were left; only his heart hung in his body. He went to the next village and ate all the people. They could not kill him, nothing would penetrate his bones.

Now his wife, carrying a little son, escaped. They went south, travelling on the grass, right on the tops of the blades of grass, so that he could not track her for a long time.[131] At last he found the tracks. The moment he found them, his wife knew it.

She travelled day and night in great fear. The husband gained on her, came nearer and nearer all the time. Far ahead of her was a blue mountain. She hurried on. When she reached the foot of the mountain, she saw a house, and went in. A very old man sat on one side making bows and arrows. His daughter sat on the other side making little tobacco sacks.

The woman called him by a kinship name, but the old man did not answer. The north wind, which had grown stronger, began to blow terribly; almost carried the house away, and threw down great trees. At last she begged so hard, that the old man said, "Hide behind me."

That moment the skeleton came in with a frightful wind, walked around the fire, and stamped on the old man's arrows, which broke into bits. The old man seized a long arrow point and thrust it into the skeleton's heart. That instant the skeleton fell to the ground--a pile of bones. The wind stopped blowing when it fell.

The old man said to the wife of the skeleton man, "Come and throw these bones outdoors."

There was plenty of tobacco growing on the hill

above the old man's house. He made arrow points all the time. And when his quiver was full, he would start out and return with it empty, but with tobacco in his hand. The old man and his daughter lived on smoke; neither ate anything. They lived on smoke from the kind of pipe that is made straight.

The old man always shot the tobacco; those whom he shot were Tobacco people. When he brought the tobacco, his daughter put it into sacks, and they smoked till all was gone. Then he went again for another hunt of these people.

The woman and child lived with the old man and his daughter a long time. When the boy got old enough, he hunted squirrels for his mother. One day when the old man went out, the boy followed him. He saw the old man shoot up a bluff of high rocks. The Tobacco people all lived on these high rocks. He crept down, sat behind the old man, took an arrow, and wished it to hit the tobacco. The arrow left the bow at the same instant that the old man's arrow left his bow, and five bunches of tobacco came down. The old man was delighted, and danced for joy. He had never shot so much in a whole day.

"You are my son-in-law," said the old man, and went home. The daughter was glad that her father had so much tobacco.

The old man said, "I don't know but that it is a death sign." The boy laughed to himself. The old man said to his daughter, "This is your husband," and added: "The people of the future will be willing to give their daughters to a good hunter, and the girl must wait till the father and mother find such a man."

The old man now rested, and the young man hunted tobacco for him. He filled the house with tobacco. The old man was satisfied. Then the young man, his wife, and mother came to the Columbia River.

When they came to the village where the young man's father had turned into a man-eater, they found only bones. The young man gathered up the bones, threw paint into the air five times, spoke five times to the sky, and the people all rose up as they were before the man-eater had devoured them.

When the mother was old, she had food given her every day by her daughter-in-law. She grew weak fast, and her son said, "It will be the duty of a daughter-in-law to care for her mother-in-law among the people to come."

The mother said, "My daughter and I will go south, and we will be guardian spirits to medicine-women, and will give authority to women to smoke. When a woman smokes, she will be a medicine-woman."

The son said, "I will be a guardian spirit to help people. Those whom I help will be good hunters."[132]

Celilo Area Indian woman (c. 1910-12). Oregon
Historical Society, Neg. OrHi 66870.

IV. TALES OF CONFLICTS AND ADVENTURES

28. A WASCO WOMAN DECEIVES
HER HUSBAND[133]

A man and his wife and four children lived at Wasco. It was the time of year when the women were cutting grass to pack their dried fish in. One day, while this woman was getting grass, a man from Tenino[134] came and talked with her. They fell in love with each other and planned to deceive the old husband. The woman said, "I will go to the creek and eat alder bark till I spit it up. He will think I am spitting blood. After a time I'll pretend to die."[135]

"All right," said the man.

She chewed the bark. At night she came to the house, apparently suffering terribly, and said, "I can't live."

"What's the matter?" asked her husband.

"Oh, I must have broken something inside." She had told the other man, "I'll die at daybreak. They will bury me, and you must be near to dig me up quickly."

At daybreak she died. Before dying she said to her husband, "When I die, take my cup and mountain sheep horn dish and cover my face. Don't cover it all up."

The husband buried her soon after sunrise. As soon as he went away, the other man dug her up, and she went with him to Tenino. The old husband built a sweathouse, sweated five days, and mourned much. He did not know what to do with his children, they cried and worried so. One day he took the children out and made pictures on the rocks to amuse the youngest child-- pictures of deer, birds, and weapons. To amuse his little girl he placed five stones in the road, one after another, and made holes in each stone.

Towards midnight of the following day the fire went out, and in the village the fires went out in every house. Next day the father said to the eldest boy, "Go over to Tenino and get fire."

The two boys started. Towards sundown they reached Tenino, peeped into the door of a house, and the youngest boy said, "That woman looks like our mother."

The other said, "It is our mother." Their father had made a stick of cedar bark for them with little cracks in it, good to hold fire. They crept up to the fire and lighted this stick.

The mother had a young baby. She saw the two boys and asked, "Does your little brother cry much?"

"Yes," said the eldest boy, "he cries all the time."

A few days after this the fire went out again. The boys went four times for fire. The fifth time they told their father that when they went for fire, they always saw their mother.

He said, "You must not talk that way."

They laughed, and he scolded, saying, "It is wrong to say that. Your mother is dead."

They said, "No, she is not. We see her every time we go."

At last he went to her grave and found it empty. Then he went to Tenino, looked into the house, and saw her with the other man. She went out for water; he followed her, touched her on the shoulder, and said, "Why have you done this?"

She threw her arms around him and begged him to save her life. She said, "I am sorry, and I want to live with you again. This man whips me all the time; I have no peace with him. I'll tell you what to do. When he puts his head on my lap and goes to sleep, you can slip in and cut his head off."[136]

This was done, and the man and his wife went home together.

Next morning, when it was time for the man to get up, he still lay covered up. People came in, took the cover off, and found that his head was gone. They could not find the head. They went up to Celilo[137] and to four different villages to hunt for it.

At last they heard that the woman's husband had stuck it up on a pole. Then they made war on the man and his people. When both sides were ready to fight, Coyote came along and asked, "What does this mean?" They told him.

"No," said he, "I'll not have such a thing. This must end here. A woman should never cause war. I'll end all such things.[138] Right here you people of Tenino become rocks, and you Wascos be rocks." Both sides are standing there to this day, all rocks.

29. A WOMAN MARRIES A PERSON WHO IS A DOG IN THE DAY AND A MAN AT NIGHT[139]

A chief of the *Ilqa'ditix*[140] people lived about four miles below The Dalles. He had a daughter whom he prized beyond anything. One time a dog came and stole away this young woman's paint. She followed the dog for four days, and was nearly dead when she came out of the woods and saw a house at the farther end of a valley.

She saw a fire there, went near, and saw a family of small dogs that were carrying fire from the house and making fires in the woods. She entered the house and found three old dogs there. One had a whole family of young dogs. Another old dog lay on one side; he had but one eye and both ears were cropped off. And still another dog lay there.

She saw a great deal of venison and wished she had some. That moment a dog jumped up and put venison in front of her. She said, "You should not do that; they will say I stole it."

Then she saw a nice buckskin, and thought, "I should like that." Another dog jumped up, pulled it down, and put it before her. She slapped him and said, "You should not do that; they will say I stole it."

After sundown she woke up--she was so tired that she had fallen asleep. She heard talking, looked around, saw that the dogs were all gone. Young men were in the house now. One of them said, "We are afraid to give you anything--you slap us so." (The dogs had all turned into young men when the sun went down.) This was the very one who had stolen her paint.

She said, "I will stay here tonight. Tomorrow I shall go home. I came for my paint."

Now the young man who had stolen the paint lay down beside her. This was the marriage; he took her for his wife. She stayed now all the time with her husband. After a while a son was born. The relatives of the man took the child, wrapped it up, opened the ashes carefully, put the baby in, covered it up, and roasted it. The mother was frightened.

The husband, seeing this, said, "You can't take care of this boy. You are fond of sleeping. I have sent him to where his grandmother and grandfather are."

Five days and five nights after the child was roasted to ashes, it walked out of the ashes. He could now walk around. He came to his mother and said, "Mother!" She could scarcely believe what she saw.

The father said, "Didn't I tell you that it was well cared for?"[141] In time a girl was born. She was treated in like manner.

When the children grew to be quite large, they seemed sad. The mother said, "They want to see their grandparents. I have told them many times about the old people." The man told his relatives to pack plenty of dried meat. The woman wondered who could carry such a load.

Her husband said, "You go ahead with the children. Camp while the sun is still up. If you hear a great noise, pay no heed to it; don't look back."

They started, travelled till near sunset, then camped. Soon she heard a great noise in the direction from which she had come. It grew louder and louder. She did not look up. Great packs of meat rolled in and stacked themselves up around the fire, kept coming till all she had seen at home was there.

The second day she camped near sunset, the meat came in the same way. Every evening, as soon as she camped, with a great roar and noise the meat came in and piled itself up around the fire. The fifth evening fresh venison came. The husband and several of his people came soon after. In the morning they all travelled on together. About night they reached her parents. The dried meat followed, and also fresh venison, newly killed.

All the time she had been gone, her father and mother had cut off their hair and mourned for her. All rejoiced at her return. She gave meat to every one. The fourth day after her return the woman called the people of the village together; all came into the house.

The husband lay on a shelf or bed and watched his wife. He was jealous. Two nice-looking men came in. She chanced to look at them. Her husband was very angry. He didn't eat for five days and nights. The fifth day he took his son and started for home. At the gathering the woman had given a skin robe to each person, and meat to all. When the man started, these robes followed him, no matter where they were or what use they had been put to, and all the venison that had not been eaten rose up and left.

When the woman's father found that her husband had gone, he questioned her. She said, "He left me because I looked at the two men who wished to buy me when I was a girl." The man, after getting home, lived many days and nights without eating. He was sorry for what he had done. At last he destroyed himself.

Since that time, if an Indian leaves his wife, he takes all he has given her people.

30. THE DISCONTENTED WOMAN AND THE *WAHK-PUCH* [RATTLESNAKE][142]

What I am telling you is a true story, not a tale like those of Coyote and others I have been giving you. They are far back in the beginning, while this happened during the time of my ancestors. My mother told it to me once when I was in trouble, when I was having trouble of a certain kind. I was unhappy as a woman could be. You will understand why my mother told it to me. She said, "My daughter, you are in trouble. Listen while I tell you a story."

One time there were two sisters who got married. The husband of the younger girl was a very jealous man. He would not live among the other Indians with his young wife. They lived apart from them, lived alone, just the two. The man built a house of logs, different from the tepee, up in the edge of the timber. Many snows they lived thus, and he would for long times leave his wife alone. A great *palout* player, he would leave her in the mountain house while he spent his time

gambling in the villages on the *n-Che-wana*. The
woman was afraid. Her husband would tell her not to go
away, not to go to anybody's house. She must stay
home all the time. He would say to her, "Do not go
anywhere. Stay here by yourself."

Once the man went to the *n-Che-wana* for two
weeks. The woman thought how badly her husband was
treating her. She cried! Cried! Cried! For three nights
and three days she cried; then in the evening she went to
bed. Soon as she lay down, she heard someone open the
door. She thought, "There is my husband. He has come
to me this night."

The man came and lay down by her side. She at
once knew that he was different from her husband.
There was a moon, and it was not dark in the house. She
looked, saw him and thought, "What a nice-looking man,
long hair, fine features!"

The man was silent for a short time then spoke,
"Why are you so sorrowful? Do not feel badly because
of the way your husband treats you. I came a long ways
to see you. I am sorry for you. I came to see if we
could not marry. Your husband is not treating you
right. I am feeling sorry for you."

There now came to the woman's nostrils a
delightfully pleasing odor. It was like the most delicate
perfumery made from the mountain seeds and herbs.
The man's blanket, everything about him was more aro-
matic and fragrant than anything that she had ever
sensed. She looked at him. He was so splendid-looking,
finer-appearing than any man she had ever seen. He said
to her, "I will come every evening, come with the night.
Then, the last time that I come, I will take you with me,
take you to my home."

They talked! He amused the woman! She was
happy! She laughed, forgetting her troubles, forgot all
about her indifferent husband. The stranger said to her,

"I will do everything for you. I will not treat you as your husband does." Finally they slept.

Early in the morning, just as it began to grow light, the man said to the woman, "I will now leave you. I must go. Your husband might come and find me here. I will go, will stay away all day, but I will come again tonight."

The man arose and left her. All day she could smell that sweet odor, the herb and berry perfume. But it was nicer than any that the Indians could make. It was of the man. All that day she was lonesome for him. That night he came again. He came every night for about seven suns; then she felt sickly at her stomach. It was from smelling the perfumery. She liked it, but it made her feel ill. She had said to him, "You ought to take me home with you. I do not want my husband. I am willing to go with you."

But the man had put her off. He would say, "I will take you, but not tonight. I will take you to my home."

The woman was lonely, did not want to stay alone. She said, "We ought to go now."

This was the last night, when she had said this. But the man again put her off. He answered, "No! Not now."

When the light came, the woman looked at the man in the early morning rays. Yes! He was a fine-looking man. He said to her, "I am lonesome for you all day. I always wish night would come so I can see you." Every morning at first dawn, he had said, "I must go!"

She never watched to see which way he had gone, but this last morning she thought, "I will see which way he goes."

The man rose up and walked, walked like a man. He opened the door, looked back at her, and smiled. He said, "Good-bye!"

He closed the door back of him. The woman jumped up as quickly as she could. She peeped through a crevice between the logs. She saw the man stand for only a space, then fall down on his stomach. She looked closely. There was a rattlesnake (*wahk-puch*). She was scared! She opened the door, watched it go. Yes! It was a rattlesnake, this, her fine-looking man.

There was a rimrock on each side of the house. She saw the Thing crawling up towards one of these rims--a white-looking Thing--crawling high up. She saw it go into a crevice of the rocks. The woman now discovered that it was a rattlesnake smell which she had thought so sweet, so much nicer than the Indian-made perfumery. Then she cried! Cried! Cried! She cried out! "It was a rattlesnake I have been sleeping with, this fine-looking man! I have slept with a rattlesnake!"

The poor woman cried! Cried! Cried! The smell made her sick. You know the smell of the rattlesnake. It is different from all other odors, different from all other snakes. It makes you sick. The poor woman could eat nothing that morning. She said, "I will go to my sister! I will go stay with her. I do not want to sleep with that man! I thought he was a fine-looking man. He is a rattlesnake!"

The woman got ready, hurried as fast as she could. She arrived at her sister's. There were lots of people there. She was ashamed to tell her sister what had happened. She only said, "I am sick! I cannot eat!" She stayed with her sister. She grew poor, only skin and bones. If she ate, she threw it up. She could smell the rattlesnake all the time. She threw up everything. At last she was nearly dead.

In time the husband returned home from the *n-Che-wana*. He found his wife gone. He looked for her. He followed her to her sister's tepee. He was mean.

The sister asked the sick woman, "What is wrong with you, my sister?"

The sick woman said, "I will tell you, my sister. I am going to die! I will tell you what has killed me. I made love with a rattlesnake!"

The husband did not know his wife; she was so poor. The sister said to him, "See your wife! It is all your foolishness. You did not take her to live like other people." The man cried. The sister knew all about what had killed her younger sister. She died from living with a rattlesnake. But she did not tell this to the husband.

The children of the older sister grew up and married. Their descendants are still living. The younger sister never had children.

This was the story told me by my mother, *An-a-whoa*, who got it from her mother, *Mo-qui-nee*. My mother advised me, "Do not worry about your husband. Everybody will know it. Evil spirits, every bad thing like the rattlesnake, will know about it. It will bring you trouble. Let it all go; forget all." This story may have occurred in the time of my grandmother, *Mo-qui-nee*; I do not know. The rattlesnake is bad. I am afraid of it.

31. *DIABEXWA'SXWAS,*
THE BIG-FOOTED MAN[143]

There was a chief who lived near the mouth of the Columbia River. His feet were three feet long, his whole body was in proportion. He had a long house with five fireplaces. The house was nicely fixed, with fish and animals carved around on every side. He had a hundred wives--fifty beds on one side of the house, and fifty on the other. A short distance to one side he had a house in which lived one hundred slaves. These slaves took great baskets every evening at sundown, brought sand from a bank at the seashore, and scattered it around the chief's house for fifty yards in width. Then they smoothed the sand perfectly. Not even a mouse could move around the chief's house without leaving tracks.

This big-footed man was chief of all the people about there. After nightfall nobody went near the chief's house. The chief went around his house every night to each one of his wives. About midnight he would be halfway around, and the sun would come when he was with the last wife. He had a great many daughters, but not one son.

News came to *Diabexwa'sxwas* that there was a chief's daughter in the Wasco country, and he made up his mind to go and buy her.[144] He had fifty canoes filled with provisions and men to take him up the river. They landed near Wasco and came on foot to the village. He brought fifty slaves to give for the chief's daughter -- twenty-five men and twenty-five women. *Nädaiet* was the name of the girl he had come for. They camped beside a bluff of rocks. He bought the girl. Her people were willing to sell her, as he was a great chief. Whatever he asked for, he got. He took her home.

Next morning, when he returned, he asked, "How many children were born while I was gone?"

"Five girls." He had no sons, because he killed them as soon as they were born, for he did not want any one to be greater than himself.[145]

Nädaiet bore him a child in time. The slaves brought sand every evening; it was perfectly level, so that no person could come near to meddle with his wives. After her child was born, he asked, "What is it?"

Five of the women had made a plan to deceive him, and they said, "It is a girl." They had been with their husband when he bought *Nädaiet*, and they sympa-

thized with her. They put girl's clothes on the baby.
The five women thought and cared for the child even
more than the mother did. Word went out that the chief
was killing all his sons. Everybody was angry. The boy
grew fast. He was large and heavy, and began to look
like a boy; he was very wise. The girls were very large;
at three or four years of age they were as large as
women. And it is from this that the Chinook people are
so large and have such big feet.

The mother of the boy, as he grew older and
began to show by his behavior that he was a boy, began
to cry. She felt very anxious. The chief noticed this,
and thought that she was homesick. He said, "If you
wish, you may take the child and go home to your father
for a visit. I'll come for you."

This was just what pleased the women. They got
a canoe ready, and the five women went with her. They
told all not to tell about the child, and they promised to
keep the secret. As they got up the river out of sight of
the old man, they took off the girl's clothes that the child
was wearing, and put on a boy's. All that were with her
were delighted, and said, "The old man shall not be our
master any longer." The boy was named after his father.

The others returned, the mother remained at
Wasco. The mother told the boy about his father and
how many boys he had killed. The boy was angry, and
hunted in the mountains for guardian spirits that he might
get strength to fight his father. The fifth night he came
home and said, "Mother, the five Thunders and Light-
nings have given me their strength."[146]

His mother said, "That is not enough."

He went again, came home the fifth day, and
said, "I have the strength of five bands of Grizzly Bears."

"That is not enough."

He went the third time, and said, "There are five bands of Elk, and the strength of them is mine; they promised it."

"That is nothing, get more."

The old chief was very bad among his people. He could walk on the water. When people were coming along on the water in a canoe, he could walk out and destroy them.

Now the boy's mother wanted him to get the power of running on the water so that he might overcome his father. She said, "Do not seek power any longer on the mountains, but seek by the water."

He went to the water and got the power of the five Whirlpools. His mother said, "That is not enough."

When he came the fifth time, he said, "I have the power of the five long-legged Water-Spiders (*tsia'xitilul*). They [had] said, 'We will give you strength to run on the water, as we do.'" His mother went to the water and saw him run on it; he already had large feet.

Now she told him, "You had better look for still another power of something that runs on the water." He got the power of five bands of yellow flies running on the water (*iq!i'naxwixwi*). His mother said, "This is enough."

The old chief had not come for his wife and daughter, as he had intended to. The young man was now half grown, and was larger and stronger than his father. He gathered fifty canoes and men and weapons, took his mother, and went down to make war on his father for killing all his half-brothers. They landed on the side of the river opposite the house of the old chief, who sent his servants to ferry them over. He did not yet know who the people were.

The young man told the men to remain with him, and all were glad to do so. At night he walked over on the water to the other side, and got to the house just as his father rose up from one of the women. As his father went to the next woman, the young man lay down at the foot of the first woman's bed. All that night, as his father went from one woman to another, he followed him. The women all wondered how it was that he came a second time to their bed. They talked together and said, "It must be the young chief, our son, who has come."

The second night he did the same. Next morning the chief saw tracks, measured them, and found that they were larger and broader than his own.[147] He now suspected that he had a son, and told his people to get ready for war. The old chief brought fifty canoes with weapons and made an attack on the young man. He came with a Chinook Wind of great force, while the young chief brought the East Wind. The young man's canoes were urged forward by the East Wind, and the Chinook Wind drove onward those of the old man.

When they met, there was a terrible crash; the canoes were broken and sank. The young man drove the old chief all the way home, and a great many men were drowned. Four days they fought in this way, the East Wind driving the Chinook Wind.[148] The fifth day the old man's strength began to fail him. The father and son did not fight in the canoes, but on the water, hand to hand. As the old man's strength began to fail, he began to sink in the water; it would not hold him up any longer. He was overcome by his son and killed. The young chief liberated all his father's wives; only ten he took for himself. His mother went back to the Wasco people and lived with them. The young chief ruled his people well.[149]

32. BATTLE BETWEEN EAGLE AND CHINOOK: ORIGIN OF THE HORN SPOON[150],[151]

It was at *Win-quat*. One old man, a big chief, had good children, had a nice daughter. This chief was rich. He had a great *Too-noon* (mountain sheep) horn. He wanted somebody to split that horn, but nobody could do it. He wanted to make a spoon, make a ladle or anything from that horn. But nobody could split it for him. The chief said, "I will put up my daughter. The man who can split the horn can have my daughter as his wife."

The chief called all the people, all the young men to try their strength for his daughter. None could burst the big horn. One big chief Chinook at the saltwater, at the mouth of the *n-Che-wana*, heard about this trial for the *Win-quat* woman. He said, "I must go see about this business. I will see what is being done."

So chief Salmon went, and on that same day Eagle, a big strong man, also came to the *Win-quat* chief's lodge. Eagle had heard about the trial of strength; so he came on the same day as chief Chinook. They both went in that lodge, a great mountain, a cave in the big mountain. I can show you that lodge, a cold place. We call it Eagle's cellar. Eagles build nests in the rocks about that cave, live there. When in that lodge, Chinook said to Eagle, "You try first! Try your strength on the horn of *Too-noon*."

Eagle did so. He squeezed that horn in his hand and split it. Eagle threw the horn on the ground, all split. Chief Chinook made that horn whole, made it sound as at the first. Five times Eagle crushed that horn. Five times Chinook made it sound and good. Chinook said, "No use trying to split the horn. We cannot split the horn."

Then Chinook took up that horn. He crushed it, threw it on the ground. Eagle could not make that horn sound again. It lay there all split, burst open. The old chief said to his daughter, "You must go with this man. You must marry him." Chief Chinook took the girl, married her.

Eagle was mad. He called all his people together. He said, "We have got war! I was the first man to split the horn of *Too-noon*! Chinook became jealous. He spoiled my work; he took the girl. We will fight Chinook; we will fight his people."

The Eagle people said, "All right! We will make a war! We will fight!"

Chinook's people were all fish, all in the water. It was below *Win-quat* where the big fight took place. Coyote (*E-tal-i-pus*) put up rocks all level on top. He made long grooves in that rock where he shot arrows straight. He shot chief Chinook in the eye, killed him. Eagle said, "We have killed the big chief Chinook! Come! We will eat!"

All the birds, all the animals ate the big chief of Salmon. They ate all but one little egg. That egg dropped down in a crevice of the big rock. It lay there several suns. No bird, no animal could get that egg. Then rain fell; water was in the rock where the egg lay. A little Salmon came out of that egg. It got into the water of the creek; it went into the *n-Che-wana*. The little Salmon grew to a big man. He found [Meadow] Lark. He thought that Lark killed his father. He tore open the leg of Lark.

Lark cried! He said, "You fix my leg, and I will tell you all about it. I will tell you who killed your father."[152]

Chinook fixed Lark's leg, made it sound and strong. Lark said, "At *Win-quat* a big chief had a fine-looking daughter. Your father won this daughter from Eagle. He crushed the big horn of *Too-noon*. Coyote shot your father in the eye and killed him. Five wolves (*Lal-awish*) got your father's wife, the handsome daughter. The youngest of the Wolf-brothers married her. They put up a lodge at *Schumn*, below *Win-quat*. They live there. Every morning the five wolves go hunt the deer. They leave the woman alone. You go see her in the morning."

Lark told all this to Chinook. Chinook now hunted for a strong spirit in the mountains. He piled up rocks, tore rocks out from the cliffs. He grew strong, stronger all the time. He came after the wolves, came to their lodge.

The next day the wolves all went to the mountains to hunt. Chinook made it warm, made it hot. All the water dried up, all in creeks, all in rivers dried up. The Wolves could not find water; they were dying for water. They came home staggering like drunk men, almost drunk with thirst. Chinook had made one spring, a big spring at *Schumn*. The water was cold, nice. The Wolves came there, put their heads in the water, and drank just like crazy men. Chinook took a bow and arrow, shot the oldest Wolf, killed him. He shot the four oldest of the brothers, the youngest running off to the mountains. He escaped with his life.

Chinook took his father's wife home in a canoe. They went just below the mouth of the Klickitat River. There Chinook grew sleepy. He slept with his head on the woman's lap. Worms came out of his mouth, his nose, his eyes and ears like he was dead. The woman was afraid, was scared! She dropped Chinook off her lap. When he dropped, he came to life. There were no worms. Chinook took up the canoe paddle, took the woman on it, threw her to a cave in the cliff along the river [Washington side]. I can show you that cave up in the rocks, up in the side of the wall-rock. It is there today.

Young chief Chinook now went home to the saltwater at the mouth of the *n-Che-wana*. He had two grandmothers. They were the Raven (*Esh-kolloh*), man and wife, always two. They looked some like the crow. They found dead people. They ate nasty things.[153]

One of them went east every day. This grandmother said to Chinook, "Our grandchild! I find a woman in the rock cave. She is nearly bones now, nearly dead. Some day we will eat her."

Chinook said, "No!" You must not eat her. Bring her here."

The grandmother replied, "All right!"

The next day the two grandmothers went to that cave. They brought the woman, all starved and poor, brought her to Chinook at the saltwater. They flew side by side, carrying her on their backs. Chinook put lots of grease, lots of fat on her body. He made her well and young again. Young chief Chinook took that woman for his wife.

33. THE *AT!AT!A'LIA* WHO WAS DECEIVED BY HER TWO SONS[154]

A Wasco man went to a dance. A Celilo woman followed him home, so they were married. One time, towards spring, the man and his four brothers killed many ducks, more than they could use. The man's mother said to his wife, "If you have any people, you had better take these ducks to them."

She packed a large number of ducks, and started off northward. She had two sons, whom she left with her mother-in-law. She travelled till she came to a lake. The ground around it was dry and cracked up; it looked like Indian bread made of roots. She thought, "I'll eat the ducks, and carry this dirt to my father and mother and give it to them for bread."

She ate all the ducks, and carried a load of the dirt. When she reached home, she gave them the bread, and they ate it all. This woman was an *At!at!a'lia*.[155]

She went back to her mother-in-law, and said, "My mother was very glad because of the ducks. She wants more." The hunters went out and killed more ducks. She went with another load; she did just as before.

She started the third time with ducks. She did as before--ate the ducks and carried dirt to her father and mother. She went the fourth time, and came home late in evening.

Early in the morning her husband arose. She was still sleeping. Her mouth was open. He looked in, and saw that her teeth were full of meat and feathers. He thought, "This is very strange," and told his brother to follow her and see what she did.

He followed, saw her eat the ducks. If even a feather escaped, she ran after it and ate it. The boy came home and told what he had seen, but the husband said nothing. The next time she went she carried a larger load than ever.

The husband said, "Follow her, brothers, and see what she does with the ducks." All four brothers followed her. When she reached the lake, the boys went around to the opposite side and watched.

Now the eldest brother called out, "Our sister-in-law is going to kill herself eating." As he said this, the woman stopped eating and listened. Then she went on eating again. He called out in the same words, louder than before. She stopped and listened, but ate again. The fourth time he called she began to change form, turned into a grizzly bear, and ran after them. Soon she overtook the youngest and ate him up. Then, she caught the next in age and ate him. She ate the third; but the fourth got into the village, and told the people that his sister-in-law was running after him and was going to eat them all up.

Now the people of the village turned out and tried to kill the woman bear, but she ate them as fast as she could. Nothing could kill her. At last she had eaten all the people except her husband. He turned himself into a decrepit old man. Finally she thought of her two children. They were already off some distance, running away from her.

She left the old man and ran after them. She was almost upon them, when the younger one said to the elder, "What shall we do?"

"We will make a village here to deceive her, and all the people will be dancing around a pole." They made the village. There were many frogs; these they turned into people, and the two boys were in the midst of the frogs dancing.

When she came in sight, she said, "Yonder is *Weditc*, my elder son, and *Wilu*, my younger son." She was delighted to see such a crowd of people. She began to dance with them, danced a long time. When she came to her mind, she found herself in the middle of a swamp surrounded by frogs, up to her waist in mud and water. The boys had run far away.

She followed her sons a second time, and was nearly upon them, when the younger said, "It is time for us to do something."

"All right! We'll make a village, and make appear to our mother that we are dancing." They did so.

As she got near, she saw her two boys, joined in the crowd, and began dancing. Now this was at the swampy side of a lake, and the people were grass and frogs. They seemed to her real people dancing, the grass waved back and forth in the dance, the frogs sang. At last the deception ceased, and she found herself in the swamp up to her neck, with reeds and grass and frogs all around her.

She ran after the boys a third time, and was about to catch them. They made a village of people. Two parties were gambling. She took part in the gambling. These were frogs. Half sat on one log, a long line of frogs, and opposite was another log full of frogs. But they seemed to the woman like men. After a time she saw things as they were, and got out of the swamp.

The fifth time she was about to catch her sons, when they made it appear that a crowd of people were playing ball on a flat. At one end she saw her elder boy, and at the other her younger. The valley seemed full of men. She joined in the play herself. When the deception ceased, she saw that the leaves of the trees, carried along by the wind, were what seemed people to her.

The boys ran on, and met Coyote, who said, "My grandsons, why do you run so fast?"

They said, "We are running away from our mother, who is an *At!at!a'lia.*"

Coyote said, "Run on up the hill. I'll meet her." He picked up a lot of mussel shells, broke them into bits, and put them into his leggings, tying the leggings tight at the ankle and below the knee. Then he began to beat time with his leg, the shells making an excellent rattle. He saw her coming, and began singing and dancing towards her. She wondered what it was that rattled so about that man. He came along on the trail, came near going over her, pretended not to see her.

She stepped off the trail, and asked, "What is the matter with you?"

"Oh, I've killed two children."

"You have killed two children?" repeated the woman. "Why, I have been following those children a long time."

"Well, I ate them long ago." He went on.

"Wait," she called, "and tell me what rattles so." He danced on. She followed, and insisted on knowing how he rattled.

At last he said, "I met a man who told me that he broke his leg bone on a great rock, and then it rattled, and still it had the same strength."

"Oh, fix mine as you did yours."

"No, you haven't strength enough. It would hurt, and you would run off."

But she insisted, and at last Coyote took her to a rock. Taking a great stone, he was about to throw it on her leg, when she drew back and said, "Oh, I can't stand it!"

He danced off again, saying, "I knew you couldn't stand it. Only great men have endured it, great chiefs."

She begged him to come back again.

He came back, she straightened out her leg. He took as heavy a rock as he could lift and broke her leg into pieces. Then he danced off. She tried to follow, but fell down.

Coyote called to her, "You've got your rattles, haven't you? And now you are satisfied?"[156] He turned her into a large rock on the north side of the Columbia River. She leans out against a bluff, as she stood when he changed her.

34. THE HUNTER WHO HAD AN ELK FOR
A GUARDIAN SPIRIT[157]

There was a man at Dog River,[158] in days gone
by, whose wife was with child. Pretty soon she gave
birth to the child. While she was sick, he carried wood,
and one day a piece of bark fell on his forehead and cut
him. When the boy was large enough to shoot, he killed
birds and squirrels. He was a good shot. One day the
father said, "You don't do as I used to. I am ashamed to
own you. When I was of your age, I used to catch
young elks. One day when I caught a young one, the
old one attacked me and made the scar you see on my
forehead."

The boy had a [*Tah*] visit from an elk. And the
elk said, "If you will serve me and hear what I say, I will
be your master and will help you in every necessity.
You must not be proud. You must not kill too many of
any kind of animal. I will be your guardian spirit."[159]

The young man became a great hunter, knew
where every animal was--bear, elk, deer. He killed what
he needed for himself, and no more. The old man, his
father, said, "You are not doing enough. At your age I
used to do more."

The young man was grieved at his father's
scolding. The elk, the young man's helper, was very
angry at the old man. At last she caused the young man
to kill five herds of elk. He killed all except his own
elk, though he tried to kill even her. This elk went to a
lake and pretended to be dead. The young man went
into the water to draw the elk out; but as soon as he
touched it, both sank.

After touching bottom, the young man woke as
from a sleep, and saw bears, deer, and elk without

number, and they were all persons. Those that he had killed were there too, and they groaned.

A voice called, "Draw him in." Each time the voice was heard, he was drawn nearer his master, the Elk, till he was at his side.

Then the great Elk said, "Why did you go beyond what I commanded? Your father required more of you than he himself ever did. Do you see our people on both sides? These are they whom you have killed. You have inflicted many needless wounds on our people. Your father lied to you. He never saw my father, as he falsely told you, saying that my father had met him. He also said that my father gave him a scar. That is not true. He was carrying firewood when you were born, and a piece of bark fell on him and cut him. He has misled you. Now I shall leave you, and never be your guardian spirit again."

When the Elk had finished, a voice was heard saying five times, "Cast him out." The young man went home. The old man was talking, feeling well.

The young man told his two wives to fix a bed for him. They did so. He lay there five days and nights, and then told his wives, "Heat water to wash me, also call my friends so that I may talk to them. Bring five elkskins." All this was done.

The people came together, and he told them, "My father was dissatisfied because, as he said, I did not do as he had done. What my father wanted grieved the guardian spirit which visited and aided me. My father deceived me. He said that he had been scarred on the head by an elk while taking the young one away. He said that I was a disgrace to him. He wanted me to kill more than was needed. The spirit has left me, and I die."[160]

35. COYOTE AND EAGLE[161]

Coyote and his younger brother, Eagle, were living together. Now Eagle used to go out to hunt, but Coyote was left at home. Coyote used to be in the house. And then Eagle always killed deer, and he carried the deer on his back, bringing about two or three to the house. They were always left outside of the house. And then he used to go inside in the house.

Then Coyote used to arrive, but he always brought merely mice. And then he would roast them in the ashes in the house. But Eagle used to boil meat.

Now then Coyote always got angry. So Coyote just secretly killed his younger brother. They [sic.] slew Eagle.

Then he never used to stay long in any place. And then he said to himself: "Never mind! I shall go to the woods. Very soon the Indians will come here."[162]

36. A DESERTED BOY IS PROTECTED
BY *ITC!I'XYAN'S* DAUGHTER[163],[164]

There was a village opposite The Dalles, and in the village lived a boy who was very quarrelsome. He whipped the other boys, killed one or two. At last the chief told the boys to take this bad one away to some distance, leave him, slip off, and come home. Then they were all to move away. The bad boy had two grand-mothers who had reared him.

The boys took him off to the place agreed upon, then slipped off and left him. He stayed till sundown, then began to shout to the boys that it was time to go

home. The boys had left their voices there to answer for
them, and they said, "No, it is not time yet." It was then
almost dark.

The two grandmothers had left fire for him
between two mussel shells hid in the ashes, a deer rib
which the Indians used to make fishhooks out of, and ten
wild potatoes. They did not want to go and leave him,
but the people forced them to go.

Now the boy discovered that he had been left,
and he ran home as fast as he could, found the village
gone, the place cleared off. He looked across to the
other side of the river, and saw the whole village camped
there. He felt very lonely, and every now then began to
cry. He searched around where his grandmothers had
lived, and found the fire and rib.

In the morning a great many magpies came
around. He set a trap and caught three of them. He
skinned them and made a robe, which he spread over his
breast at night. Next day he caught three more. He ate
one potato a day as long as they lasted. Each day he
caught three magpies. On the fourth day he had twelve
skins, his blanket now came to his knees.

He made a fishline out of his trap strings and
went fishing. He threw his line out, and said to the
river, "Give me all kinds of food." He fished five days,
caught a fish each day. The people saw him from the
other side.

All at once, on the fifth day, he jumped up and
ran back and forth from the bank to the water. Then he
danced along the river and sang very loud. The words
he sang were, "Now I'll make my magpie robe fly, now
I'll make my magpie robe fly." They heard his words on
the other side. They watched, and saw him draw something long and white out of the water. He threw it on
his back and went to his camp. The bundle was made of
different kinds of wood, and was full of roots, salmon,

and all kinds of Indian food.   Towards evening the people saw that he had a large fire and was eating.

That night he slept warm and well. After a time he felt something cold under his head, and then something cold between his feet. He woke up, and felt a person lying at his side.

The person said, "Are you awake?"

"Yes." He raised up his robe, thinking that it was his robe. As he raised it, he found he had a blanket of mountain sheepskin over him, the blanket of the chief's daughter. He looked, and found a woman at his side. He was in a house, and everything was beautiful with skin and carving around him.

Early next morning the people on the other side went out, and, looking across the river, saw that the boy had a nice house where their village had been. *Itc!i'-xyan's* daughter had come out of the water in the night, while he slept, made the house, and lain down by his side. Towards sunrise he and she arose. His people saw all this.

The chief called the people together and told them to go over and see the young woman, and say, "The chief of the village had a purpose in leaving you. He left you so that you might get this house. Now that you have the house, he will come back."

When the messengers came, they were astonished at what they saw. The house was much greater than they had expected. While *Itc!i'xyan's* daughter was sleeping with the young man that one night, food was brought out of the river. "All right!" said the boy. "Let him come with his people, but he must come last."

The next day the boy's two grandmothers came, then the whole village. Last of all came the chief. But as he was crossing the river, the young man raised a storm and drowned him. The young man then became chief and fed all the people for years with the food which came out of the river for his wife.

Even now the Indians on the Columbia River send their boys to fish after dark to get the spirit of *Itc!i'xyan*. She lives in the water and helps people yet.

37. AN *AT!AT!A'LIA* HAS HER ARM PULLED OFF[165]

At Wasco there was a boy who cried all the time. Nobody could quiet him. At last everybody got tired of him and went to bed, left him. He was near the fire. The others had gone up on the beds, and were trying to sleep. The boy cried away till at last he grew quiet. He saw an arm reaching out for him, all striped and painted. As it caught hold of him, he screamed with all his might, "Something has got me." The arm reached down through the smoke hole to the ground.

He struggled and struggled and screamed. At last he pulled the striped, painted arm off, threw it down by the fire, and said, "I've pulled off somebody's arm." They got up then and saw the arm.

The old *At!at!a'lia* ran to tell her four sisters that she had lost her arm. Now all the people living around came to the house where the crying boy was, to see the arm.

Two or three mornings after that, Coyote said to the boy's parents, "Let us have a great dance." On the night of the dance the five *At!at!a'lias* came; one of them had lost an arm. With the five were two little *At!at!a'lias*.

Coyote hired Bat, Ground Squirrel, and Gray Squirrel to put dry grass around the house and smear it with pitch. When the house was ready, the five sisters came, but the two young ones would not go in. They came because they saw the people assembled. Coyote went out and invited them in; he urged them to dance first. They danced and sang. One sang, "Give me my arm."

Now Coyote told the little boy to run and get the arm. All the people slipped out. The boy brought the arm and put it on the woman. Then all five of the women got excited dancing, and did not notice that the people had gone out. They were shut in tight.

Then Coyote set fire to the house. As it blazed up, they still danced. The two *At!at!a'lia* girls outside screamed, "Oh, you are burning!" Coyote slapped their tongues with his hand and cut them off. They could not scream then. As the flames went higher and higher, the women danced. The house fell in, and they were burned up. The two girls went home.[166]

38. A JACK RABBIT BOY TRICKS AN *AT!AT!A'LIA*[167]

A Jack Rabbit boy once played below Wasco near a sandbank. He played around in this way for four days. The fifth day he went off some distance from the house, playing and jumping. At last he ran against a woman all painted in stripes. She was a human being, and acted like one, but lived on people. She was three times as large as men are at the present day. When the boy ran against her, she reached out to catch him; but he ran away from her as fast as he could, ran towards home. She followed him.

When he came to a rock, he ran around it. On the rock was a mountain sheep's horn. He ran into this horn, and she ran on. She ran around the rock, looked into the horn, saw the boy's eye, and thinking, "I'll get you," put in her hand, but couldn't reach him.

Then she sat down with her back to the sun and waited. The sun was getting hot. She felt something on one side of her neck, and put her hand on the place. It was a wood tick. She pulled it off. Then there was one on the other side. At last she felt ticks all over her body. She pulled off her buckskin robe; inside it was a mass of wood ticks. While pulling off the ticks, she would often look at the horn.

At last the boy put his hair up on top of his head, blackened his nose, and came to the opening of the sheep's horn. He looked at her and rushed back into the horn. She roared with laughter, and said, "Have I ever seen so ugly a boy!" And she rolled and laughed.

Then she said to the boy,"If you could look worse than that, I should die."

He pulled his hair over his face; it came to his breast, and his great eyes were looking through the hair. He came to the opening of the horn again. She laughed harder than ever, took her dress, made a hole in it, and put it over the horn so that if he came out, she could catch him.

While she was laughing, he came out and ran away with her dress. The boy and dress were gone before she knew it.

The woman called loudly, but the boy would not stop. She shouted and screamed, "I'll let you off, if you will bring back my dress."

The boy went on till he came to a lake. He made ice over the whole lake, then walked over. Soon the woman came in pursuit. He threw the dress away in the middle of the lake. She tried to cross; put her foot on the ice. It cracked. She stood on the other side and teased him to get her dress for her, made all sorts of promises.

He said, "The ice is strong." He threw two great rocks on the ice; the rocks broke--the ice was so hard.

This convinced the woman. She crept onto the ice, went out onto the lake, and got near her dress. The boy caused the ice to grow thin and break. She sank in the water and was drowned. This woman was a man-eater.

39. THE FIVE *AT!AT!A 'LIA* SISTERS STEAL A BOY[168]

On the right side of the Columbia River, fifteen miles below The Dalles, lived a woman who had a child. She had also five sisters-in-law who lived in another house. The woman sang every night. When the sisters-in-law heard the singing, they took the child, carried it home, and kept it till morning.

Now five *At!at!a 'lia* sisters said, "If we pretend to be the sisters-in-law, we can get the child."[169] These five sisters could not speak Wasco well. They had their own language, but nobody knows what it was. All tried, and at last the youngest could speak best. They heard the mother singing.

The youngest went to the door, and without showing her face called out, "I want the child." The child was given to her, and the five went off.

They were hardly out of sight when the sisters-in-law came and said, "Give us the child."

"You have it already," was the answer.

"No, we have not."

They struck a fire and looked at the tracks. They were the tracks of the five *At!at!a'lia* sisters. While running off, the four sisters tried to get the child from the youngest sister, but she held to it. They wanted to eat it as they ran. When they were home, the eldest sisters would often beg to eat the boy; but the youngest kept them off, and the boy grew up with her. The mother mourned long for her son.

He grew to be about twelve years old. He used to go hunting, and brought in rabbits, squirrels, and other game. The woman like him more and more. The other sisters wanted to feed him on frogs and snakes, such as they gave their own children to eat and ate themselves, but she always gave him good food. They often begged of her to let them eat him, but she would say, "No, he brings food.. You'll eat me first." At last they all called him son.

He began to wonder why the other children were striped and spotted. An old man, Sandhill Crane, lived near the five sisters. He knew all about this, and it troubled him.

Once in a while the woman gave the boy snakes, and he ate them. One day the woman said, "You may hunt on every side except the north." Old Crane lived in the north not far away.

One day the boy determined to go north and see why they did not want him to go there. He came to a creek, and on the other side he saw a tall old man. The man called to him, "Come over here!"

"I can't," said the boy, "I have no way to cross."

The old man sat down and stretched his leg across the river. It was a wide stream. He said, "Now cross, but don't step on my knee. If you do, you will slip."[170]

The boy went over, and old Crane told him that he did not belong to that people, but to one that lived far away. "Now you must escape," said the old man. "Make five creeks, and at the last creek make choke-cherry bushes, very thick and covered with berries. Go on a little farther and you will find hung on a tree the board on which you were when a baby, and your little blanket. Take them and go on."

That night he went back and told the sisters that he had found a creek and lots of berries. While the boy was on his way back to them that day, the eldest sister said, "I told you that that boy should be eaten. Now he has gone north." The youngest sister said nothing. At dusk the boy came in loaded with chokecherries on the boughs, and told the sisters where he had found them.

Next morning they started; he remained at home. They crossed the five creeks, found the berries, and ate so many that they could hardly move. They began to spit blood. They looked in their baskets to see how many cherries they had gathered. The baskets were full of blood. They had put cherries on their blankets; they found only a mass of blood. Blood ran out of their mouths.

The boy made the sun very hot. And when they started to return home, all the streams dried up. They had to go up and down the deep [steep?] sides of can-yons. Four of the sisters died one after another. Only the youngest reached the house. She found the house burned and her boy gone. She put the blame on old Crane, and hurried to his house. She came to the bank and accused Crane.

After quarreling a long time, she wanted to be reconciled, and asked him to ferry her over. "All right, if you are not afraid." [She intended to eat him and then follow the boy.]

Crane said, "Step on my knee when you come over." She started, then drew back; she did this two or three times. Old Crane got very angry, threatened to

take his leg away. Then she started, and in the middle
of the stream she stepped on his knee. He turned his leg.
She fell into the river and was drowned.

40. TWO CHILDREN ESCAPE FROM
AN *AT!AT!A'LIA*[171]

Two *Ikinickwai*[172] children went out to gather
flint. A boy and his sister went every day for this purpose. They had each five good paddles, the sixth was
full of holes its entire length. The little girl said, "Hurry
and pick up the flints. The *At!at!a'lia* may come."[173]

And sure enough, she was right there. The
moment the words were out of the girl's mouth, she
looked behind, and there was *At!at!a'lia*. The brother
and sister ran with all their might. The boy had one of
the flints in his hand. He held it tight.

The *At!at!a'lia* caught them, put them in her
great basket, and tied the mouth of it with buckskin
strings. She was all spotted and striped, a terribly ugly-
looking creature, and very large. She lived on people,
and was especially fond of eating children. She hurried
along with the two children. The girl was larger than the
boy. She sat on his foot in the basket. His foot was
tender from the itch which he had had on it. She hurt
him greatly, and he said, "Sister, you hurt my foot where
I had the itch."

The woman said, "What is the matter? My
children are burning up, surely."

The girl heard what she said, and felt that she
could frighten her. She repeated the *At!at!a'lia's* words:
"Your children are burning up, surely."

The woman was terrified at this, and said, "Somebody tells me my children are burning up." She called over their names on her fingers.

The fourth time the girl called out very loud, "Your children are burning up!" The woman put down the basket and ran towards home. But she came back, and hung the basket up on an oak tree, one of the trees near The Dalles on the *Wi'cxam* side. The two children were hung up, could not get out of the basket. The boy gave his sister the flint. She cut the strings of the cover, and they got out. They filled the basket with stones and dirt, and hung it up again. Then they ran to the river.

The woman hurried home, found her children all safe, and said, "Oh, I thought you were burned to ashes! I have a nice pair of children out here," and she told how she had got them. Then she started to bring the brother and sister. She pulled down the basket; it was heavy. She put it on her back, went home, and took off the basket. All her children got around it. She unstrapped it. Behold! There was nothing but stones and dirt. She knew they had gotten out and had run away. She put the basket on her back and started after them.

The boy now made five rivers, for he was very powerful. The old woman jumped over the first river. She went over so nicely that she said, "I must try that again." She jumped over the first river five times. When she came to the second, she leaped over that too. High in the air she jumped this river five times. She jumped the third river five times; the fourth river the same way, also the fifth.

She saw the children now about a mile ahead. She drew in her breath, and the children came in with it. They were almost in her jaws when she stopped, for she had to blow out again. That sent the children off about as far as they were before. She drew in her breath; they were nearly at her mouth, but she could not draw in another bit. She had to blow them away.

They reached the Columbia River, jumped into a canoe, and pushed it way out. They told the crawfish, the turtles, and all the fish in the water to eat her, and the big rocks to roll on her. When the old woman came to the river bank, she drew in her breath, and the canoe came almost to her hand. Then she had to blow out, and it went far out again. She tried many times to draw them in, but her breath was not long enough.[174] Then she ran into the water and waded out part of the way. The fish began to eat her body all over, and the rocks came rolling down from the cliffs on to her. At last, barely alive, she waded out of the water, and the children escaped.

41. OLD MAN GRIZZLY BEAR DECEIVES THE FIVE BROTHERS[175]

In *La'daxat*[176] lived five brothers who were known far and near. One evening about dark they heard the voice of an old man, who asked, "Have the young men of this village gone to bed? If they have not, I'll tell them something which has happened today."

The young men answered, "We are all awake."

"A great bear came on our island today," said the old man, "and I want you all to come and hunt that bear tomorrow." All the young men were willing.

Next day they went out. The chief of the village stood on the very spot on the island where the bear had first been seen. He had all his feathers on, had his shield and his quiver full of arrows; he looked very well. The evening before, the old man had given them arrowpoints, had told the chief to use them and give them to his men. He did so.

The people saw the bear, and drove it toward the chief, who was the eldest of the five brothers. He shot at the bear, but the arrow did not penetrate, and the bear devoured the chief. All the people went home, left the bear on the island.

The brothers sweated five days and nights,[177] for that was the custom if a relative died. Then they were ready for another attack on the bear. The fifth night the voice of the old man cried out and asked, "Are the young men ready to hunt the great bear again?" A still whiter one has been seen on the island today. Have they arrowpoints enough?"

Now this voice was the voice of the great bear himself, who was deceiving the people. And the first arrowpoints were the points of fern leaves that looked like arrowpoints; the great bear made them look so. The old man brought another bundle of arrowpoints. He was very old, and as he gave them he cried. These second points were made of the leaves of the wild grape, and had been turned into points by the bear. The people were mourning more and more.

All kinds of birds came and received arrowpoints, and were helping the brothers. All shot at the bear. The second brother stood on the trail, the others drove up the bear. He shot. The bear fell and pretended to be dead. As the brother went towards him, he sprang up and swallowed him.

They sweated five days for the second brother. Then the old man's voice was heard. It was low, and seemed to be drowned in tears, it trembled with sorrow, and at last, choked with tears, he cried so loud that the whole village heard him. He brought a great bundle of arrowpoints to the three chiefs, poured them down and wept. This time the points were made of dried grape leaves. The people rejoiced to get them, they seemed so beautiful and sharp.

They went out the third day. The third chief was killed, though all the birds of the air came to assist him, and all shot at the bear. The chief shot at him, he fell over. The chief went up and pushed him with his bow; the bear sprang up and devoured him.

Again they sweated for five days and nights. The voice of the old man was heard on the fifth night. It seemed weaker and sadder. Another bear had been seen. The old man brought another bundle of arrow-points, and he cried all the time. They were long, sharp, and beautiful. They were made of willow-leaves turned yellow. The fourth brother was killed as the third had been. Only the youngest was left.

He sweated five days and nights. He was going around mourning for his brothers, when he came upon the leg bone of a meadowlark. He couldn't step over it or crawl under it; finally, he slipped on it and broke it.[178] Then Meadowlark appeared to him, and told him that the bears did not come to the island, that it was their home, that the arrowpoints were nothing but leaves, and that the old man who brought them was himself one of the bears.

"Go to your grandfathers way over on that mountain," she pointed southward. "They will give you arrowpoints there that are real points. And when you go to fight, put a stump on the place where your brothers were killed. Put feathers on it as on a man, then stand on it; and when the bear rushes up, shoot him."

The young man went to the mountain, and from the rattlesnakes received their teeth made into arrowpoints. He came home and gave them to his men.

Now the old man called out again, and asked if they had arrowpoints. They said, "We have none." He brought a bundle and gave them to them; they were made of cottonwood leaves. The old man cried bitterly as he gave them. As soon as he left, the young man threw them into the fire, and they burned up. Sure enough, they were nothing but leaves.

Next day all went out, drove the bear as before. All the birds screamed and whooped and shot at the bear. This time he felt every arrow, for the points were made of the teeth of rattlesnakes. His nose and eyes puffed up, and he went into the water and lay down. He drank much water. A fish with long sharp fins behind his head came there and was swallowed, and he cut through the bear's stomach.

The bear came out of the water, and again the birds shot at him, and each said, "I've hit him, I've hit him."

Razor Snake said, "I am doing the best I can under his feet."

Frog said, "I have done best. I jumped on his foot and frightened him."

At this moment the young chief, the fifth brother, shot and killed him.

All the people came together around the dead bear, the chief at the head. He said, "Give five whoops!" They did so and then skinned the bear. The white part of the skin the chief took, and also the front claws. Then the people took the meat and went home. A small bird, the smallest of all, found a drop of the bear's blood on a leaf. He took that for his share. The chief said, "Take a shoulder to the old man Grizzly Bear." There were five of these bear brothers.

Blue Jay said, "I'll take it." He threw it over his shoulder and went to the house of the five brothers. They were crying. Blue Jay pushed the door open and said, "Here, old man, take this," and he threw the shoulder in.

They said, "Oh, our house smokes terribly. We can scarcely see."

42. EAGLE, A KLAMATH MAN, GOES TO THE COLUMBIA RIVER TO GAMBLE[179]

Eagle was a Klamath man, and he came to the Columbia River on a sporting expedition--to gamble. At first he won all the games. He gambled with Crab, Crow, Hawk, Raven, and many other people. Towards the end, luck turned against him. Crab was called on to take part in the game.

After that Eagle lost everything that he had won and all that he had brought with him. He gambled off his buckskin dress, his moccasins, arrows, everything. Then he bet one arm, lost; lost the other arm; bet one leg, lost; bet the other leg, lost. He lost one whole side of his body, one eye, one ear, all of one half of himself. Then he played and lost the other half of his body. His life was now in the hands of those with whom he gambled. They cut off his head. Then his people at home discovered where he was and what had become of him.

He had two sons, and they looked for guardian spirits to get supernatural power to help them avenge their father. The younger brother received the strength of twenty-five grizzly bears. The elder received the power of five double fires [five two abreast, ten in all]. They started with these powers and hunted for their father's tracks. After five years they found them, and followed them to The Dalles.

They stood on the hill overlooking the village, saw their father's head stuck on a pole. They saw a house at one end of the village. "We will go there," they said. They reached the house where they found two old women. The young men asked, "Who is the chief of the village?"

The old women said, "We must not tell you. If we mention his name, that moment he will sneeze and say, 'My name is mentioned in the old house at the end of the village,' and he will send to see who is here." But the brothers insisted.

At last the old women told him, and that instant the chief sneezed and sent to the house. The first messenger came. In an instant his face was burned from the power of the elder brother. Five came; all were served in the same way. Then the chief sent and invited the young men to come and gamble with him. [And this is one of the sayings of the Indians now, from this story: If a person sneezes, he says, "Somebody is talking about me."][180]

They played and won back all their father's body, and brought him to life by putting the pieces together and stepping over them five times.[181]

The people now wanted to fight with them. They agreed. The brothers placed the five double fires on one side of the village, and the twenty-five grizzly bears on the other side. Not one person escaped. All were killed and burned to ashes. The father and sons went home. They scattered the grizzly bears over all the mountains. When they came home to Klamath, they lived happily and well.

147. NATIVE AND DUGOUT CANOE, CELILO, COLUMBIA RIVER.

Native and dugout canoe, Celilo, Columbia River (c. 1897).
Oregon Historical Society, Neg. CN 018927.

NOTES TO THE NARRATIVES

PART ONE
INTRODUCTION: LOCUS AND CULTURE

1. See Spier, Leslie and Edward Sapir, 1930. *Wishram Ethnography*, UWPA 3/3. Seattle: University of Washington Press:160. Spier notes, "The Wasco were located on the south bank [of the Columbia River] directly opposite the Wishram at the Dalles [sic]. They probably also had villages on the south side of Ten-Mile Rapids, at Celilo Falls, and as far upstream as the mouth of the Deschutes [River]. They also laid claim to the country as far east as the John Day River, but never occupied it." DH

2. In our *Tragedy of the Wahk-Shum: The Death of Andrew J. Bolon, Yakima Indian Agent, As Told by Su-el-lil, Eyewitness; Also, The Suicide of General George A. Custer, As Told by Owl Child, Eyewitness* (Issaquah, WA: 1995), p. 25, *Su-el-lil* relates, "The Indians had returned from the mountains, and our party was on its way to The Dalles to get dried salmon." This same group of Indian travelers was met with by Indian Agent Bolon, cut his throat, and buried him under some dirt, limbs and brush--his body has never been found. DH

3. See Strong, William D. & W. Egbert Schenck, 1925. "Petroglyphs Near the Dalles of the Columbia River," *American Anthropologist* 27:76-90. Also, Strong, W. Duncan & W. Egbert Schenck, Julian H. Steward 1930. *Archaeology of the Dalles-Deschutes Region*, UCPAAE 29:i-vii, 1-154, plates. Also consulted: Hodge, Frederick W. ed., 1959. "Wasco," *Handbook of American Indians North of Mexico* II, BAE 30. New York [repr. Pageant Books, Inc.]: 917-918. Swanton, John R. 1952. "Wasco," *The Indian Tribes of North America* BAE 145. 1952:475. DH

4. Joseph Schafer ed., 1940. *Memoirs of Jeremiah Curtin*. Madison: State Historical Society of Wisconsin. DH

5. Schafer:501 ff.

6. Schafer:354 f..

7. Curtin's wife served as his faithful secretary-stenographer. DH

8. Schafer:360.

9. Sapir, Edward 1909. *Wishram Texts, Together with Wasco Tales and Myths, Collected by Jeremiah Curtin*, PAES 2. Leyden, Brill:314 pages. DH

10. In the preparation of this volume, the author journeyed to the American Philosophical Society's library in Philadelphia. There, APA librarians kindly called his attention to a list of Wasco words written in a fine hand, evidently Curtin's wife's labor. DH

11. Works which we have previously published and which draw on materials from the McWhorter Collection appear in the Selected List of Readings hereafter. DH

12. We understand that on the Warm Springs Reservation some six or eight Wasco tale texts have been collected. Our queries about these texts have not been answered. DH

13. Spier, Leslie and Edward Sapir, 1920. *Wishram Ethnography*, UWPA 3(3). Seattle WA 1930:299 pages. DH

14. Ault, Nelson A. 1959. *The Papers of Lucullus Virgil McWhorter*. Pullman: Friends of the Library, State College of Washington:101-106. DH

15. We have employed the best Folklore scholarship to aid in defining these categories of folk narrative, and then in aiding us to place individual narratives within a particular area of likeness. Listed hereafter are some critical terms, used in their particular folkloric or traditional sense, plus definitions:

VERSION ". . . a distinctive , usually a geographically limited, type of a (narrative) which exists. . . in several variants with characteristic common elements, such as motifs, structure, etc., by which it is distinguished from other versions of the type." (See Bødker, p. 312, cited hereafter. [See TYPE below].

VARIANT ". . . a variant may be a mutation, but usually it constitutes, with other variants of the same tradition, a type, which may be divided into several versions. . . ." (Bødker, p. 310).

MYTH ". . . myth (means) a tale laid in a world supposed to have preceded the present order. It tells of sacred beings and of semi-divine heroes and of the origins of all things, usually through the agency of these sacred beings. Myths are intimately connected with religious beliefs and practices of the people." (Thompson, *Folktale*, p. 9, cited hereafter).

LEGEND   ". . . an account of an extraordinary happening believed to have actually occurred. It may recount a legend of something which happened in ancient times at a particular place--a legend which has attached itself to that locality, but which will probably also be told. . . in remote parts of the world." (Thompson, *Folktale*, p. 8).

TALE OF MAGIC   ". . . an <u>ordinary folktale</u> about supernatural adversaries, supernatural helpers, magic and marvels, and other supernatural objects and happenings. . . . (Bødker, p. 291).

TRICKSTER TALES   ". . . (relate) deeds of a trickster. Sometimes the buffoon is a human being, but more often he is an animal endowed with human characteristics. . . . Most culture heroes are also tricksters and that even in their most dignified moments they are prone to show something of their dual nature." (Thompson, *Tales of North American Indians*, p. xviii, cited hereafter).

TALES OF BEAST MARRIAGES ". . . In stories of beast marriages, animals carry off human girls or marry human husbands. They have offspring--sometimes human, sometimes animal, sometimes capable of becoming either at will. Sometimes the animal spouse is a transformed person. The tales regularly end with the transformation of the animal spouse to human form, or with an escape from the animal." (Thompson, *Tales of North American Indians*, pp. xix-xx).

TALES   COMPARABLE   WITH   EUROPEAN MÄRCHEN ". . . tales widely found over Europe appear, may exhibit European phraseology, background, and ideas. More than fifty European tales are current among the American Indians, who usually recognize them as borrowings." (Thompson, *Tales of North American Indians*, p. xx).

TYPE ". . . a traditional tale that has an independent existence. It may be told as a complete narrative and does not depend for its meaning on any other tale. It may indeed happen to be told with another tale, but the fact that it may appear alone attests its independence. It may consist of only one motif or of many . Most animal tales and jokes and anecdotes are types of one motif. The ordinary <u>Märchen</u> (tales like "Cinderella" or "Snow White") are types consisting of many motifs. (Thompson, *Folktale*, p. 415).

MOTIF ". . . the smallest element in a tale having a power to persist in tradition. In order to have this power it must have something unusual and striking about it. Most motifs fall into three classes. <u>First</u> are the actors in a tale. . . ; <u>second</u> come certain items in the background of the action--magic objects, unusual customs, strange beliefs, etc.; <u>third</u> are single incidents (these comprise the great majority of motifs, can have an independent existence, may therefore serve as true tale-types.") (Thompson,

Folktale, p. 415-416). DH

16. Bødker, Laurits 1965. *Folk Literature (Germanic)*, Vol. II of *International Dictionary of Regional European Ethnology and Folklore*, ed. Åke Hultkrantz. Copenhagen: Rosenkilde and Bagger. DH

17. Thompson, Stith 1946. *The Folktale*. New York: Holt, Rinehart and Winston. DH

18. Thompson, Stith 1966.*Tales of the North American Indians*. Bloomington, Indiana: Indiana University Press. DH

19. We understand that authorities of the Confederated Tribes of the Warm Springs Indian Reservation have employed linguists to reconstruct the tribal languages in order to provide language instruction to Wasco or other reservation youths. But the traditional languages on the reservation are beyond our focus here. DH

20. Thompson, Stith 1955. *Motif-Index of Folk-Literature, A Classification of Narrative Elements in Folktales, Ballads, Myths, Fables, Mediaeval Romances, Exempla, Fabliaux, Jest-Books, and Local Legends*. Bloomington, Indiana: Indiana University Press, six volumes. DH

PART TWO
THE TRADITIONAL TALES OF THE WASCOS

I. TALES OF THE ORIGINS OF MAN,
ANIMALS AND PLANTS, PHENOMENA

21. From Edward Sapir, *Wishram Texts, Together with Wasco Tales and Myths*. . . pp. 267-269 [hereafter cited as Sapir]. The Wasco narratives collected by Jeremiah Curtin during a visit to the Warm Springs Reservation, Oregon, during the winter of 1885 appear on pages 239-314 of Sapir. See also "Coyote and *Itc!I'xyan*" (Monster):41-43 from the Wishrams, the same volume. DH

22. Other instances wherein Coyote asks advice of his excrement include Sapir, "Coyote and Antelope:"67; "Coyote Enslaves the West Wind:"99. Coyote also seeks advice from his "five sons" or excrement in *Tales of the Nez Perce*: "Coyote the Expeditioner:"5; "Bears and Coyote:"71;"Coyote and Hummingbird:"79.

See also Boas, Franz 1901. *Kathlamet Texts*, RBAE 26. Washington, D.C., U.S. Government Printing Office:45-49. [This work is cited hereafter as *Kathlamet Texts*]. Also, Boas, Franz 1894. *Chinook Texts*, RBAE

20. Washington, D.C., U.S. Government Printing Office: 101-106. [This work is cited hereafter as *Chinook Texts*]. On the coast of British Columbia similar acts are told of the raven. DH

23. Eagle and Weasel appear as elder and younger brothers also in Sapir:117 ff.

24. In *Tales of the Nez Perce*, "Coyote and Monster:"43-46, *Itc!-i'xyan* is described as a gigantic animal monster residing near Kamiah, Idaho. By his powerful inhaling he swallowed people who subsequently died of starvation and confinement in his stomach. According to the Nez Perce, these people were revived from the dead by Coyote who also cut up portions of the monster's carcass, threw the portions in all directions, and thus created the several Indian nations.

But Sapir identifies "*Itch!-e'yan*" as a Merman residing in the waters of the Wishram or the Lower Chinook, the Columbia River above the Dalles, Oregon. "Even today the imagination of the Wishram peoples certain bodies of water with mermen; e.g., a lake in the mountains south of Fort Simcoe (the former headquarters of the Yakama Indian Reservation) is said to be *ayatc!-E\xyanix* (peopled with mermen)." DH

25. Sapir:303-307.

26. The "arrow chain" episode related here is often told as part of the Star-husband narrative. See tales 2B "Sky-Rope;" also 21 "Five Stars Visit the Earth," hereafter. See also 5 "Legend of the Great Dipper" hereafter. See especially Stith Thompson 1965. "The Star Husband Tale," in Dundes, Alan, ed. *The Study of Folklore*. Englewood Cliffs, N.J.:414-474. DH

27. In *Tales of the Nez Perce* an episode of obtaining a rope from the spider(s) by which to descend from the sky appears in 8 "Coyote Causes His Son to be Lost:"61-65. See also Sapir, "The Boy that was stolen by *At!at!a'liya*:"165-173, which contains many similar motifs describing the upper world.

28. Spier and Sapir:277. Related by Frank Gunyer about 1924-1925.

29. According to Leslie Spier, "Sky Rope" is a long tale of which the opening given here is not the beginning.

30. See "Coyote Causes His Son to be Lost," esp. p. 62, in *Tales of the Nez Perce*. DH

31. This superstitious belief or omen was also current among the Wishram who made reference to "rainbows" around the moon.

32. Sapir:308-311.

33. According to Sapir, there are no published Chinookan cognates of this myth. That it is not Chinookan in origin is further made probable by the fact that Sun and Moon are here male characters, whereas the Wasco words for "sun" and "moon" are both feminine in gender. Contrast Sapir, "Coyote and the Sun:" 46-49, where Sun is a female character.

34. Sapir notes that *tawna, tawna* is evidently a customary conventional ending, to show that the story is finished. Compare *k!anik!ani'* in line 28 of Sapir's language notation to his text 11 "The Five East-Wind Brothers and the Five Thunder Brothers:"121-131, esp. the very last lines. Also, see *k!one'-k!one'* in *Chinook Texts*:110, line 9.

35. This is probably a misspelling for the modern town of *Prineville*, Oregon. DH

36. McWhorter: a Wasco tale heard during October, 1921. Narrator not named.

37. The *tahmahnawis* spirit was first acquired by youths, both boys and some girls, at about 12 years of age during a lonely quest and vigil far in the mountains. An animal, seen in a dream, imparted to the young person some of the magical power unique to that animal, also may have taught the youth a song. The magical powers gave to the young person marvelous abilities to heal, or to locate game during the hunt, etc. For descriptions of some of the magic powers acquired on the youthful quest, see our *Magic in the Mountains, The Yakima Shaman: Power & Practice*, cited hereafter. DH

38. McWhorter: a Wasco tale collected during October 1921. Informant not named.

39. For another example of the magical arrow-chain from the sky to the earth, see 2A "The Ascent to the Sky and Return to the Earth" above. DH

40. This probably refers to the constellations Ursa Major, Ursa Minor-- if the Indians' lore of the constellations approximated ours. See Gibbon, William B. 1964. "Asiatic Parallels in North American Star Lore: Ursa Major," *JAF* 77:236-250. DH

41. These constellations probably include Ursa Major, Ursa Minor, and Canis Major. DH

42. McWhorter's notes about the *Whoch-whoch* have been lost or misplaced. DH

43. The 'big white road across the sky' is the "Milky Way' as we know it today.

44. The "knife of stars," to the west in the evening, over the mountains, probably refers to the _forepart_ of Leo. Interesting, not the first star to be seen of an evening as we believe; but the Indians believed this "knife of stars" was lucky, a good omen for their gambling, horse-racing, etc.

45. McWhorter: a Wasco legend narrated by _An-a-whoa_ (Black Bear) September 1914.

46. References to Thunderbird appear in our _Ghost Voices, Yakima Indian Myths, Legends, Humor and Hunting Stories_, cited hereafter. The five mountains likely include the highest peaks of the Cascades Mountain Range: Mount Rainier, Mount St. Helens, Mount Hood, Mount Adams. DH

47. At this point in the narrative _An-a-whoa_ handed me [L.V.M.] a small plume of downy eagle feather, plucked from under the wing, as typical of the one presented Coyote by _Why-am-mah_. Of course the down of the young eagle is more pronounced than that of the matured bird.

48. The Klickitats tell me [L.V.M.] that long ago, when passing up or down the _n-Che-wana_ [Columbia River] by canoe, the occupants, excepting those necessary to man the oars, would land when the Bridge was approached, and walk around to the opposite side where they would again re-embark. Those who took the canoes through the tunnel, or bridge, always bade their friends good-bye, for it was believed that the great natural structure would sometime fall, as prophesied by the ancient seers. The catastrophe might take place during transit of the boats. The final destruction of the Bridge formed the Cascades, the first real salmon trap to be met with in the _n-Che-wana_, or Columbia River.

49. This last statement by the narrator, who must then have numbered close to her century milestone, was confirmed by her daughter _Yes-to-la-lema_ who was acting as interpreter. She said, "I had never heard all of this story as given you by my mother. She never told it to her children in full as she has told it today. One way that I have heard it--not from my mother--is that when the five mountains were destroyed, the Bridge, which was in the first mountain, was also broken down. Most Indian stories are rehearsed in various ways by different tribesmen. It is the same as with white people, the preachers. But my mother, who is the oldest living member of her tribe, must have it correct as the Wascos knew it. She has always had a good memory, and her mind today seems as clear and strong as when I was a child.

At this point _Yes-to-la-lema_ conversed with her mother for a few moments, when the aged woman again spoke for interpretation. "Do not go to the young Indians for these old stories. Do not depend on the young people to tell them in the true way. They do not know. They do not listen to the stories, as did the old Indians when they were young. The wisdom of my people will soon be forgotten.

50. McWhorter: a Wasco legend collected July 1918. Narrator not

named.

51. McWhorter locates the "Tumwater" at what is now Fall Bridge, the Columbia River, the upper point of the great rapids. It has no connection with the familiar, and well-advertised springs and brewery near Olympia, Washington. DH

52. This was a Wasco spy who married the Wishom [Wishram] girl.

53. This is, perhaps, the most pronounced declaration to be found in any of the legends peculiar to the *n-Che-wana* where a particular tribe or tribes of Indians are designated as coeval with the age of Animal People. In other legends where "Indians" are mentioned, it is in allusion to the Animal People rather than the actual Indian race. If interrogated on this point, the legend narrator [raconteur] usually explains, "They were real people, real Indians; yet, they were animals and birds with a language. They could talk the same as actual people talk."

54. Compare also the Wishram narrative of the release of the salmon: Sapir, "The Origin of Fish in the Columbia:3-7. DH

55. McWhorter: A Wasco rendition of a popular theme. The date and informant were not given.

56. Spier and Sapir:277-278. Related by Frank Gunyer, a middle-aged Wasco, about 1924-1925.

57. McWhorter: a Wasco legend told by *I-Keep Swah* (Sitting Rock), July 1918.

58. The *Chi-col-lah* is a small bird of the swallow variety, like the Cliff-swallow, the *tic-teah* of the Yakimas.

59. Another narrative of a "people without mouths" appears hereafter as 16 "Food Smellers." For still another narrative about men without mouths, see Sapir, "Coyote and the Mouthless Man:"18-25. Perhaps the same "small-mouthed" people are recounted in *Ghost Voices, Yakima Indian Myths, Legends, Humor and Hunting Stories*, 20 "The *Pach-an-a-ho*."

60. Sapir:264-267.

61. According to Sapir, two absolutely distinct myths [sic] have here been welded into one. For the first part (the struggle between Eagle and Coyote) compare Gatschet, Albert S. 1890. *The Klamath Indians of Southwestern Oregon*, CNAE 2,1. Washington, D.C.:94-97. "Eagle and his Grand Father [sic], respectively correspond to *A'ishish* and his father *K'mukamtch* of the Klamath myth. See also Teit, James A. 1898. *Traditions of the*

Thompson River Indians, MAFLS 6. Boston, MA:21. And see Teit, James A. 1900-09. *The Shuswap*, PJE 2. New York, NY:622,737. [This work is cited hereafter as *Shuswap*.] This is distinctly a myth of the Plateau region, and presumably adapted by the Wasco to the Coyote and Eagle cycle. For the second part, compare Sapir, "The Origin of Fish in the Columbia:"3-7. Also see Spinden, Herbert J. 1908. "Myths of the Nez Perce Indians," *JAF* 21:15-16. Also, in our *Tales of the Nez Perce*, cited hereafter, see "Coyote Causes His Son to be Lost:"61-65, esp. p. 65.

62. Recounted here is the episode wherein the mischievous women are transformed into birds, the harbingers of the salmon. This narrative is frequently told to include segments often related separately: a) distribution of salmon into streams, past fishing sites; b) origination of means of taking salmon; c) meat stolen from sleeper. DH

63. Spier and Sapir: related by Frank Gunyer, a middle-aged Wasco, about 1924-1925.

64. Spier and Sapir: Related by Frank Gunyer, a middle-aged Wasco, about 1924-1925.

II. TALES OF THE LEGENDARY

65. Sapir:294-298.

66. The motif of the two blind crones each of whom has 5 firebrands is interestingly similar to F512.1.2. See also K333.2. Theft from three old women who have but a single eye among them. The hero seizes their eye. DH

67. According to Sapir, this word is evidently the same, though different in gender, as the Wishram *ickcu 'tcien* [adz]. Perhaps it is to be read as *asksk!u 'tsian*, the diminutive form of the word. See Sapir:153-165. And in *Kathlamet Tales* Lynx (*ipu'koa*), cognate with the Wasco *ipkwa'* (wildcat), uses an instrument called *e'qa-itk* (translated: adz).

68. For a similar fight--in midair between Eagle and buzzard, who hold on to each other until each is nothing but a mass of bones, see Sapir, "The Adventures of Eagle and his Four Brothers:"75-93. See also the fight between Panther and Owl in *Kathlamet Texts*:138-141.

69. McWhorter: a Wasco tale narrated by *I-keep-swah* (Sitting Rock) during July 1912.

70. McWhorter: A Wasco tale told by *I-keep-swah* (Sitting Rock) during 1918.

71. *Wasco* comes from the Wasco word *wacq!o* (cup or small bowl of horn), the reference being to a cup-shaped rock a short distance from the main village of the tribe. From the tribal name *Galasq!o*, "those that belong to Wasco," or 'those that have the cup,' are derived many of the forms of the name that follow in the synonym. The derivation of the name from the Shaphtian *wask!u*, 'grass,' lacks probability. See "Wasco" in Hodge, Frederick Webb 1907/1959. *Handbook of American Indians North of Mexico*. New York: Pageant Books, Inc. 2: reprint. See pages 917-918, esp. p. 917 [L.V.M.].

72. This spring, so rich in tribal legendary lore, was completely buried under the grade of the Union Pacific railroad when it was built down the Columbia [on the Oregon side]. So I have been informed by older tribesmen who were well-acquainted with its locality. [L.V.M.]

73. McWhorter: told by the Klickitat, Cascade (*Watlala*), Wishom (Wishram) and Wasco tribes, heard July 4, 1918. No informant named.

74. *At-te-yi-yi*, "cold northeast wind," is the most deadly of all winds. It is sometimes called *Ta-ye-a*.

75. McWhorter consistently employs the spelling "Wishom" for the tribal name and, here, the modern town-site, "Wishram," also nearby the mammoth BN railroad yard.

76. *Wah-pe-us* is literally "catching fish with a dip net." It is located at/or near *Skein*, "cradle-board," in the *n-Che-wana* not far from Celilo. Salmon were also gaffed at *Wah-pe-us*, those that "jump."

77. The oils of the dog-salmon, and of the eel, possess the property of preventing slipping on the ice. Either of these oils applied to the sole of the moccasin insures the wearer a secure footing on the smoothest of ice. The dog-salmon is the *Qee-nut*, or royal chinook salmon, at a certain period. The *um-to-li*, or *m-to-la* is the *Qee-nut* at spawning.

78. *We-now-y-yi*, "Young Chinook-wind," is a powerful warm wind from a distance. In the legend young Chinook-wind is personified as *Qee-nut*, the chinook salmon, and the son of *To-qee-nut*, the Chief of Salmon, Chief of all the fishes.

79. In some versions of this legend, even in the same tribe, as with the Klickitats, this slave woman held by the *At-te-yi-yi* was *We-now-y-yi-ats*, a sister to *We-now-y-yi*, a young Chinook wind.

80. In this narrative it is noticeable that *Ats-te-yi-yi*, the crippled sister, does not pour water for the purpose of forming ice that the enemy of her brothers might not stand as she does in 15B "The Battle of Cold-Wind and

Chinook-Wind" hereafter. DH

81. The peculiar cry or call is rendered by placing the hand over the mouth and by rapid vibrations of the palm, breaking into sharp staccato a long-drawn, quavering yell. It is a signal of triumph, or victory and defiance, and is never used by the vanquished in either games or in war. Such was Coyote's "ruling" when the world was yet young, when the Animal People held sway.

82. McWhorter: a Wasco tale told by *An-a-whoa* (Black Bear) 1917.

83. An aged woman of the *Wan-a-pums* or *Sokults* of the Priests Rapids, on the *n-Che-wana*, averred that there were ten Cold Wind brothers, which is the only instance coming to my notice of a claim that there were more than five. This last is the mystic numeral pervading the philosophy of the Yakimas and kindred tribes, embracing the *Sokults*. Vary rarely, the number seven appears, as where *We-now-y-yi* (see the previous text) kills the youngest and last of the *At-te-yi-yi* brothers at the seventh turn or whirling. At the funeral of Chief *Sluskin We-owikt*, the cortege circled the residence three times and the cemetery seven times, making ten (circuits) all told.

84. The Nez Perce version of this legend has it that the Cold-wind People powdered the snow, and in the battle this snow was used on the ground for the purpose of making it too slippery for Warm-wind, or Chinook-wind, to stand. In the big snowstorms you see a bare place on the mountain where the snow is melted. This is the work of Warm-wind. The young Chinook-wind, in his practicing and exercising, pulled up great trees, carried them on his shoulder to his mother's tepee or lodge, and cast them on the ground with such force as to shatter them into firewood.
The great sturgeon [cf. in the previous version the mother's instruction: *salmon*] from which the oil was made to be cast on the ice so as to prevent the feet of Chinook-wind from slipping was caught by the old grandparents. Chinook was lying in the bottom of the canoe, and when they were pursued by Cold-wind who had always robbed them of their fish, coming near the boat; Chinook shook himself and the boat darted away from the pursuers.   Cold-wind said, "*Eh*! That was never done before."This happened five times, and the Cold-wind gave up the chase, saying, "Let them go with their fish. Just this one time they can go."
All Cold-winds, the five brothers, were killed by the youngest. He begged to be let live, promising that when he was lonely, he would make it cold only five years. Chinook would not agree. The period was shortened to three years, two years, one year, five months, and finally to one moon. This is the generally prevailing ruling now. Formerly it was cold <u>ALL</u> the time. [The source of the Nez Perce version and other details referred to by McWhorter here is not given.]

85. See "Gusty Wind and Zephyr," in *Tales of the Nez Perce*:120-

126. This version details not wrestling to the death, but the entertaining of the surviving Wild Geese brothers as possible husbands for the five daughters of North Wind, then of South Wind. Depicted here not only are the tensions of securing husbands for many daughters, but also of obtaining food and warmth during the cold time. DH

86. A noted spring, location not determined. The name means, literally, "a place out of the ground," as explained further on in the text. The scene of the legend is laid about the Tumwater, more recently known, perhaps, as Celilo Falls, above The Dalles, Oregon.

87. *Sko-lus, Skoo-lus,* or *Sco-lus*: an edible root. The name is applied to a "rim-rock" on the lower *n-Che-wana*, between Lone Rock and Rooster Rock [Multnomah County, OR] as pointed out by *An-a-whoa* while steaming up the river in September, 1911. It is nearly opposite Multnomah Falls.

88. The salmon and the sturgeon are often referred to as one and the same fish. In "The Battle of *At-te-yi-yi* and *Qee-nut*" above, salmon oil was poured on the ice by the old aunt that *Qee-nut* might be enabled to stand.

89. *Ta-man-tow-lee*: "dragging," is near the mouth of the Yakima River. The scar in the earth from the sturgeon's tail dragging [in the dust] is to be seen just above the mouth of the Yakima River.

90. It is notable that not until this point of the story was reached did the narrator refer to the hero as Chinook-wind. Emphasis apparently was placed on the fact that he was a mere boy, although endowed with supernatural strength.

91. *His-to mah*: "place of mussels." As set forth in note 86 above, the exact location, while not definitely determined, is in close proximity to the Tumwater. The name applies also to both the clam and the oyster.

92. Spier and Sapir:279. Related by Frank Gunyer, middle-aged Wasco, about 1924-1925.

93. McWhorter: told by *I-keep-Swah* (Sitting Rock) during July 1918.

94. This tale is fascinating, relating of the volcanic eruption of Mount Hood sometime in the past. Many residents of the Pacific Northwest experienced the eruption and fallout of volcanic ash from Mount St. Helens during May 18, 1980. But, there have been no eruptions of Mount Hood recorded in modern times; thus, the strict chronology of the story (of three white men and three Indians as guides) seems incorrect. What is more likely correct is that where once there was fire, there could be fire again. Of interest here is Dorson, Richard M. 1972. "The Debate Over the Trustworthiness of

Oral Traditional History," *Folklore: Selected Essays*. Bloomington, IN:199-224. Especially on pp. 202-205 he reviews the arguments over the value, the historicity of American Indian oral narratives. Modern researchers tend to find a correlation between the traditional oral text and the geological or other phenomenal past. DH

95. McWhorter: told by *An-a-whoa* (Black Bear) or Mrs. Mary Pilkins. The story of *Nihs-lah* was narrated to McWhorter when coming up the Columbia River on a steamboat from Portland to The Dalles, September 12, 1911. The aged woman seemed to live her younger days over again as she pointed out the different scenes of interest along the river, once the home of her people. *Yap-pi-lute* (Standing in the Water), she declared, is the Wasco name of Castle Rock. When the image of *Nihs-lah* would appear, Castle Rock was half-submerged by the angry waters.

96. Multnomah Falls is located alongside the Columbia River c. 28 miles east of Portland, Oregon. DH

97. Wasco accounts of a specifically water-dwelling monster mention a water creature, "*Itc!i'xyan*" or his daughter. See 36 "A Deserted Boy is Protected by *Itc!i'xyan's* Daughter," hereafter. Similarly, in Sapir, "The Deserted Boy:"139-145, the banished youth is aided by "*Itc!E'xyan's* virgin daughter."

98. McWhorter: told by *Et-Wa-mish* in the Chinook jargon, 1906.

99. That there was some such serpent as described by the aged *Et-Wa-mish* of the Tumwater [Celilo?] and in the accompanying legends, is believed by many of the more enlightened Indians. The fearsome hole under the cliff where the monster was destroyed by fire, and in the depths of which its body was found by the slave boy, is still in evidence. The canyon and other distinguishing features of land over which the men were pursued are to this day pointed out by the old Indians. There are characteristics which separate it [the narrative] from the creative and Monster period legends. Captain Martineau, a half-blood of the Cascade tribe, who at one time was the best swift-water pilot of the Northwest, held that the *Gy-u-boo-kum* was not altogether a mythical production. He gave me this description of it, as he had gathered from the various tribesmen.

It resembled in part the sturgeon, with its mouth similarly located. The body was short, compared to relative thickness, possessing neither fins nor legs. The tail terminated in a great castanet of rattles. Exclusively a denizen of dry land, it haunted the caverns of cliffs, from which it sallied forth only in search of food. Carnivorous and voracious, after gorging it would seek its subterranean den, where it remained in a semi-dormant state until again driven by hunger to seek the light of the upper world. At such time, it pursued its prey with an appalling swiftness, giving vent to a frightful bleating bark, unnerving and paralyzing [with fright?] its victim. The name *Gy-u-boo-kum* or "terrible noise" was /is suggestive of the dread and terror in which this monster was held by the Indians. Besides the three dealt with in the legends proper, there was one seen at Celilo on the *n-Che-wana*. The Captain did not believe that the legends could have dealt with the ordinary rattlesnake of that region.

However, there are grounds for the supposition that the rattler could have figured in the tragedy at the camas patch. This reptile has been known to grow to almost fabulous dimensions, devouring young fawns and other animals of similar size. Chief *Houh Sluskin* of the Yakimas saw one swallowing a full grown woodchuck at the mouth of the Cowiche Creek, near Yakima. A gruesome story is told of a papoose being devoured by a rattler in the Kittitas Valley. The mother left the infant on the ground while she went a short distance to gather chokecherries. The vicious proneness of the male rattler to attack and even pursue a man during a certain moon is recognized by the tribesmen. Even the writer [McWhorter] can attest to the danger attendant on an invasion of their den-infested or "village" dwelling areas.

100. McWhorter: told by *I-keep-swah*, Sitting Rock, 1918.

III. TALES OF MAGIC AND THE MARVELOUS

101. Sapir:302-303.

102. According to Sapir, the Wasco myth, as given here, is evidently a mere fragment of a fuller myth that filtered in from the east. It is known from the Pacific coast from Southern Vancouver Island [see Boas, Franz 1895. *Indianisch Sagen von der Nord-Pacifischen Kuste Amerikas*. Berlin:62.], and from southern Alaska [see Boas, Franz 1898. "Traditions of the *Ts'ets'aut*," *Journal of American Folklore*, 10:39].

103. The Star-rock is also related of in 7 "The Star Rock of the Tumwater" above. DH

104. The Wasco cup is mentioned in 14 "Wasco" above; also in 7 "The Star Rock of the Tumwater" above. DH

105. Other Wasco versions containing folkloric motifs found in this narrative include above 1A "The Ascent to the Sky and Return to the Earth;" 2B "Sky-Rope." DH

106. Sapir:269-273.

107. According to Sapir, this is a composite myth. The first part consists of two episodes of the wide-spread story of the unsuccessful imitation of the host. The second part is a string of four loosely connected anecdotes.

108. With this episode compare Jones, William 1907. *Fox Texts*, PAES 1. Leyden:263-267. [This work is cited hereafter as *Fox Texts*].

Kingfisher and the trickster *Wisa'ka* of the fox myth closely correspond to the Wasco Fish Hawk and Coyote. Compare also Boas, Franz and George Hunt, 1906. *Kwakiutl Texts*, PJE 10. New York, NY:153.

109. Compare Sapir, "Coyote and Deer:"145-147, also the version in *Chinook Texts*:180 for similar procuring of food from one's nose and body. In these versions Mountain Sheep is replaced by Deer, and by Black Bear.

110. Compare *Kathlamet Texts*: 152-153; also Sapir, "The Raccoon Story:"153-165, especially Sapir's note concerning "*wala'lap*," 'some kind of mythical being.' The Wasco *wala'lap* corresponds to the Wishram *wala'lap*, and the Kathlamet *wa'laxlax*, according to Sapir.

111. This rolling rock episode is perhaps to be considered a variant of the rolling skull myth motif. Compare Grinnell, George B. 1892. *Blackfoot Lodge Tales*. New York:165; also Lowie, Robert H. 1909. *The Northern Shoshone: Part II, Mythology*, PAAM 2. New York, NY:262-265. See also 24 "Wild Goat Carries Away a Woman," *Tales of the Nez Perce*, esp. pp. 114-115. DH

112. The Bungling Host is frequently related among North American Indian tribes. See especially the study done by Boas, Franz 1916. *Tsimshian Mythology*, RBAE 31. Washington, D.C.. [This work is cited hereafter as *Tsimshian Mythology*.] And see Thompson, Stith 1966. *Tales of the North American Indians*. Bloomington, IN: Indiana University Press. See pp. 71-73, especially notes on pp. 301f.. DH

113. Sapir:287-290.

114. According to Sapir, this narrative contains two evidently distinct myths [texts] which have been connected into one. The first part, Eagle's successful contests with Fish Hawk, is paralleled by [in *Wishram Texts*] "Eagle's Son and Coyote's Son-in-law," pp. 133-139, wherein a footrace takes place between Fish Hawk and Jack Rabbit, one of Eagle's men. The second part deals with Eagle's generous treatment of poor Skunk, who makes himself ridiculous in his attempt to imitate the dancing and hunting feats of Eagle.

115. The characteristic modesty of Eagle in laying no claim to great running or diving prowess, although he wins out in this instance, is illustrated also in Sapir, "The Adventures of Eagle and his Four Brothers:"75-93, especially that portion where Eagle claims to have no power in gambling, yet defeats his opponents.

116. Sapir:311-314.

117. According to Sapir, this dance festival narrative corresponds, in a general way, to [in *Wishram Texts*] "Coyote's People Sing:"95-99. The dance referred to is perhaps to be compared with the Nez Perce Guardian

Spirit dance described by Spinden, Herbert J 1908. *The Nez Perce Indians*, MAAA 2. Lancaster, PA:262-264. [This work is cited hereafter as *Nez Perce Indians*.]

118. Compare Sapir, "Coyote as Medicine Man:"11-19, especially which relates of deer or elk as singers *par excellence* among the animals.

119. The idea of an increase in heat with the advance of the song is found also in Sapir, "The Five East Wind Brothers and the Five Thunder Brothers:"121-131.

120. See *Nez Perce Indians*:263 cited above.

121. Sapir:290-292.

122. According to Sapir, this is translated by Jeremiah Curtin as "a root," and the species is not known. In the Nez Perce version, "Weasel," *Tales of the Nez Perce*: 117-120, the opening episode recounts of a maiden, a plant entity, a sunflower. She wrestles and defeats suitors who would be her husband, but is defeated by Weasel, the least likely, informidable suitor, and leaves Coyote out-of-sorts at having not won the maiden. DH

123. According to Sapir, this was translated by Curtin as "Tobacco-Man," but this can hardly be the literal meaning of the name.

124. Sapir:244-245.

125. According to Sapir, a similar tale occurs in *Kathlamet Texts*:216-220. In that version a trivial but forbidden act done by a child [a boy plays with his excrement] brings on an unusually severe storm. {Here, in this Wasco version, a girl has struck a bird.} See also *The Shuswap*:744.

126. Sapir:259-260.

127. According to Sapir, the visit of human beings to the land of the whales, seals, or other food animals, and their return to the people of this earth, to whom they grant power to obtain a large food supply, is a characteristic type of tale or myth [sic.] among the Coos of Oregon. See St. Clair, Harry H. and Leo Frachtenberg, 1909. Traditions of the Coos Indians of Oregon, *JAF*. 22:25-41. Compare also a similar tale of a visit to the salmon in Swanton, John R. 1905. *Haida Texts and Myths*, BBAE 29. Washington, D.C.:7-14.

128. According to Sapir, the implication doubtless is that he becomes a guardian spirit for seal hunters. Compare the ending of the tale with *Kathlamet Texts*:166-174.

129. Sapir:246-248.

130. According to Sapir, this narrative is evidently a composite of two distinct stories. The first part of the tale as here given is a variant of the widespread Rolling Skull tale. See, for example, Curtin, Jeremiah 1898. *Creation Myths of Primitive America*. Boston:325-335 for a Yana parallel. See also 24 "Wild Goat Carries Away a Woman," *Tales of the Nez Perce*:109-114, esp. p. 113f.. The second part of the tale, the hunting of the Tobacco people as game, is only loosely joined on to the first.

131. Travelling on the tops of blades of grass in order to avoid making tracks is also found in Sapir," Coyote and Antelope:"67-75.

132. The last paragraph, in which arrangements are made for the world to come, helps to give this narrative much of the character of a myth [mythic text], or so Sapir felt.

IV. TALES OF CONFLICTS AND ADVENTURES

133. Sapir:242-244.

134. According to Sapir, Tenino (or *Te'naino*), a village of the *Wa'yam* Indians (known to the Wasco as *Itk!a'umamt*), was situated nearly five miles above The Dalles, being the first Sahaptin village on the south side of the Columbia River east of Chinookan territory.

135. According to Sapir, the episode of pretended death in order to satisfy forbidden lust, appears also [in *Wishram Texts*] "Coyote and his Daughter:"105-107. In 24 "Wild Goat Carries Away a Woman," *Tales of the Nez Perce*:109-115, the original husband and the wife tryst, plot means whereby she will betray and do in the second or abductor husband. The tryst occurs while she is cutting grass, and she pretends to cut herself. DH

136. Similarly as in the Nez Perce version, the original husband cuts off the head of the second husband, and then escapes with the wife. DH

137. Celilo (*Si'lailo*) was a *Wa-yam* village about eleven miles above The Dalles. Hereabouts the river began a horrendous mass of rapids and white-water, certain death to any boatman, for the river appeared to literally turn on its side in its downriver course of anguish.

138. According to Sapir's notion, this particular text was to be included with five other narratives that deal with the doings of human beings as such. In other words, the idea of a mythic or Pre-Indian age, the people of which are the untransformed prototypes of present-day animals or plants, is either absent or kept in the background. [The word "tale" should be employed rather than "myth"]. See 25 "A Hard Winter Near The Dalles;" 27 "An Arrow Point Maker Becomes a Cannibal;" 31 "*Diabexwa'snwas*, the Big-Footed Man;" 29 "A Woman Marries a Person Who is a Dog in the Day and a Man

at Night." The word "tale," as contrasted with "myth," is not meant to imply that supernatural or mythical elements are lacking, but merely that such elements are thought in these tales to have entered into the life of human beings as now constituted [the main emphasis in the tale lies elsewhere].

With these tales as a class, Sapir finds comparable in *Wishram Texts* "IV. Non-Mythical Narratives:"201-233. See also *Kathlamet Texts*:155-230.

139. Sapir:253-256.

140. According to Sapir, Curtin's manuscript has *Ickaditiq*, to be read probably as *Ilqa'ditix*; *iqa'ditix* is the Wasco word for "cinnamon (?) bear." (Since the black bear can appear in several different hues, the narrative may have wished to differentiate black bear from the grizzly bear).

141. Compare *Chinook Texts*: 189. The same kind of adventures are told by the Chinook of a woman who married the Salmon-Harpoon.

142. McWhorter: told by *Yes-to-lah-lemy*, April 1919.

143. Sapir:248-253.

144. According to Sapir, the similar Kathlamet tale begins with an incident of a woman giving birth to dogs which later become human beings, when their dog-blankets are burned. This is evidently an absolutely distinct story in origin. See the Wasco text 29 "A Woman Marries a Person Who is a Dog in the Day and a Man at Night" above. Sapir finds a connection between the two tales: loosely established by having *tia'pexoacoac*, the Kathlamet correspondent of the Wasco *Dia'bexwasxwas*, woo one of the dog-children, a daughter of the woman.

145. For the killing of one's male children, compare also *Kathlamet Texts*:187.

146. Compare the natures of the five Thunder brothers here with those in Sapir 39 "The Five East-Wind Brothers and the Five Thunder Brothers:"121-131."

147. In the Kathlamet tale the son's feet are of the same length as his father's, but are broader.

148. Compare the fight here with that between the Chinook and the East Winds in Sapir, The East Wind and the West Wind:"103-105.

149. For a study of this tale, AaTh 931, "Oedipus," an American Indian telling of the folktale adapted by Sophocles into the tragedy, *Oedipus Rex*, see Hines, Donald M. 1995. " Of big Foot, The Oedipal Tale Told along the Columbia River," *Fabula, Journal of Folktale Studies* 36(1/2):98-104. DH

150. McWhorter: told by Sitting Rock, *I-keep swah*, October 1921. *I-keep-swah* was born at *Win-quat*, "moving sands" or "washing sands," the Wasco name for what is now The Dalles, Oregon, about 1828. His father was half Klickitat and half Wasco. His mother, *Goos-hpah*, was half Wasco and half Wishom. Both these tribes were warlike, speaking much the same language. *I-keep-swah* was baptized in youth by the Roman Catholics and christened Jim Peter. "Peter" was the Christian name of his father. Both were warriors in their day. *I-keep-swah* is also known as "Wasco Jim." Of this name, when questioned, he said, "That is only fun-making name, whiskey name. Used to I drink lots whiskey. Injuns give me that name, shame name." DH

151. The "Horn Spoon" is likely the same as the Big Dipper. DH

152. A similar motif occurs frequently in Nez Perce texts where as a result of accident the leg of Meadowlark is broken, but is usually repaired with "brushwood." And grateful Meadowlark supplies the hero with needed directions into the future. DH

153. The raven is truly a bird of ill-omen with the *n-Che-wana* tribes. It appears ahead of coming epidemics, such as smallpox and other scourges. Traveling alone or in pairs, it is ever on the watch to pick out the eyes of the exposed dead. The raven winters on the *n-Che-wana*. And for accounts of the "wormy dead," see 13 "The Dead Canoeman of the *n-Che-wana*" above.

154. Sapir:282-286.

155. An *At!at!a'lia* woman was a child-stealing woman-fiend or monster.

156. The rattling ruse employed by Coyote is similar to that in Sapir, "Coyote and *At!at!a'lia*:" 35-39.

157. Sapir:257-259.

158. Dog River is now generally known as Hood River, a southern tributary of the Columbia River which enters the Oregon side of the Columbia.

159. According to Sapir, this tale and others like it, [*Wishram Texts*]:257-264, deal with the acquisition of supernatural power, and with the idea that moderation must be exercised in the use of magic. This latter point comes out strongly in *Fox Texts* I:183-193.

160. The fact that the young man divulges his guardian spirit is itself indicative of approaching death, for only upon the deathbed was it customary to communicate this, the greatest secret of one's life.

161. Sapir:233. This short Wasco text was collected by Dr. Franz Boas in 1892 at the Grand Ronde Reservation near Yamhill, northwestern Oregon. The informant was not identified.

162. The sense of the last sentence implies: "When the Indians come to inhabit the country, things will be as told in the narrative. Eagles will always get large game, but coyotes will have to wander about and content themselves with rodents."

163. Sapir:260-263.

164. Compare Sapir, "The Deserted Boy:139-145. Compare also *Chinook Texts*:221. According to Sapir, *Itc!I'xyan* is the protector of fishermen and hunters of water animals.

165. Sapir:281-282.

166. The burning of the *At!at!a'lia* by Coyote is comparable to the episode found in Sapir, "Coyote and *At!at!a'lia*:"34-39.

167. Sapir:279-280.

168. Sapir:276-279.

169. With this tale compare *Kathlamet Texts*:9-19. See also Sapir, "The Boy That was Stolen by *At!at!a'liya*:165-173. According to Sapir, the last portion of the Kathlamet-Wishram mythic/narrative, evidently a distinct story in origin, is closely related to a separate tale in Jeremiah Curtin's Wasco tale here, 2 "The Ascent to the Sky and Return to Earth," above.

170. The motif of the crane's leg bridge occurs often in *Tales of the Nez Perce*, and in other collections of Plateau tribal narratives. DH

171. Sapir:274-276.

172. According to Sapir, *Ikinickwai* was translated by Jeremiah Curtin, collector of the Wasco tales, as "a kind of fish."

173. The *At!at!a'lia* is a frightful, child-stealing ogress characterized by immense size, a stripped body, fondness for children's flesh, and stupidity. She feeds frogs, lizards, and such other food to her children. Her Kathlamet correspondent is called *Aq!asxe'naszena*.

174. Other powerful breathing-in monsters include the monster-creature in 1 "Coyote and Monster," *Tales of the Nez Perce*:43-46. See also above, 1 "Coyote is Swallowed by *Itc!i'xyan*"; and see also Sapir, "Coyote at Lapwai, Idaho:"43-47; "Coyote and *Itc!E'xyan*:"41-43. DH

175. Sapir:298-301.

176. *La'daxat* was a winter village of the Wishrams, situated on the Washington side of the Columbia River about ten miles below The Dalles, and a short distance above Memaloose Island, an Indian burial ground. Many suckers (fish) were caught at *La'daxat* in the winter.

177. They purified themselves for the hunt by sweats in the sweat house.

178. For similar advice given when repairs are made to Meadowlark's broken leg, see Sapir, "The Boy That was Stolen by *At!at!a'liya*:"165-173.

179. Sapir:292-294.

180. See Sapir, Edward 1907. "Notes on the Takelma Indians of Southwestern Oregon," *American Anthropologist* 9:251-275. See also Hand, Wayland D. ed, 1964. *Popular Beliefs and Superstitions from North Carolina*, in *The Frank C. Brown Collection of North Carolina Folklore*, vols. 7 & 8. Durham, N.C.: Duke University Press, especially belief no. 3506. Among Euroamericans this widely held folk belief holds that not sneezing but an "itchy ear" presages that someone is gossiping about oneself. DH

181. The motif of reviving the dead by straddling the corpse five times occurs often in traditional tales of the Plateau Indians. For instance, in *Tales of the Nez Perce* see Motif E13, "Resuscitation by jumping (stepping) over" in "Coyote and Elbow-child:"48; "Coyote and Fox:"95; "Weasel:"117. Often, arrangement of disassembled limbs plus straddling are combined to bring the dead to life. DH

Indians fishing at Celilo Falls, Special Collections Division, University of Washington Libraries, Neg NA 715.

INDEX OF MOTIFS

For each oral narrative in this volume the *motifs* have been noted hereafter. By *motif* we mean that ". . . smallest element in a tale having a power to persist in tradition. . . . Most motifs fall into three classes. First are the actors in a tale. . .; second come certain items in the background of the action, magic objects, unusual customs, strange beliefs, and the like; . . . in the third place there are single incidents--and these comprise the great majority of motifs" (Thompson 1946: 415.) We have employed Thompson's *Motif-index of Folk-literature*, also his *Tales of the North American Indians*.

PART TWO

THE TRADITIONAL NARRATIVES
OF THE WASCOS

I. TALES OF THE ORIGINS
OF MAN, ANIMALS AND PLANTS, PHENOMENA

1. COYOTE IS SWALLOWED BY
ITC!I'XYAN
A. Mythological Motifs

A522.1.3. Coyote as culture hero

B. Animals

B11.2.9.1. Heart of Monster, cut
B211.8.1. Speaking monster(s)
B810. Eagle(s)
B810. Weasel
B810.3.3. Coyote(s)

D. Magic

D908. Coyote finds himself in dark place, swallowed up by Monster
D1001. Magic spittle
D1002. Magic excrements
D1213. Magic bell. Cf. E545.14.1. Bell heard by the dead
D1312.1.1. Excrements as advisors
D1602. Self-returning magic object(s). Cf. D1686. Magic object(s) depart and
return at formulistic command

D1610.6.4. Speaking excrements
D2061.1.1.1. People reduced to bones, hair over many years
D2143.1.4.1. Rain produced by throwing spittle in the air; cf. D15641.1.9.
        Magic spittle causes storm; cf. D1776. Magic results from spitting

E. The Dead
E402.1.1. Vocal sounds of ghosts of human beings

F. Marvels
F911.6. All-swallowing monster
F912. Victim kills swallower from within; see also K952. Animal (monster)
        killed from within
F964.6. Fire made inside monster
F1041.1.6.2. Hero (Coyote) faints away
F1088.5. Coyote and people escape, are blown from out Monster by a tremen--
        dous breath

G. Ogres
G332. Sucking monster
G427. Monster swallows Coyote while he is unconscious

K. Deceptions
K615.1. Coyote would prevent Monster from swallowing him by carrying a
        long log across his shoulders

L. Reversal of Fortune
L434.1.1. Arrogance of Coyote as"know-it-all"

M. Ordaining the Future
M301.22. Five old men warn Coyote that he will be swallowed
M340.5. Prediction of danger

P. Society
P672.5. Taunting Monster with insults

Z. Miscellaneous Groups of Motifs
Z71.0.3. Two; 2 "Cayuse Girls" [excrement sisters] of Coyote
Z71.2.2. Direction: east - up river; travels "up the river;" Coyote warned not
        to "go along up the river"
Z71.2.2.1. Direction: west--Eagle travels west
Z71.2.2.2. Direction: south--Coyote is blown six miles south past Celilo hills
Z71.2.2.3. Direction: north--Coyote looked north
Z71.3.3. Five; five men

2A. THE ASCENT TO THE SKY
AND RETURN TO EARTH
A. Mythological Motifs

A220.1.1. Sun-goddess: origin of the sun

A290. Twin sons as the shadows

A711.1.2. Sun as traveler along a road

A736.3.1. Sun and moon as twin brothers

A736.3.1.1. Two grandchildren of sun are siamese twin brothers who will be cut apart

A950. Hollow in ground near "Wasco spring" where boy landed upon descent from heaven

A1172.4. Day and night determined: when bundle of night is opened, there will be darkness as long as it lasts--then light will come

A1174.1. Bundle containing night--when opened all becomes darkness

A2355.1.2.1. Why ants and yellow-jackets have small waists

B. Animals

B810.7.3. Ground squirrel(s)

B810.8.4. Bluejay

B810.14.2. Flea(s)

B810.17.1. Spider(s)

B810.17.2. Body-louse (lice)

B810.17.3. Nits (crowd of nits)

C. Tabu

C835.2.7. Tabu: Shooting arrows high into the air

D. Magic

D991. Magic hair

D1331.1.6. Magic hair restores sight

D1799.1.1. Magical power from cleaning house and burning "sweet stuff" five times each; cf. V81. Baptism [see esp. notes]; also V81.5. Sea bath as purificatory rite

D1812.5.1.4. Eclipse (of sun) as evil omen; cf. F961.1.ff. Extraordinary behavior of sun; also F965.1.1. Premature darkness at time of execution of innocent people

F. Marvels

F12.2.1. Grieving mortal taken by Sun and daughter to return to earth

F51.0.1. Sky-rope shot by means of arrows

F51.1.1. Spider-web sky-rope

F51.2. Sky-basket

F53. Ascent to upper world on arrow chain

F56.1. Sky-window from digging or uprooting plant(s) (tree) in upper world; cf. F92.1. Visit to lower world through hole made by lifting clumps of grass

F56.4. A hole scratched in the "ground" enables hero to see world below

F163.8. Nice road with many tracks on other [upper] side of sky

F171.2.1. Broad road in otherworld

F529.1.1. Man has arrow through body--as he passes by, he falls dead

F661.7.3. One arrow shot into end of last one to make rope of arrows

F771.1.12. Two houses nearby: first shines brightly [sun] while second is all
          darkness [death]; cf. D1645.3. Magic castle shines from afar

F827.7. Many feathers, much paint found at side of road

F989.25. Mountain sheep has arrow through body--falls dead as it passes by

G. Ogres

G11.10.2. Cannibalistic "people" in upper world, intent on eating blood of
        people

H. Tests

H1221.2. Following road across other side of sky leads to adventure

N. Chance and Fate

N747. Accidental meeting of people who declare/discover they are related; cf.
        N730. Accidental reunion of families [two instances]

P. Society

P322.4. Guest hospitality received

P681.1. Sister of Coyote mourns excessively

P681.2. People of Boy's village mourn excessively--hunt for his bones

P681.4. Mourning customs: to lie at length in bed

P715.2. Crowds of assorted people are met on road across the sky

S. Unnatural Cruelty

S302.2. Siamese twins are killed in attempt to separate them

T. Sex

T111.1.3. Daughter of Sun is taken as wife by boy

T299.1. Sleeping with head in wife's lap as sign of tenderness

T550.8. Siamese twin boys born; cf. F523. Two persons with bodies joined;

T587. Birth of twins

W. Traits of Character

W46. Personal hygiene: man and wife wash heads in river

W193.2. Occupants of black house attempt to kidnap the boy

W230.2.2. Beautiful girl

W231.1.1. Man [men] [man with hair tied on head, carrying bow and quiver
        of arrows]

W230.2.2.2. Sister(s); cf. P. 252.1. Two sisters

W230.4.2. A boy and his mother

Z. Miscellaneous Groups of Motifs

Z71.3.5. Five. [5 days and 5 nights in bed] [5 times each, clean house, burn
        "sweet stuff"] [on the 5th day]

Z111.0.1. Death as traveller carrying an arrow along road

2B. SKY ROPE

A. Mythological Motifs

A522.2.1. Blue Jay as culture hero

A736.5.3. Sons of Sun-daughter taken back to sky-home

A738.5. Sun and her sons appear (sundog?) as death omen

B. Animals

B810.8.4. Bluejay(s)

C. Tabu

C610. The one forbidden place

D. Magic

D1184. Magic thread; cf. D1313.1.1.1. Magic thread breaks as sign of misfortune; cf. F877. Extraordinary threads

D1799.1.1. Magic power from cleaning

F. Marvels

F10. Journey to upper world

F51.1.1. Spider-web sky-rope

F56.1. Sky-window

F523. Two persons with bodies joined--Siamese twins

F961.1.3.3. Sun with bright light on each side as omen of a death or severe illness

L. Reversal of Fortune

L54.1.1. Youngest daughter of sun marries a mortal

M. Ordaining the Future

M341.0.4. Sun-dog is sign of death or serious illness

M341.0.5. A star near the moon is a sign of death or serious illness: cf. A787. Relation of planets to human life

W. Traits of Character

W230.1.2. A boy [a little boy]

W230.1.2.1. A brother

W230.2.1. A woman

W230.2.2.1. Youngest daughter of the sun; cf. A220.1. Sun-goddess

W230.4. People, cannibals [eat human eyes]

W230.5. Siamese twins

Z. Miscellaneous Groups of Motifs

Z71.3.5. Five [clean house 5 times (5 days?)] [5 daughters]

3. TWO BROTHERS BECOME
SUN AND MOON

A. Mythological Motifs

A221.1. Sun killed with arrows by brothers

A240.2. Moon killed with arrows by brothers

A240.2.2. Old Moon and lame daughter

A711.5. Elder brother becomes the sun

A720.2.1. Sun formerly stayed directly overhead and its heat was too great for living beings

A736.3. Two brothers become sun and moon after they kill the Sun, the Moon

A741.4. Younger brother becomes moon, marries its daughter

A754.2.1. Moon lives in house on left side of house of sun; cf. A721.0.1.

A2686.4.4. Origin of camas-roots: when brothers wrestle and Spider-boy is thrown

B. Animals

B810.17.1. Spider(s)

D. Magic

D1052. Mother makes two beautiful robes trimmed with shells

D1810.2.1. Information received through dream by younger brother

D1962.4.1. Lulling to sleep by "sleepy" stories (songs)

F. Marvels

F11.4. Two brothers journey to upper world

F292.3. Younger brother has belly containing snakes, frogs, lizards, etc--all come out when belly is stomped on

F556.5. Young brother persists in singing one song

F601.5.1. Extraordinary brothers: oldest is dull, youngest has magic wisdom --they become sun and moon; cf. P251.5.4. Two brothers as contrasts

F699.2. Marvelous powers of youngest brother: tells of things past and to be; sees visions of absent father

J. The Wise and the Foolish

J1223.1. Rebuke for telling a story that is too short

J2175.2.1. When old man only tells a short tale to restive child, he is scolded and left behind

Q. Rewards and Punishments

P231.4.1. Mother [and elder brother] dislike youngest child

P681. Excessive grieving--an elder boy

S. Unnatural Cruelty

S12.8. Mother orders sons to make arrows and to go kill Sun

S112.7. Death by falling onto hot rocks

S192. Younger brother's distended belly is stomped on to make it smaller; cf. F959. Marvelous cures--miscellaneous

S482. Ridicule of the lame

W. Traits of Character

W127. Petulance: elder brother is abusive with younger brother

W138. Elder brother is stupid-- only cries or laughs

W230.2.2. Girl(s): crippled girl

W230.4.2.1. A mother and two sons [children]

W231.1.1. Man (men): an old man

Z. Miscellaneous Groups of Motifs

Z71.2.2. East; travel eastward

Z71.2.2. South: travel south-ward

Z71.3.5. Five: [5 times brief tales told] [5 quivers of arrows]

4. THE SUN-LODGE
A. Mythological Motifs

A522.1.3. Coyote as culture hero

A538.1. Culture hero builds circular lodge about sun

A710.1. Creation of sun: Rockperson changed into sun

A721.0.3. A sun-lodge built about sun

A736.5.3. Two children of sun live/can be seen inside circular lodge surrounding the sun

B. Animals

B560.2.1. Meadowlark advises youth on cause of death of brothers; cf. D1814.5. Magic advice

B810.3.3. Coyote(s)

D. Magic

D293.1. Transformation: Rock-person into sun

D432.1.1. Transformation: stone to person, who then has two children; cf. D1776. Magic results from spitting

D1001. Magic spittle

D1731.3. Youth finds strong *Tahmahnawis* spirit; Cf. B500. Magic power from animal; B560. Animals advise men

N. Chance and Fate

N339.17. Four children of old woman die

P. Society

P681.1. Excessive grieving -- mother

W. Traits of Character

W230.1.2. Boy(s)

Z. Miscellaneous Groups of Motifs

Z71.0.1. Two: [2 children]

Z71.2.0. Four: [4 children die]
Z71.3.5. Five: [5 children]

5. LEGEND OF THE GREAT DIPPER
A. Mythological Motifs

A522.1.3. Coyote as culture hero
A530.2. Culture hero, Coyote, creates constellations
A700.9. All stars come from the Grizzlies [Ursa Major] and Wolves [Pleiades]
A703.1. Excess stars threaten to fall down; earth to be covered with frost
A766. Origin of constellations
A766.1. Constellations arranged into present order by Coyote
A766.2. From the Grizzlies and the Wolves come all the stars
A769.6. At the first there were no stars
A771. Origin of the Great Bear [Ursa Major, Ursa Minor]
A773. Origin of the Pleiades
A774.1. Origin of the North Star and the Great Dipper
A778. Origin of the Milky Way
A778.2.1. Milky Way as a trail

B. Animals

B39.2. *Whoch-Whoch* bird
B182.1.0.4. A dog kept by the five Wolves
B235. Secrets discussed in animal meeting
B435.4.1. Helpful youngest wolf
B561.1. Animals tell hero of the sky phenomenon
B810.3.2. Wolf(s) [5 wolf brothers]
B810.3.3. Coyote
B810.3.5. Grizzly Bear(s) [2 grizzly bears]

C. Tabu

C0.1. Wolf brothers warned not to approach the Great Bears (Ursa Major /
     Ursa Minor)
C411.2. Tabu: Asking about sky marvel
C423.7. Tabu: speaking of extraordinary sky phenomenon

D. Magic

D1092. Magic arrows

F. Marvels

F53. Ascent to upper world on arrow-chain
F167.1. Animals in otherworld
F661.7.3. One arrow shot into end of last one to make rope of arrows; cf. F53.
     Ascent to upper world on arrow-chain
F794. Two animals sighted high in the sky

P. Society

P414. Wolves spend each day hunting

Z. Miscellaneous Groups of Motifs

Z71.2.0. Four [4 brothers refuse to tell Coyote]

Z71.3.5. Five [5 Wolf brothers] [5 quivers of arrows]

Z71.16.17. Innumerable [Coyote and Wolves climb for *many* days]

6. BRIDGE OF THE GODS
A. Mythological Motifs

A162.9. God blinds eyes of Thunderbird that Coyote can kill it

A172.1. "Great Man" instructs Coyote words to speak to Eagle to obtain magic feather

A182.1.1.1. God (Great Man above) instructs Coyote in wisdom

A183.2. Coyote pleads to "Great Man" for power to recover his dead sons, to best Thunderbird

A185.1.1. "Great Man" aids Coyote in overcoming power of Thunderbird; cf. A185.9. Covenant between God and mortal

A189.1.2. "Great Man" aids Coyote overcome Thunderbird

A189.2. God summoned by weeping

A200. God of the upper world

A284.2. Thunderbird

A284.4. Thunderbird fears for his life at sign--when he hears another making sound of thunder

A507. Some animal people are great, can do mighty wonders, kill people

A522.1.3. Coyote as culture hero

A879. When earth was first made, Animal and Bird people lived over the land; cf. A1101.2.3. Formerly men were dumb: birds and animals talked

A986. Bridge of the Gods

A986.1. Body of slain Thunderbird forms a great bridge across the *n-Che-wana* at the Cascades Mountains

A986.1.1. After standing for many years--the bridge fell into the river

A995.13. Islands in *n-Che-wana* formed of fragments of the shattered five mountains

A1142.10. Thunder made henceforth by a Thunderbird never to be as great again

A1580.3. First law: tabu against people travelling westward--given by Thunderbird

B. Animals

B31.6.3. Thunderbird

B172.4.1. Bird [young eagle] with magic feathers

B505 Magic object (feather) received from animal (young eagle)

B810.1.3. Cougar(s) [panther]

B810.3.2. Wolf(s)--five wolf brothers

B810.3.3. Coyote(s)

B810.3.5. Grizzly Bear(s)

B810.4.2. Beaver(s)

B810.9.1. Eagle(s)

B810.9.1.1. Young Eagle

C. Tabu

C42.1. Offending Thunderbird [directed to the Wolves, Bears, Cougars, Beavers]

C333.1. Tabu: looking up, at the bridge or the rocks of the bridge

C426.1. Tabu: telling entire story or narrative about circumstances of the Bridge of the Gods

C526.1. Tabu: touching first of five mountains with left foot [death results for Wolf and Bear brothers]

C614.1.3.1. Forbidden direction: towards the sundown/in the West [animals: wolves, bears, cougar, beavers, coyotes; mankind]

C614.3. Tabu: staying away from home overnight

C617.1. Forbidden to cross over the five high mountains [especially the Wolves, Bears, Cougar, and Beavers]

C650.2. Coyote must go to "land above" in order to regain his five sons

C921.1. Immediate death for breaking Tabu [to step with left foot on forbidden mountains--Wolves and Bears] [jumping over forbidden mountains--Cougars] [going under the forbidden mountains] [using magic to attempt to destroy the five mountains--five young Coyotes]

C617.2. Mankind forbidden to come to place where Thunderbird lives [Wolves, Bears, Cougar, Beavers, and Coyotes]

C643.1. Tabu: touching with left foot first of five mountains [Wolves and Bears]

C899.2. Tabu: to go under five forbidden mountains

C899.2.1. Tabu: jumping over forbidden mountains

C920. Death [by Thunderbird] for breaking tabu

D. Magic

D421.1.2. Transformation: Coyote to a feather, small, fine and invisible

D532. Transformation by putting on claw, feather, etc. of helpful animal

D556. Coyote transformed into a feather by going without food and drink for ten days and ten nights

D910. Magic body of water--its depths protect from lethal thunderbolts

D995.2. Magic right foot [right foot touches mountain, nothing happens]; cf. D996.0.1.1. Magic power of right hand for good

D995.3. Magic left foot. [left foot touches mountain, death results]; cf. D996.0.2.1. Magic power of left hand for evil

D1021.1. Magic bird's power [strength of heart] in one feather

D1402.33. Magical thunderbolt from Coyote destroys five mountains, kills Thunderbird

D1719.4.1. Elder brother possesses magic power

D1741.3.1. Silence or not telling culture hero of plans nullifies magical powers

D1811.2.1.1. Magic wisdom received from god; cf. D1726. Magic power from deity

D1813.0.3.2. Father knows of sons' death when they have been absent five nights

D1814.3. Advice from god (or gods)

D1834.1. Magic strength from small wing feather of Young Eagle

D1980. Magic invisibility [Thunderbird must remain unseen]; cf. B11.5.2. Dragon's power of magic invisibility

D1983.1. Invisibility conferred by a god

D2093.1. Five Forbidden Mountains made to shake, to dance up and down by Elder Brother in effort to break open a trail westward

D2149.1.2. Coyote, transformed, creates noise like Thunder

D2149.1.3. Thunderbird and Coyote attempt to slay each other with thunderbolts

E. The Dead

E68.1. With death of Thunderbird, five sons each of Wolf, Grizzly Bear, Cougar, Beaver, and Coyote all come back to life

F. Marvels

F1041.21.8. Coyote grieves, wails and prays for dead sons a lengthy time among lonely caverns and rocks

H. Tests

H1049.5. Task: testing tabu [by Wolves, Bears, Cougar, Coyotes, Beavers]

M. Ordaining the Future

M201.7. As directed by "Great Man," Eagle promises Coyote his strength and power and a feather in the fight against Thunderbird

M202.3. Eagle plucks magical small downy feather from his son for Coyote

N. Chance and Fate

N817. Deity as helper

Z. Miscellaneous Groups of Motifs

Z71.22. Direction: West [where Thunderbird lived {forbidden to locate}] [attempt made to break trail westward]

Z71.3.5. Five--[5 mountains] [5 Wolf brothers] [5 Grizzly Bear brothers] [5 Cougar brothers] [5 Beaver brothers] [5 Coyote brothers] [absent 5 nights] [travels 5 days and 5 nights] [5 children of Eagle] [thunders 5 times]

Z221.1. Eldest brother, powerful leader

7. THE STAR ROCK OF THE TUMWATER
A. Mythological Motifs

A1.5. *Schoc-o-les tom* (Su-preme power-deity)

A7.2. *Schoc-o-les Tom-e-yah-kon* (Son of the Supreme power-deity)

A185.7.1. Deity tears down tepee, lets bison go free for all people

A530.2. Coyote stops fighting between the Wascos and the Wishrams

A541.3. Coyote and Son of Supreme being Deity give free to all mankind bison, fish of all kinds

A541.3.3. Coyote relates how "at the sundown" he tore out dam allowing fish now to migrate to all the Indians

A541.4. Demigod relates how "at the sunrise" he tore away great tepee, freed bison for everyone

A692.2. Otherworld at the sunrise and contains in one tepee all bison and all mankind

A965.2. Origin of present location of Mount Hood and Mount Adams

A1182.1.1. The sundown as place of origin of fish

A1182.2.1. The sunrise as place of origin of buffalo

A1202. Origin of man--when people got life; when "big time" came

A1231.2. Coyote or son of supreme-power deity as first man on earth

A1832.1. Silver fox was created when residue from treasure rock was rubbed on dog

A1878.2. Origin of bison at sunrise where they were held all in one tepee

A2100.1. Origin of fish--at "the sundown"

A2100.2. Origin of buffalo--at "the sunrise"

B. Animals

B810.3.3. Coyote(s)

D. Magic

D931.0.5. Large rock of Wascos opened, contains silver and diamonds; cf. D1466. Magic stone furnishes wealth

D931.0.6. Large star rock of Wishoms in water of the *n-Che-wana*

D1021. Magic Eagle feather; cf. D1205. Magic shovel

D1275. Magic song sung by Coyote

D1466. Magic stone furnishes wealth

D1546.2. Magic stone of Wishoms shines brightly as a star

D1733.6.1. Magic song by Coyote sends Eagle feather to attempt to move two mountains--but failure

D2136.3.2. Two mountains moved by prayer

F. Marvels

F969.7. Mount Hood and Mount Adams made to move about to their present locations by magic spell

H. Tests

H900.1. Coyote is assigned task of moving two mountains. If successful, he will be the "first man"

H911.2. Task assigned Coyote by his rival, Son of supreme-power deity; cf. H927.1. Task as trial of prowess of mortal by gods

H975.2. Task performed with aid of supreme-being deity

H1010.1. Impossible tasks: moving two mountains

K. Deceptions

K359.6. Wishom Indians steal away at night with rock of Wasco Indians

M. Ordaining the Future

M202.3. Coyote, failing to move two mountains, acknowledges Son of Supreme-power deity as First Man; cf. P525. Contracts

P. Society

P210. Wasco man marries Wishom girl

P213.1. Husband, loyal to his tribe, informs them that the Wishoms have the treasure rock

P716. Wasco Indians ponder how to retrieve their treasure rock

Q. Rewards and Punishments

Q212.5. Theft punished; for Wishoms' theft of treasure, Wascos steal the Wishoms' star-rock

W. Traits of Character

W151.8. Wascos and Wishoms quarrel over boulder containing diamonds and silver

W151.8.2. Wishoms and Wascos wage war over the magic or precious rocks stolen by each tribe from the other

Z. Miscellaneous Groups of Motifs

Z71.2.2. West [Coyote sent to the sundown] [two mountains each moved toward the sunset]

Z71.2.2.2. East [Son, Supreme power deity, goes to sunrise] [Coyote travels towards the sunrise]

Z71.3.5. Five [magic feather sent 5 times] [each mountain shakes 5 times]

8A. COYOTE' BIG MISTAKE

A. Mythological Motifs

A522.1.3.1. Coyote chief as culture hero

A592.2. Virgin daughter of culture hero

B. Animals

B810.3.3. Coyote(s)

C. Tabu

C331.4. Tabu: looking back or stopping while packing box back to Coyote's valley

C731.1. Tabu: stopping during journey

C905.3.When Coyote opens Box containing Life, he discovers only decayed corpses--his daughter scolds him

C920.3. Death comes to man-kind when Coyote cannot resist opening the Box of Life; cf. Q411. Death as punishment

C929.7. For opening Box too soon, Coyote has lost chance to bring immortality to life

C953.1. Coyote's daughter must return to and remain in Other World when he violated tabu

D. Magic

D1174.2. Magic bundle contains spirits of the dead; cf. D1520.2.4. Transportation by magic box

D1687.1. As Coyote nears the end of his journey, Box containing Life grows heavier, voices talking and singing are heard

E. The Dead

E13. Resuscitation by stepping over

E62. Resuscitation by letting body lie for five suns

E64.1.1.1.2.1. Resuscitation by carrying Box containing Life

E156.1. Gradual resuscitation as Coyote carries Box of Life, human spirits begin to materialize

E162.3. Resuscitation and eternal life to occur after traveling many days, carrying the Box back to valley of Coyote

E186.2. Resuscitation fails when corpse is "dead beyond life"; cf. E162. Resuscitation impossible after certain length of time

E361.4. Coyote's daughter returns from dead that he will stop weeping; cf. E324. Dead child's friendly return to parents. Frequently to stop weeping; E381. Ghost summoned by weeping

E363.4.1. Ghost of daughter meets him on a high mountain, reassures him

E374.2. Coyote's daughter returns from dead, to be with Coyote always

E379.6. Coyote's daughter returns from dead if he will promise to do as she directs

E481.4.2. Land of dead is a pleasant place: always light, no distress of any kind

E721.7.1. Soul leaves body during sleep and visits his *Tah*

F. Marvels

F55.2. Coyote's daughter talks with him on highest mountain

F1041.21.4.1. Coyote grieves mightily, calls to his daughter at her death

M. Ordaining the future

M325.1. Prophecy: the people will come soon, a higher race and different (from animal-people)

N. Chance and Fate

N339.18. Coyote's daughter sickens, dies

P. Society

P234.3. Coyote mourns too much at death of his daughter; cf. C762.2. Tabu: too much weeping for the dead

Z. Miscellaneous Groups of Motifs

Z71.3.5. Five [corpse lays for 5 days] [step over 5 times to revive corpse] [5 days Coyote calls]

8B. ORIGIN OF DEATH
A. Mythological Motifs

A521. Culture hero [Coyote] as dupe or trickster

A672.1.2. Ferryman takes the drowned in his boat to place of death; cf. F129.7. Voyage to the Isle of the Dead; E481.2.2. Boat to land of the dead

A1174.5. Darkness comes when frog leaps up to swallow the moon; cf. A751.3. Frog in moon; F911.6.2. Frog as swallower of moon

B. Animals

B810.3.3. Coyote(s)

B810.9.1. Eagle(s)

C. Tabu

C929.7. For opening Box too soon, Coyote has lost chance to bring to life immortality

C952.1.1. Spirits of dead come out when Box is opened, return to land of dead

D. Magic

D1174.2. Magic Box contains spirits of the dead; cf. D1520.2.4. Transportation by magic box

D1273. Coyote practices making 5 jumps, wearing skin of frog

E. The Dead

E122.3. To obtain the dead, the frog must be killed--his skin and body used to capture the moon; cf. S114.1.1. Skin of flayed frog to be used to regain the dead

E155.3.1. Children revive from dead at night, visit parents and island

E155.4.2. The dead come out when it is pitch dark

E156.2. Gradual resuscitation: as Box is carried on boattrip, people are heard talking inside

E481.6.2. Land of dead in west; cf. F129.7. Voyage to island of the dead

E481.2.0.1. Island of the dead

E483. Abode of dead in big house where a huge frog looks after them; cf. B876.1. Giant frog

F. Marvels

F167.12.2. Inhabitants of otherworld are two old people

J. The Wise and the Foolish

J2752.1. Trickster Coyote's ineptness gives him away: fails to jump high enough, fails to swallow all of the moon

J2752.2. Coyote insists on being allowed to carry the Box

T. Sex

T51. Wooing by emissary

T257.12. Jealous husband hears wife having a good time with someone in place of the dead; wishes to apprehend them both

Z. Miscellaneous Groups of Motifs
Z71.2.2. West [downriver, to place of death]
Z71.2.5. Yonder [way over there]
Z71.3.5. Five [5 jumps to reach moon]

9A. COYOTE AND THE TWO SISTERS OF THE *N-CHE-WANA*
A. Mythological Motifs
A916. Coyote builds many fish traps in *n-Che-wana*
A993. Huge dam at mouth of *n-Che-wana* [Columbia] River
A1316.7. Coyote cuts open a mouth in the mouthless people
A1316.8. Mouthless people cut mouths for each other
A1421. Hoarded game released--runs of salmon begin
A2484.2. Coyote drives salmon and all fish up the *n-Che-wana* when dam is
     wrecked

B. Animals
B810.3.3. Salmon [Chief] (and all fish) or salmon people
B810.3.5. Coyote

D. Magic
D55.2.7. Coyote transforms self into crying infant in a cradleboard, usually
     found floating downstream
D55.2.8. Coyote transforms self to and from form of infant as he works to
     destroy dam across river
D151.1.1. Transformation: two sisters into the *Chi-col-lah* which always her-
     alds coming of the salmon
D267. Coyote transforms self into a piece of [nicely carved] alder wood
D1092.0.2. Magic flint arrowhead; cf. D1175.2. Magic fire-steel (flint, strike-a-
     light); cf. also Type 562
D2489.2. Small swallows are ordained by Coyote to be heralds of the coming
     of the salmon

F. Marvels
F513.0.3. Mouthless people
F561.9. Mouthless people take in nourishment by smelling of the food--then
     throwing it away [eat by smell]

P. Society
P252.1.1. Two sisters rescue infant from river; raise, feed and succor it
P252.8. Older sister warns other sister(s) against picking up piece of driftwood

Q. Rewards and Punishments
Q40. Chief of Mouthless people would reward Coyote for his kindness
Q115.2.1. Chief offers his daughter as reward to Coyote

R. Captives and Fugitives
R219.3. Coyote escapes confinement of marriage by refusing Chief's daughter-

-to be free

W. Traits of Character

W230. People sans mouths (take in food by smell only) found by Coyote; cf. F513.3. Mouthless people

W230.2.2.1 Two sisters

Z. Miscellaneous Groups of Motifs

Z71.2.2. East [Coyote travels up the river]

Z71.3.5. Five [digs for 5 days] [digs with 5 arrow-wood sticks]

Z252.1. Coyote refuses to give name to Chief of Mouthless People; cf. C436. Tabu: disclosing own identity; K1831.0.1. Disguise by changing name

9B. COYOTE DECEIVES EAGLE, AND STOCKS THE COLUMBIA WITH FISH

A. Mythological Motifs

A993. Huge dam at mouth of *n-Che-wana* (Columbia River) bars salmon from migrating upstream

A1421. Hoarded game released--start of salmon runs

A2484.2. Coyote drives salmon and all fish up the *n-Che-wana* when dam is wrecked

B. Animals

B211. Old Thunder

B455.3. Helpful eagle--as hunter

B810.3.3. Coyote(s)

B810.9.1. Eagle(s)

B810.18.1. Salmon [Chief] (and all fish, or Salmon people)

D. Magic

D55.2.7. Coyote transforms self into crying infant in a cradleboard, usually found floating downstream

D55.2.8. Coyote transforms self to and from form of infant as he works to destroy fish dam

D151.1.1. Transformation: two sisters into the *Chi-col-lah* which always heralds coming of the salmon

D267. Coyote transforms self into a piece of [nicely carved] alder wood

D421.2.3. Transformation: two slain bucks to hanging bushes

D457.7.1. Transformation: Eaglet feathers to coyote entrails

D575.2. Transformation: two sisters are transformed to swallows when ashes are blown on them; cf. D931.1.2. Magic ashes

D902. Magic rain

D953.4. Coyote makes a (two) long stick(s)--when told to be strong, stick is used to break the fish dam

D1223.1.1. Magic flute of Eagle

D2489.2. Small swallows are ordained by Coyote to be heralds of coming of the salmon

J. The Wise and the Foolish
J641.2.2. Coyote moves his camp often to avoid detection by Eagle

K. Deceptions
K700.1. Coyote captured by deception--wives of Eagle pretend their husband
is not near

K1039. Coyote duped into fetching two fat bucks [deer]--killed by Eagle

K1200.1. Eagle persuaded to remove all his clothes before climbing rock

K1810.2.1. Disguise of Coyote by putting on fine clothes of his grandson,
Eagle

K2310.1. Deception by equivocation--Eagle is lured by news of [false] nest of
eagles which Coyote supposedly found

P. Society
P252.1.1. Two sisters rescue infant from river and raise, feed and succor it

P252.9. Younger sister warns other sister(s) against picking up piece(s) of
driftwood

Q. Rewards and Punishments
Q115.4. Two wives of Eagle plus his clothing given as reward to Coyote

R. Captives and Fugitives
R49.4. Eagle held captive for many days on high cliff

R51.1.1. Eagle grows thin during captivity

R111.1.2.1. Rescue of two wives of Eagle from Coyote--following [trail of]
the campsites

R151.1.2. Husbands rescues two wives stolen by Coyote

R211.6.1. When Thunder shatters rock, Eagle works himself down to the
ground

R219.3. To escape his desolate place, Coyote swims over four gulches filled
with rushing streams

T. Sex
T423.1. Coyote seduces two wives of his grandson, Eagle

W. Traits of Character
W230.2.2.1. Two sisters

Z. Miscellaneous Groups of Motifs
Z71.2.3. West. [Coyote carried downstream to great ocean]

Z71.3.5. Five [crosses 5 gulches] [transforms self 5 times

10. CHIPMUNK'S STRIPES
A. Mythological Motifs
A2217.2.3. Chipmunk's back scratched; hence his stripes. A cannibal woman

grabs at him, her fingers scratch the marks onto his back

B. Animals
B810.4.1.1. Chipmunk(s)

G. Ogres
G312.8. Cannibal woman

11. RACCOON
A. Mythological Motifs
A972.1.1.1. Marks near Columbia River caused when Raccoon rubbed his buttocks along the rocks--while grieving

A2217.2.1. Raccoon's back scratched; hence his stripes. When his grand mother whips him with a stick, welts are left which made marks Raccoons have today

B. Animals
B810.3.4. Raccoon(s)

D. Magic
D231.1.1. Grandmother transformed into a rock near the Columbia River; cf. A974.1. Rocks from transformation of people to stone

D981.10.2. Magic ball(s) of berries with thorns sticking out

K. Deceptions
K331.3.1. Raccoon steals acorns from 5 holes; defecates in them as substitute

P. Society
P292. Grandmother

Q. Rewards and Punishments
Q212.5. Raccoon's theft is punished when he is whipped with a stick

W. Traits of Character
W122.19. Stingy Raccoon deliberately gives his grandmother inadequate water to drink

W125.6. Raccoon eats grandmother's share of acorns as well as his own

W152.18. Stingy grandmother gives Raccoon scant food

W230.2.3. A grandmother

W231.1.2. Young Raccoon

Z. Miscellaneous Groups of Motifs
Z71.3.5. Five [5 potholes filed with acorns] [5 balls of berries]

II. TALES OF THE LEGENDARY

12. PANTHER AND WILDCAT FIGHT
WITH THE GRIZZLIES

A. Mythological Motifs

A970. Origin of particular rocks and stones [bodies of four grizzlies transformed into rocks ca. 2 1/2 miles below The Dalles: "the great bears and the wolves"]

A1812. Origin of Panther and Wildcat--transformed from being "animal people"

A2412.1.7. Origin of black spots on Wildcat's head

B. Animals

B810.1.3. Cougar(s) [Panther]

B810.3.3. Wildcat(s)

B810.3.5. Grizzly Bear(s) [5 Grizzly Bear brothers]

C. Tabu

C221.3.2.1. Tabu: Eating shin-bone of buck deer

D. Magic

D113.2.1. Two blind sisters transformed: become 5 Grizzly Bears

D271.1.1. In fight between Grizzly and Panther, nothing remains finally but pieces of flesh; cf. D2061.1.1.1. Person magically reduced to pile of bones

D705.2. Disenchantment of residence--house moved, dead bodies of bears thrown across river

D838.14. Magic fire-brands stolen from two old sisters

D905.1. Magic storm(s): hail and rain, lightning and thunder, great wind

D1013.2. Magic shin-bone of a buck deer

D1091. Magic bow

D1097.1. Magic battle-axe falls trees with little effort [hold axe aloft, to cause trees to fall]

D1271.1. Magic fire [2 firebrands] [scorches thief's ears]

D1293. Magic color(s): Panther paints self with yellow, red, black in readiness for battle; cf. Z65. Color formulas; also D1293.1. Red as magic color; D1293.4. Black as magic color

D1311.17.4. Magic bow breaks, streams blood as sign of something wrong at home

D1381.15.1. Particular colors painted on warrior guards against danger

D1419.5. When magic bone is broken, the fire is extinguished

D1720.3. *Tah* power(s) acquired from Wildcat, from Panther [Cougar]; cf. B500. Magic power from animal(s)

D2001.0.1. Death of Grizzly by burning scraps remaining of his flesh, bones, heart

E. The Dead
E80.3.1. Resuscitation: remnants of Panther's flesh, heart, put in water
E183. Panther returns to life on sixth day, is fed

K. Deceptions
K333.6. Theft of magic firebrands by substituting two bundles of cedar splints

P. Society
P251.5.7. Two brothers: one hunts, the other keeps the home
P252.2. Two sisters accuse each other of stealing
P414.1.1. Wildcat as neophyte hunter, kills small animals near home

S. Unnatural Cruelty
S162.0.1. Grizzly bear(s) are killed when their hind-legs are cut off

W. Traits of Character
W230.2.2.2. Sister(s) [two old and blind sisters]; cf. P252.1. Two sisters

Z. Miscellaneous Groups of Motifs
Z71.0.1. Two [2 old and blind sisters]
Z71.2.0. Four [Wildcat retreats 4 times]
Z71.3.5. Five [5 magic firebrands] [5 trees felled] [5 times Old Grizzly calls]
[5 times storm of rain and hail increases] [5 Grizzly Bears] [5 days
and nights pass]

13. THE DEAD CANOEMAN OF
THE *N-CHE-WANA*
A. Mythological Motifs
A989.5. Origin of cave in river cliffs near Lyle, Washington
A1224. Days of Animal People preceded man

D. Magic
D192. Transformation: man to worm(s); cf. E734.9. Soul of man in form of
worms; cf. Q551.3.2.5. Punishment: man transformed to a mass of
worms
D1021. Magic feather
D1520.35.1. Magic transport of wife on eagle feather
D1960.4. Deathlike sleep; cf. D1962.3. Magic sleep by hairdressing. Head
laid on another's lap

E. The Dead
E11.4. Resuscitation: by being pushed off wife's lap

W. Traits of Character
W230.3. A man and wife

14. WASCO
A. Mythological Motifs
A941.0.1. Origin of a particular spring - *Wasco*

D. Magic
D928.2. Deep hole with magical power
D931. Magic rock; cf. F800. Extraordinary rocks and stones
D1318.1.1.1. Stone reveals guilt of the very bad boy, a lesson to others
D1542.1.8. When stick is thrust into magic hole-in-ground, rain comes; cf.
        D1541. Magic object controls storms; D2141. Storm produced by
        magic

F. Marvels
F809.10. Extraordinary rock seizes fingernail from bad boy; cf. D1413.17.
        Magic adhesive stone

W. Traits of Character
W230.1.2. Boy(s)

15A. BATTLE OF THE *AT-TE-YI-YI* AND *TO-QEE-NUT*
A. Mythological Motifs
A101.2. Spirit which rules
A522.1.3. Coyote as culture hero
A536.2. Coyote (culture-hero) fights as ally of the Wolf brothers; cf. N810.
        Supernatural helpers
A536.2.1. Coyote aids Salmon-youth in struggle against the Wind brothers
A546.1. Coyote regrets killing of Salmon-Chief, who was "a good man"
A950. Dual tracks where wolves stood set into rocks on Washington side of
        Columbia River, at Wishram, near the Tumwater
A1135.1.2. Origin of cold: Sister of winds escapes into river
A1136. Origin of warm weather: hero [Salmon-youth] defeats Wind brothers;
        Chinook winds to blow instead
A1599.17. Origin of the victory call in games or battles
A2433.3.13.1. Why wolves live in Cascade Mountains
A2484.2. Why salmon come plentifully as they do

B. Animals
B264.6. Representative single combat between animals [between Salmon and
        the Winds]
B810.3.2. Wolf(s) [5 Wolf brothers
B810.3.3. Coyote(s)
B810.13. Birds
B810.18.1. Salmon [Chief] (and all fish or Salmon people)
B810.18.2. Salmon-Youth
B810.24.2. Animal people(s) [Wolf, Coyote, Fox people kill Salmon people]

D. Magic

D124.2.4. Magic oil

D1017.2. Magic salmon oil

D1242.1. Magic water

D1335.18. Magical oil poured underfoot gives strength

D1810.14. Magic knowledge of identity of Salmon-youth; cf. F643. Marvelous presentiment of coming of Salmon-youth

D1832.1. Magic strength and growth come by cold water baths in winter

D1832.1.1. Magic strength by bathing, by sweating, cold water

D1835.7. Magic strength from "practicing his strength while going"

D2144.2. Contest of heat and cold. Hero [Salmon] and the Wolves [Winds] wrestle. If the Winds win, ice and cold will be everywhere always

F. Marvels

F436.1. The North [Northeast] Winds [5 brothers and a sister]

F436.2. Chinook wind [Salmon-wind], a warm wind

F610.2.1. Remarkably strong youth [Salmon-youth]

F611.1.14.1. Salmon-youth, son of Salmon-chief, as strong hero

F611.3.1. Strong hero practices uprooting trees; cf. F621. Strong man: tree-puller

F611.3.1.1. Strong hero practices uprooting trees, lifting, pulling, running, jumping, throwing rocks

F617. Mighty wrestler(s)

F642.2.0.1. Strong youth throws enormous stone great distance [to middle of the Columbia River]

F645.3. Marvelously wise grandmother [relates to young salmon mishaps suffered by parents] [marvelous presentiment of coming of Salmon-youth]

F645.4. Marvelously wise grandmother tells magical actions Necessary to obtain revenge

F715.10. Frozen *n-Che-wana* as site of wrestling

F757.2.1. Five wind brothers live in cave [at *Wah-pe-us*, near Celilo]; cf. A1122. Cave of winds; R315. Cave as refuge

F930.9. Heavy rains cause Salmon egg to hatch, to slip into the water

F962.13.1. Extraordinary darkness and heavy rains; cf. D2140. Magic control of elements

H. Tests

H1381.2.2.3. Grandmother sought [found] by young Salmon

H1562.9. Test of strength: wrestling

J. The Wise and the Foolish

J321.5. Wolves fail to lick up last salmon egg, so abandon it

J641.2. Salmon advises his wife and children to flee in event of his defeat

K. Deceptions

K619.2.1. Oil put on ice [or applied to feet] prevents slipping

L. Reversal of Fortune

L101. Unpromising hero; cf. L111.2. Foundling hero
L101.2. Unpromising hero: Third brother bests Salmon-chief
L431.4. Sneering brothers disregard power of young challenger
L311. Weak (small) hero overcomes large fighter
L333. Sister escapes by diving through hole in ice into river

M. Ordaining the Future

M325.1. Prophecy of coming of the human race

P. Society

P555.4. Two Wind brothers are defeated in wrestling by *Toque-nut*
P555.5 *To-Que-nut* defeated and killed by third Wind brother
P555.5.2. Five Wind brothers are killed in wrestling with Salmon-youth hero
P556.3. Challenge made to wrestle on frozen river ice [wolves challenge Salmon-chief to battle] [Wolves challenge Salmon-youth to battle
P557.4.4.2. Youngest Wind brother afraid, must fight slayer of his four older brothers

Q. Rewards and Punishments

Q469.14. Punishment; lame sister struck hard on naked buttocks with thorny rosebush
Q471.3. Punishment: defecating in old slave woman's hair; cf. R51. Mistreatment of prisoners; cf. P672.3. Rubbing shaved head of hero with cow dung as insult

R. Captives and Fugitives

R51.1.1. Slave woman denied food, clothes, warmth
R327.1. One salmon egg rolls into deep crack in rocks--escapes destruction

S. Unnatural Cruelty

S110.6. Children of Salmon-Chief murdered by the Wolves
S116.7. Eggs of Salmon-woman are destroyed by being crushed; cf. C544. Tabu: crushing eggs; Cf. J622. Preventing the birth of enemies
S139.1.1. Murder of Salmon-chief's wife by "bursting her open"; cf. P555.2. Corpses of dead foes dismembered
S302.2. At defeat of hero, all his children are killed/beheaded

T. Sex

T500. Wife of slain hero with child [filled with eggs]

W. Traits of Character

W212.3. Salmon-youth shows strength, heart, eagerness for combat
W230.2.1.1. A slave [woman]; [sister to grandmother]
W230.2.2.2. Sister(s) [crippled sister]
W230.2.3. Grandmother

Z. Miscellaneous Groups of Motifs

Z71.0.1. Two [2 Wind brothers defeated]

Z71.2.0. Four [4 whirls of foes]

Z71.3.5. Five [5 Wolf brothers] [5 days] [5 days, 5 baskets of oil] [5 Wind brothers] [5 whirls {wrestling "falls"} of foe]

Z71.4. Six [6 months or "moons"]

Z71.5. Seven [7 times foe whirled]

Z71.16.15. Fifty [stronger than 50 men]

15B. BATTLE OF COLD-WIND
AND CHINOOK-WIND
A. Mythological Motifs

A522.1.3. Coyote as culture hero

A545.1. Culture-hero as executioner of loser of contest

A972.8. Origin of mark in rock near mouth of Yakima River

A974.3. Origin of two large rocks at the Tumwater [mid-Columbia River]: from Coyote and lame sister of Cold-wind

A1129.4. Origin of Chinook-wind [warm southerly wind of late winter]; cf. A1136. Origin of warmer weather

B. Animals

B264.6. Representational single combat [between Winds and the Eagles]

B810.3.3. Coyote(s)

B810.9.1. Eagle(s) [Eagle, wife, one son]

D. Magic

D231.3. Transformation: Coyote and *Tah-mat-tox-lee* [lame sister of Cold-Wind] to very large rocks at the Tumwater, mid-Columbia River

D815.6.1. Magic object received from daughter-in-law

D904. Magic ice formed on ground

D1017.2. Magic salmon oil

D1021. Magic feather

D1242.4. Magic oil

D1293.3.1. White feather signifies birth of future hero

D1323.16.1. Magic feathers (red/white) signify whether a girl or boy infant has been born

D1832.1.1. Magic strength by bathing-sweating and cold water

D1835.7. Magic strength from "practicing your strength while going"

D2144.2. Contest of heat and cold: hero and Winds wrestle; if Winds win, ice and cold will be everywhere, always

F. Marvels

F436.1. North [Northeast] Winds [5 brothers and a lame sister]

F436.2. Chinook wind [Salmon-wind], a warm wind [5 brothers]

F610.2.1. Remarkably strong youth

F611.3.1. Strong hero practices uprooting trees; cf. F621. Strong man: tree-puller

F611.3.1.1. Strong hero practices uprooting trees, lifting, pulling, running, jumping, etc. and throwing rocks to become strong
F617. Mighty wrestler(s)
F624.2.0.1. Strong youth throws enormous stone great distance [to middle of the *n-Che-wana* river]
F645.4. Marvelously wise mother, tells magical actions necessary
F757.2.1. Five wind brothers live in cave [at *Ta-mant-towla*]; cf. A1122. Cave of winds; R315. Cave as refuge
F986.6. Chinook-youth catches the biggest sturgeon

H. Tests
H1381.2.3. Child seeks unknown grandparents
H1562.9. Test of strength: wrestling

K. Deceptions
K619.2.1. Oil put on ice [or applied to feet] prevents slipping

L. Reversal of Fortune
L101. Unpromising hero; cf.L111.2. Foundling hero
L311. Weak (small) hero overcomes larger fighter
L432.5. Youngest of cruel brothers begs for his life; cf. P555. Defeat in battle

M. Ordaining the Future
M311.0.2. Prophecy: birth of hero at certain time

N. Chance and Fate
N822.1. Lame sister as helper

P. Society
P253.0.5.1. Helpful sister and five brothers
P555.5. Five Wind brothers are killed in combats with [Salmon-youth] hero
P555.5.1. Five Chinook-Wind brothers are slain [beheaded] for losing contests
P556.3. Cold-wind shouts challenge to wrestle
P557.4.4.1. Chinook-youth accepts challenges to wrestle by deed: show of great strength
P557.4.4.2. Youngest Wind brother, afraid, must fight slayer of his four older brothers

Q. Rewards and Punishments
Q421.0.9. Beheading as punishment for losing wrestling match
Q467.6. Dousing with cold water as humiliation / punishment of grandparents
Q471.4. Punishment: pouring cold water over old grandparents; cf. R51. Mistreatment of prisoners

S. Unnatural Cruelty
S110.7. Son of Eagle defeated by Cold Wind [beheaded by Coyote]
S302.2. At defeat of hero, all his children are killed / beheaded

T. Sex
T500. Wife of slain hero with child

Z. Miscellaneous Groups of Motifs
Z71.3.5. Five [5 brothers] [5 baskets of water] [5 Chinook Wind brothers] [5 days infancy] [5 days travel] [5 baskets of oil] [5 times youngest brother begs for life] [5 times Coyote asks]

16. FOOD SMELLERS
A. Mythological Motifs
A522.1.3. Coyote as culture hero
A530.2. Coyote, as culture hero, opens eyes and mouths of the Food Smellers

W. Traits of Character
W230.5. People sans mouths (take in food by smell only) found by Coyote; cf. F513.0.3. Mouthless people

17. *AH-TON-O-KAH* OF *SHE-KO-UN*,
A WASCO LEGEND OF MOUNT HOOD
A. Mythological Motifs
A497.2. Echo, on Mount Hood
A1195. Origin of Echo

F. Marvels
A451.4.4.4. Es-cho-likes cause fire to come from Mount Hood to deter people away from where they lived; cf. F451.3.4.2. Dwarfs as smiths
F556.5. *Ah-Ton-O-Kah's* voice so loud that leaves and pine needles fall to the ground
F701.3. Lodge of *Ah-Ton-O-Kah* contains plentitude of food of all kinds
F753. Mountain of fire [volcanic eruption]
F823.5. Spiked shoes

J. The Wise and the Foolish
J2635. Mountain climbers frightened away by eruption

K. Deceptions
K1887.1. Echo answers

P. Society
P322.1.1. Giantess with long breasts forces lost man to accept her long term hospitality; cf. T281. Sex hospitality

R.Captives
R11.2.2.1. Abduction by Echo; cf. D2065.6. Person abducted by Echo crazed and dumb

W. Traits of Character

W230.1. Men [three Indians] [three white men]

W230.2. Woman [very large woman [giantess?] with long breasts; cf. F460.1.2. Mountain-wife has breasts so long that she throws them over her shoulder; F531.1.5.1. Giantess throws her breasts over her shoulders. Her two sons can run after her and suck

W230.5. Dwarf people [*Es-cho-o-likes*] on Mount Hood; cf. F451.4.18. Dwarfs live in the high banks of the seashore

Z. Miscellaneous Groups of Motifs

Z71.1.1. Three [3 white men] [3 Indians]

Z71.3.5. Five. [5 dwarfs] [calls 5 times]

18. *NIHS-LAH*, A WASCO LEGEND OF MULTNOMAH FALLS

A. Mythological Motifs

A522.1.3. Coyote as culture hero

A530.1. Bridge of Gods caused to fall by Coyote's fit of madness at creation of *Nihs-lah*

A530.3. Coyote (culture hero) creates fish-human monster

A546.1. Coyote accompanies girl to protect her

A546.2. Coyote pronounces enmity between upriver people and downriver people

A968.3. Origin of *Sko-lus*, the tall cliff or rimrock above the *n-Che-wana* at Multnomah Falls

A1131.2.1. Origin of violent storms of wind and rain near Multnomah Falls-*Nihs-Lah*; cf. F420.1.3.2. Water-spirits as fish; cf. B70. Fish-beasts; F420.5.2. Malevolent water-spirits

A2687.2.2. Origin of roots and berries about Multnomah Falls

B. Animals

B82. *Nihs-Lah*: half-human (man), half-fish

B810.3.3. Coyote(s)

D. Magic

D199.4. Transformation: man to large monster, half-human, half-fish

D1002. Magic excrements

D1312.1.1. Excrements as advisers

J. The Wise and the Foolish

K1771.10. Sham threat of lethal hail and rainstorm

T. Sex

T61.1.1. Betrothal of lovers by means of travel to his parents' lodge

T71.1. Girl scorned to be accepted as wife

T71.3. Scorned as wife, woman is sent home

T131.1.3.1. Marriage without both parents' knowledge

W. Traits of Character

W230.1. A Chief's son
W230.2.2. A beautiful girl

Z. Miscellaneous Groups of Motifs

Z71.3.5. Five. [waits 5 nights] [5 sisters]

19. STORIES OF THE *GY-U-BOO-KUM*
B. Animals

B16.5.1.2. Devastating (man-eating) sea-monster (serpent) [devours infant]
B16.5.1.3. Devastating monster serpent leaves print in dust like a log that's
been dragged
B16.5.1.4. *Gy-U-Boo-Kum*, monster snake half as long as a tepee pole, with
a large belly and large rattles like a rattlesnake
B211. *Gy-U-Boo-Kum*, monster serpent
B875.1. Giant serpent; cf. X1321.1.The great snake

F. Marvels

F913. Victims rescued
F913.3. Victim [dead infant] rescued from dead serpent's belly.

H. Tests

H1161.1. Task: killing ferocious beast [giant serpent]

K. Deceptions

K812.4. Pursuers set large fire, burn to death giant serpent in its cave

N. Chance and Fate

N271.8.1. Giant serpent traced by trail it leaves
N773.3. Adventure following giant serpent into cave

P. Society

P173.5. Slave boy [from Snake Indians]
P716. Particular places: near the great village of the Wishrams

R. Captives and Fugitives

R315.1. Deep cave as refuge of great serpent

W. Traits of Character

W230.2.2. A young woman and her infant sister
W231.1.2. A slave boy

Z. Miscellaneous Groups of Motifs

Z71.1.0. Two (2 bow shots)

20. THE *GY-U-BOO-KUM*

B. Animals

B16.5.1.2. Devastating (man-eating) sea-monster (serpent) [devours girl]

B16.5.1.4. *Gy-U-Boo-Kum*, monster snake half as long as tepee pole with large
        belly; has short legs in front like a lizard, has a bell on its tail]

B765.23.1. Giant snake with legs

F. Marvels

F913.3. Victim(s) [dead girl] rescued from dead serpent's belly

K. Deceptions

K812.4. Pursuers set large fire; drive giant serpent from its cave

N. Chance and Fate

N773.3. Adventure of following giant serpent into cave

R. Captives and Fugitives

R315.1. Deep cave as refuge of great serpent

W. Traits of Character

W230.2.2. Beautiful girl [on spirit quest into mountains]

21. FIVE STARS VISIT THE EARTH

A121. Stars as deities; cf. A125.1.1. Five stars assume forms of men

A762. Stars descend as human beings

A762.1. Star-husband. Star takes mortal maiden as wife

A769.6. Stars now stay in heaven [people learned of their visits to earth]

C. Tabu

C15.1. Wish for star-husband realized

D. Magic

D231.3. Transformation: Star-man to the Star-rock

D439.5.2. Transformation: star(s) to person(s)

D861.2.1. Magic stone (of Wasco tribe?) stolen by enemies

D1741.2.1. With theft of Star-rock, tribe loses "superior" powers--become very
        common people

D1761.1. Wishing by stars

P. Society

P716. Particular Places [right bank of Columbia River]

R. Captives and Fugitives

R227.2.1. Flight from old man husband; cf. J1457. The gray fox; cf. also,
        K2213.12. Young queen murders her old husband in order to get
        a new

T. Sex

T91.3. Love of mortal and supernatural person

T91.4.1.2. Old Star-man marries young girl; cf. J445.2. Foolish marriage of old man and young girl

T111.1.1.1. Maiden chooses Star-man as husband

W. Traits of Character

W230.1.1.1. An old man [old Star-man]

W230.1.3. Stars [5 men]

W230.2.2. Girls [5 girls]

Z. Miscellaneous Groups of Motifs

Z71.3.5. Five [5 Star-men] [5 girls]

22A. COYOTE IMITATES FISH HAWK AND MOUNTAIN SHEEP, AND MEETS WITH VARIOUS ADVENTURES.

B. Animals

B182.1. Magic dog(s)

B810.3.2. Wolf(s) [5 Wolf brothers]

B810.3.3. Coyote(s)

B810.5.2. Deer [Deer people {5 brothers}]

B810.5.3. Buffalo cow

B810.5.4. Mountain Sheep [and wife]

B810.9.2. Fish hawk [and wife]

D. Magic

D1431.1. Rock (stone) pursues person; cf. D93. Magic rock (stone); cf. R261.1. Pursuit by rolling head; cf. E261.1. Wandering skull pursues man

D2092.1. Pursuing rolling rock gets stuck in mud

D2105.8. Provisions magically furnished--blood, fat, meat from nose or sides of wife of Mountain Sheep; cf. D2161.2.1. Steaks cut from live cow who heals herself by magic

D2105.8.1. Mountain Sheep lops steaks from his own sides

D2105.8.2. Buffalo cow lops steaks from about her body

F. Marvels

F365.3. Coyote as unwilling servant

F679.10. Remarkable fisherman; cf. D2105. Saint causes fish to come out of lake to satisfy guests for whom he has no food

F696.1. Marvelous diver [Fish Hawk]

J. The Wise and the Foolish

J2411.3. Unsuccessful imitation of magic production of food

J2425. The bungling host

K. Deceptions

K11.10. Race won by deception: magic hounds entered

K624.1. When magic hound wins race, Coyote flees

K833.1. Deer family lured into aiding Coyote against an imaginary foe--are killed

W. Traits of Character

W151.2.2. Hospitable host impoverished by greedy guest; cf. Q272. Avarice punished

Z. Miscellaneous Groups of Motifs

Z71.2.2. Direction: East [Coyote travels to the East]

Z71.3.5. Five: [5 times food given to Coyote] [5 different kinds of fish caught] [5 deer slain]

22B. EAGLE DEFEATS FISH HAWK, AND PITIES SKUNK

B. Animals

B281.12.1. Coyote's daughter wed to Fish Hawk

B810.2.3. Skunk(s)

B810.9.1. Eagle(s)

B810.9.2. Fish Hawk

B810.17.2. Body louse (lice)

B873.1. Giant louse

D. Magic

D1013.2. Magic fish bones

D1021. Magic feather(s)

D1766.9.1. Magic results from singing

D2061.1.1.2. Louse destroyed by increased heat of sun's rays; cf. D2144.4.1. Person burned [slain] through magic wishing [curse]

D2143.1.1. Rain produced by magic causes racer to lose race

F. Marvels

F696.1. Marvelous diver [Fish Hawk] [Eagle]

F989.24. Band of deer driven from mountains are all killed by one man

J. The Wise and the Foolish

J1706.2. Skunk as stupid beast

J2411.3. Unsuccessful imitation of magic production of food

J2443. Bungling hunter. A dupe (animal) attempts to imitate great hunter but fails. He brings a ludicrous catch, is humiliated

L. Reversal of Fortune

L101. Unpromising hero: youngest brother

L201. Modesty (lack of knowledge or ability) professed about doing feat

P. Society

P250.2. Elder brother takes object from younger

P556.3. Challenge to runners: appearance of unknown man
P716. Particular Places (as setting) [The Dalles]

T. Sex

T251.2.5.1. Ungrateful wife driven from home--she reforms, is taken back
T288.2. Wife refuses to sleep with stupid husband

W. Traits of Character

W230.2.1.2. Wife(s)
W230.5. A voice

Z. Miscellaneous Groups of Motifs

Z71.3.5. Five. [5 strings of fish] [5 tail feathers]

23. A SINGING AND DANCING FESTIVAL

A. Mythological Motifs

A962.11. At foot of Mount Hood: site of magic rites
A1234.3. Coming of people prophesied

B. Animals

B810.1.1. Wildcat(s) [5 brothers]
B810.1.3. Cougar(s) [5 Panther brothers]
B810.2.4. Marten [5 brothers]
B810.3.1.1. Fox, Black Fox [as messenger] [5 brothers
B810.3.2. Wolves [5 brothers]
B810.3.3. Coyote(s)
B810.5.2. Elk [5 brothers]
B335.6.1. Fox warns Coyote not to sing, not to enter fire; cf. B521. Animal
   warns of fatal danger

D. Magic

D62. Transformation: each of animal brothers carried into fire--become great
   hunters
D699.2. Midnight as best time for transformation; cf. E587.5. Ghosts walk at
   midnight
D1271. Magic fire; cf. D1330. Magic object works physical change
D1766.9.1. Magic results from singing
D2108. House magically enlarged, with 5 fireplaces

E. The Dead

E1.3. Coyote, dead, comes to life

J. The Wise and the Foolish

J951.6. Coyote passes himself off as a Nez Perce

P. Society

P250. Elder brother
P251. Brothers [sets of five Brothers]
P716. Particular places (as setting): at foot of Mount Hood

S. Unnatural Cruelty

S112.8. Victim burned alive in ritual fire

Z. Miscellaneous Groups of Motifs

Z71.1.1. Three [Elk sings 3 times]
Z71.3.3. Five [5 brothers, many sets] [5 fireplaces] [5 Elk brothers carry each of 5 animal brothers] [5 songs sung, stop 5 times] [5th night]

24. EAGLE HAS TOBACCO MAN AND WILLOW WRESTLE WITH *ABU'MAT*

A. Mythological Motifs

A1438.2. Pipe-Scrapings become great spirit for future people seeking to become medicine-men

B. Animals

B810.3.3. Coyote(s)
B810.9.1. Eagle(s)

D. Magic

D431.2.1. Transformation: willow twig with long root to man
D439.7. Transformation: pipe scrapings to a man
D451.1.0.2. Transformation: willow-man back to old form
D1212. Magic rattle
D1739.3. Magic strength from soaking in water

E. The Dead

E29.8. Resuscitation by gathering up pieces, rolling them between the hands

F. Marvels

F601.2.1. Extraordinary companions help in suitor test
F617.1. Girl as mighty wrestler
F759.9. Eagle and *Abu'Mat* travel to mountains where Coyote cannot go

H. Tests

H217.5. Strongest is determined by wrestling contest
H331.6.1. Suitor contest: wrestling with bride; cf. H332.1. Suitor [Coyote] [Pipe-Scrapings Man] [Willow-man] in contest with bride; Cf. T58. Wooing the strong and beautiful bride

P. Society

P716. Particular Places (as setting) [The Dalles]

T. Sex
T75.0.3. Suitor defeated in wrestling match is rejected [Coyote] [Pipe-Scrapings Man]

W. Traits of Character
W230.6.1. Plant as character
W230.6.1.1. Willow [man]
W230.8.1. Pipe-Scrapings [ash] man

Z. Miscellaneous Groups of Motifs
Z71.1.1. Three [3 companions]
Z71.3.3. Five [5th day] [5 days] [5 times twisted]

25. A HARD WINTER NEAR THE DALLES
B. Animals
B563.6. Bird as scout; cf. A2221.7. Dove returns to ark in obedience to Noah: receives sheen of Raven; cf. B450. Helpful bird

D. Magic
D1841.4.2.1. People live beneath huge snowfall
D2125.1.1.2. Magic transport by waves--brings girl up river after long voyage
B2141.0.11.2. Extraordinary snowstorm caused by striking bird; cf. C537. Tabu: touching certain animals; cf. Q228. Punishment for trying to harm sacred animal

F. Marvels
F1.3. Person comes to life unaided
F569.4. In summer girl wears many clothes; in winter goes naked
F962.11.2. Extraordinary snow-storm--snows for seven months
F962.11.3. Lack of snow all about site of immense snowfall; cf. D2145.1.1. Local winter

P. Society
P716. Particular Places (as setting): [Dog River, 25 miles below The Dalles]

Q. Rewards and Punishments
Q466.0.3. Punishment: setting the guilty adrift on an ice floe

W. Traits of Character
W115.4. Stench of humans kills girl
W230.2.2. A girl

Z. Miscellaneous Groups of Motifs
Z71.3.3. Five [5 years]
Z71.5. Seven [7 months]

26. THE BOY WHO WENT TO LIVE
WITH THE SEALS
B. Animals

B223.2. Kingdom of seals described by youth

B537.1. Seals adopt youth who lives among them; cf. R10.3. Children abducted

D. Magic

D2188.2 Person vanishes [a boy]

H. Tests

H1385.2.1. Quest for vanished son

R. Captives and Fugitives

R13.0.2. Youth carried off by seals

R13.5. Seals abduct boy

R46.1. Captivity in sea

R86. Freed captive slowly regains powers of speech, human behavior

R111.1.3.1. Rescue of boy from among seals

R169.17. Youth rescued from among seals by people

R228.1. Youth leaves home to rejoin seals

R317.1.1. Youth will remain with the seals underwater hereafter

W. Traits of Character

W230.1.2. A boy

W230.3. A man and wife

W230.4. Some people [Chinook people]

Z. Miscellaneous Groups of Motifs

Z71.0.1. Two [2 or 3 years]

Z71.2.2. East (Going east - travelling up river)

27. AN ARROW POINT MAKER
BECOMES A CANNIBAL
A. Mythological Motifs

A452.1. Origin of guardian spirit of hunters

A454.1.1. Origin of guardian spirits for medicine women (and women who smoke); cf. D2161. Magic healing power

A1555.2.1. Origin of custom of selecting worthy husbands, of awarding daughters as wives

A1579.2. Origin of duty of daughters-in-law to care for elderly mothers-in-law

D. Magic

D965.17. Magic tobacco plant(s)

D1039.3. Magic smoke of tobacco as food; cf. D1472. Food and drink from magic object

D1092.0.1.2. Magic arrowhead; cf. F831. Extraordinary arrow

D1092.0.2. Magic arrow gathers *five* bunches of tobacco

D1261.1. Magic pipe

D1322.3. Obtaining large amount of tobacco a death-sign; cf. E761.7.3. Life token: leaves fall from tree

D1653.1.5.1. Unerring arrow by wish from youth

D1857.3. Cannibal cannot be killed

D2061.1.1.1. Person (skeleton) magically reduced to pile of bones

E. The Dead

E79.4. Resuscitation: throwing paint into air; speaking to the sky brings revival of slain group of people

E607.1.1.1. Bones of dead man collected and thrown outdoors

F. Marvels

F561.4. Person lives by smoking tobacco; never eats

F661.13. Youthful marksman shoots large amount of tobacco

F677.1. Skillful tracker infallible on land or sea

F679.5.4. Skillful hunter obtains large quantity of tobacco

F815.8. Plants are Tobacco People; cf. F445.1.1. Tobacco spirit

F963.5. Extraordinary Northwind accompanies skeleton-cannibal

F973.3. Walking on tops of blades of grass (to leave no trail)

G. Ogres

G11.7.1. Cannibalistic man

G36.3. Taste of blood from own cut finger brings desire for human flesh

G51.1. Person eats self up

G79.2. Skeleton-cannibal eats people of next village

N. Chance and Fate

N832.3. Boy as helper--named son-in-law; cf. T61.6. Grateful father of girl declares relationship

N836.1.1. Woman seeks protection by establishing a relatedness with old man and daughter; cf. H1233.2. Relation as helper on quest

P. Society

P716. Particular Places (as setting) [3 miles below The Dalles, on right side of the Columbia River] [the Blue Mountains?]

T. Sex

T53.6. Father awards daughter as wife to worthy youth

W. Traits of Character

W230.1. A man [an old man]

W230.4. Some people

W230.4.2. An old man and his daughter

W230.4.2.1. A mother and her son

Z. Miscellaneous Groups of Motifs

Z71.2.4. South [Woman travels southward to become guardian spirit]
Z71.3.3. Five [5 bunches] [5 times: throws paint, speaks to sky]

28. A WASCO WOMAN DECEIVES
HER HUSBAND
A. Mythological Motifs

A522.1.4. Coyote as culture hero

B. Animals

B810.3.3. Coyote(s)

D. Magic

D231.1.1.1. People of Wasco and Tenino villages transformed to rock forms
as punishment for waging war
D1271. Magic fires, all extinguished same time throughout village; cf. F882.
Extraordinary fires
D1273.1.5.1 Midnight as magic time

H. Tests

H487. Sons recognize long-absent mother
H1210.1.1. Quest for fire assigned by father
H1385.3. Quest for vanished wife

K. Deceptions

K1501. Cuckold-Husband deceived by adulterous wife
K1538.3. Death and burial feigned that wife and lover might be together; cf.
K1860. Deception by feigned death (sleep)
K1549.2.1. Wife feigns illness and death by eating alder bark (and spitting
"blood")
K1860. Deception by feigned death; cf. K1884. Illusion of death
K1862.1. Wife feigns death to be united with lover; cf. N343.3. Woman
feigns death to meet exiled lover
K1889.7. Burial with cup and horn dish covering face [to prevent suffocation?]

N. Chance and Fate

N741. Unexpected meeting of [former] husband and wife

P. Society

P235. Father entertains mourning children
P681. Mourning Customs: husband takes sweats for five days, mourns much
P685. Seasons of the Year: "the cutting of grass"
P716. Particular Places (as setting) [at Wasco] [at Tenino]

Q. Rewards and Punishments

Q305. War-making punished

R. Captives and Fugitives

R151.1. Husband rescues stolen wife; cf. R227.2. Flight from hated husband

S. Unnatural Cruelty

S139.2.1. Head of murdered man displayed before his own house

T. Sex

T217.1. Unfaithful wife begs husband to take her back--he does

W. Traits of Character

W230.1.1. Man (men) [an old man]

W230.3.2. A man and wife and four children

Z. Miscellaneous Groups of Motifs

Z71.0.1. Two [2 boys]

Z71.2.0. Four [4 children]

Z71.2.2. Direction: East [toward Tenino]

Z71.3.3. Five [5 days' sweats] [5 errands]

29. A WOMAN MARRIES A PERSON
WHO IS A DOG IN THE DAY
AND A MAN AT NIGHT

B. Animals

B182.1.0.4. Magic family of dogs, old and young

B182.1.8. Magic dog is followed by woman

B531.1.1. Dog serves up meal of venison

B601.2. Marriage to dog; cf. B641.1. Marriage to person in dog form

B631. Human offspring from marriage to animal

B635.4.1. Son of dog and human mother

B810.3.6. Dog(s), dog family

C. Tabu

C313.2. Tabu: married woman looking at other men; cf. C180. Tabus confined
   to women

C331.4. Tabu: looking back during travel at great noise

C735.2.4.1. Tabu: making camp after sun is down; cf. C752.1. Tabu: doing
   thing after sunset

D. Magic

D141. Transformation: man to dog; cf. B641.1. Marriage to person in dog
   form

D313.0.1. At sunset, dogs are transformed into young men

D457.5.3. Deerskins and dried meat follow after when jealous husband departs

D561.1. Transformation by rolling--dried meat. Pack of dried meat rolls; as
   packs of meat in the evening fresh and dried meat rolls in and
   stacks itself up about the fire

D561.1.1. Transformation by rolling--fresh venison [packs of fresh venison]

rolls; fresh venison, like dried meat, in evenings rolls into camp
and stacks itself about the fire

D576.1. Transformation of infant(s) by roasting in fire

D1193.1.1. Magic bundle(s) of dried meat transport themselves after travellers;
cf.D1652.1.9. Inexhaustible meat; cf. D1652.5.9. Inexhaustible
food bag

D1271. Magic fire [fire carried from house, them fires made in the woods]

D1430. Packs of dried meat pursue [follow after] travellers {with fresh
venison included on fifth night}

D1733.1.1. Magic power from being covered with ashes, roasted in fire--
enables infants to walk and to talk

D1739.3. Infant(s) sent "where their grandmother, grandfather are"

D1787.1. Magic results by burning; cf. D1851.1. Immortality by burning [a
boy and a girl are both treated similarly]

F. Marvels

F899.4. Extraordinary large pack of dried meat

F1041.21.6.3. Cutting off their hair by father and mother as token of mourning

F1061.5. After being roasted to ashes, youth revives, walks about [when sister
is born, she is treated in like manner]

H. Tests

H1229.4. Quest after stolen body paint

H1239.6. Quest accomplished with aid of thief

J. The Wise and the Foolish

J369. Small inconvenience, large gain--miscellaneous [Great fatigue - "nearly
dead"; then, house found in forest; cf. J356]

K. Deceptions

K366.4.1. Thieving dog steals woman's paint

L. Reversal of Fortune

L226. Heroine refuses gifts lest she be suspected of having stolen them

M. Ordaining the Future

M223.0.1. Wish granted before uttered

N. Chance and Fate

N340.1. Suicide in remorse over hasty condemnation

P. Society

P206. Children are sad because they wish to see grandparents

P640. Custom: at divorce the husband reclaims all that he has given his wife
and her people

P678.2. Cutting off hair as sign of mourning

Q. Rewards and Punishments

Q1.1. Hospitality at return home rewarded with food gifts; cf. Q45. Hospitality rewarded; cf. P324.1.1. Guest gives gifts of food to villagers

Q535.4. Lone fasting as penance

T. Sex

T15.1.1. Love at first sight (upon setting eyes on two men); cf. T61.4. Betrothal when maiden gazes directly at a man

T135. Wedding ceremony -- bride and groom "marry" by bedding down together

T257. Jealous husband

T688.1. Children pine to visit grandparents they've never seen

W. Traits of Character

W5. Wife tells truth: but husband departs because of her wanton glances

W11.15.1. Generous animal refuses no many anything

W111.3.7. Wife too fond of sleeping--her son is taken from her, sent to grandparents

W230.1.2. Man(men): two young men, a new-born infant son

W230.2.2. Infant girl, a daughter

W230.3.4. A chief and his daughter

W230.4.4. Grandmother and a grandfather

D230.4.5. Dog-youth taken as husband

Z. Miscellaneous Groups of Motifs

Z71.0.1. Two [2 men][two children born]

Z71.1.1. Three [3 old dogs]

Z71.2.0. Four [4 days] [4th day a gathering held]

Z71.3.3. Five [follows thieving dog 5 days] [camps 5 days] [5 days and nights roasted] [5 days travel] [5 days jealous husband fasts] [husband leaves on 5th day]

30. THE DISCONTENTED WOMAN
AND THE *WAHK-PUCH* (RATTLESNAKE)

B. Animals

B613.1. Snake paramour

C. Tabu

C311.1.8.3. Interloper flees at approach of dawn

C600. Unique prohibition: woman must stay home--may not go anywhere

C735.1.1.1. Tabu: resting apart during days (animal-lover leaves, returns as man at night)

C940.3. Woman's sickness, vomiting due to breaking tabu: sexual intercourse with rattlesnake

D. Magic

D191. Transformation: man to serpent (snake).

D621.1. Animal (rattlesnake) by day; man by night
D658.2.1. Transformation to handsome man to seduce woman

F. Marvels
F687. Remarkable fragrance (odor) of person
F1041.9.4. Smell of perfume of Rattlesnake-man attracts but makes ill discontented woman

H. Tests
H44. Recognition by perfume
H44.1. Perfume recognized as emanating from rattlesnake

K. Deceptions
K1501. Cuckold. Husband deceived by adulterous wife
K2215. Jealous husband deserts wife for long periods

N. Chance and Fate
N.1.0.2. Husband gambles in villages along the *n-Che-wana*
N699.7. Wife believes that husband has returned
N741.4.1. Husband and wife meet after extensive separation

P. Society
P252.0.9. Refuge sought at home of sister

T. Sex
T11.0.1. Woman falls in love with youth never seen before
T24.1.1. Love-sickness--woman's health fails as result of sex with rattlesnake
T24.9.3. Inattentive husband meets wife as she is dying
T35. Lovers' rendezvous: youth comes to the wife's bed
T56.5. Wife attracted/enticed by "perfume" of her suitor
T57.2. Youth consoles sorrowing wife, tells he wishes to marry her
T57.2.2. Youth pledges to treat the sorrowing wife better than her husband has; cf. T91.4.1. Mature married woman in love with callow youth
T69.6. Youth pledges to come to wife every night, at dark; but the last night he will take her away with him
T92.3.2. Wife wishes youth to take her away with him--now
T165.8. Youth puts off wife, delays taking her away [marriage]
T230. Faithlessness in marriage
T257.1. Jealous husband [of younger girl]
T257.12. Jealous husband lives with wife apart from all Indians and in a house of logs
T383.4.4. Youth must leave at daybreak, stay away all day--will return at nightfall
T465.6. Bestiality: sexual intercourse with a rattlesnake
T475. Unknown (clandestine) paramour
T481. Adultery

W. Traits of Character

W230.2.2. Two sisters [who got married]

Z. Miscellaneous Groups of Motifs

Z71.1.1. Three [wife cries for 3 days and nights]

Z71.5. Seven [7 nights youth comes to the wife] [on 7th morning woman observes lover's departure]

31. *DIABEXWA'SXWAS*,
THE BIG-FOOTED MAN
A. Mythological Motifs

A1311.4. Origin of big feet and stature among Chinook people: offspring of *Diabexwa'sxwax*, the Big-Footed man

B. Animals

B500.1. Five water-spiders, Guardian Spirits--offer hero their ability to walk on water; cf. D1834. Magic strength from helping animal

B500.2. Five bands of yellow flies, Guardian Spirits--offer hero their ability to walk on water. Cf. D1834. Magic strength from helping animal

B501.5. Five bands of Grizzly Bears, Guardian Spirits--offer hero their strength; cf. D1834. Magic strength from helping animal; cf. B746. Bear could formerly lift mountain

B501.6. Five bands of Elk, Guardian Spirits--offer hero their strength; cf. D1834. Magic strength from helping animal

C. Tabu

C752.1.3.1. Tabu: single person male] to enter Chief's house after sunset

D. Magic

D905.1. Thunder and Lightning as Guardian Spirits--offer hero their strength

D906.1. Magic winds. East Wind and the Chinook Wind employed as weapons in war; cf. D1400.1.23.1. Magic wind sinks five pursuing demons in sea

D911.1.3. Five whirlpools, Guardian Spirits--offer hero their ability to walk on water; cf. F931. Extraordinary occurrence connected with sea

D1402.26.1. Magic wind causes many men to drown in warfare

D1726.3. Magical strength from Guardian Spirits in the mountains

D2125.1. Big-footed Chief able to walk on water

D2125.1.1. Son able to walk on water

F. Marvels

F531.3.7. Giant has feet "three feet long;" cf F517.1. Person unusual as to his feet; also G365. Ogre monstrous as to feet

F781.3. Immense room

F932.13. Atop river is site of combat between father and son; cf. D2125.1. Magic power to walk on water

H. Tests

H35.4.2. House of Chief features carvings of fish and animals

H36.1. Recognition by footprints as large or larger than Chief's

H1216.1. Mother sends son to mountains in search of super strength with which to fight father

H1216.1.1. Mother sends son to seashore in search of magic power of walking on water

H1241.2. Hero returns from in adequate quest for Guardian Power--is sent on another quest to the mountains [later, is sent repeatedly to the seashore]

H1300.1. Quest for super strength from Guardian Spirits

H1556.6.1. Test of fidelity of wives: sand is spread nightly bout house to show footprints of any intruder; cf. T381.0.2. Wife imprisoned in tower (house) to preserve chastity; also T383. Other futile attempts to keep wife chaste

J. The Wise and the Foolish

J1146. Detection by strewing sand. Trespasser [son of chief] leaves huge footprints in the sand

K. Deceptions

K1836.5. Deception by substitution (infant boy dressed as, passed off as girl infant to escape death); cf. K514. Disguise as girl to avoid execution

L. Reversal of Fortune

L142.3. Son surpasses father in [war] skill

N. Chance and Fate

N731.2.1.1. Son sets out to combat father, avenge murder of half-brothers; cf. J675.1. Son slays father in order not to be slain himself; also P233. Father and son

P. Society

P10.2. A Chief, lives (rules) near mouth of Columbia River

P178.3. Son frees all but ten of father's wives--keeps these for himself

P675. Old Chief's strength fails in fight; he begins to sink in water--is slain by son

Q. Rewards and Punishments

Q211.4.3. Murder of hero's half-brothers punished

R. Captives and Fugitives

R228.1. Infant clad in boy's clothing taken to Wasco to save his life

S. Unnatural Cruelty

S8.0. Cruel Chief walks across water to incoming canoe--destroys occupants

S11. Cruel father

S11.3.3.3. Chief kills all sons as soon as they are born
S11.4.7. Father wages war against unknown son
S22. Parricide
S322.1.5.3. Chief, fearful of a   son as rival, puts all infant sons to death

T. Sex

T52. Upriver [Wasco] bride purchased
T52.3.1. Bride purchased for 25 men and 25 women slaves plus 50 canoes laden with provisions
T167. Husband services each of 50 wives every night, requires from nightfall to dawn
T224.1. Chief wishes to cure new wife's homesickness, allows her to return to her home for a visit
T252.8. Five wives of Chief refuse to acknowledge him as their master
T412.5. Son copulates (?) with 50 wives of his father
T586.2.1.1. Chief has many daughters, but not one son
T615.3. Precocious wisdom of infant boy
T689. Mother is frightened that her son will be discovered and killed by his cruel father

Z. Miscellaneous Groups of Motifs

Z71.0.0.1. Two [2] nights son copulates with his father's wives]
Z71.1. Three [youth goes to mountains on 3 quests] [youth goes to seashore on 3 quests]
Z71.3. Five [5 fireplaces in longhouse] [5 wives] [5 nights] [5 Thunder and Lightnings] [5 bands of Grizzly Bears] [5 bands of Elk] [5 whirlpools] [5 water spiders] [5 bands, yellow flies] [5 days at war] [5th day Chief is killed]
Z71.12.5. Fifty [50 wives' beds on one side of room and 50 beds on other side] [50 yards width of sand "trap"] [50 canoes] [50 slaves: 25 men and 25 women] [50 canoes] [50 war canoes]
Z71.15.5. Hundred [100 wives] [100 slaves]

32. BATTLE BETWEEN EAGLE AND CHINOOK: ORIGIN OF THE HORN SPOON

A. Mythological Motifs

A969.10. Cave on mountainside, a cold place: "Eagle's Cellar"
A989.5. Flat place made of rocks by river by Coyote who cut long grooves in the rock with his arrows; cf. A522.1.3. Coyote as culture hero

B. Animals

B264.2. Fight between eagle and fish [Chinook Salmon]
B451.1.1. Helpful meadowlark
B563.2.1. Meadowlark informs young Salmon of dangers to be met on quest
B601.19. Five wolf brothers steal girl--youngest wolf marries her
B603.3. Marriage of girl to Chinook Salmon Chief

B623.6. Chief Eagle as suitor
B625.1. Chief Chinook Salmon as suitor

D. Magic

D192.3. Young Salmon sleeps--worms begin to come out of nose, eyes, ears; cf. D192.0. Transformation: demon (in human form) to worms; cf. F10. Journey to Upper World
D902. Magic rain (causes salmon egg to hatch)
D909. Magic drought--Young Salmon causes hot weather, all creeks and rivers to dry up
D927.6. Magic spring produced by Young Salmon at *Shumn*
D995.2. Magic leg, broken, is fixed--Meadowlark tells Young Salmon who killed his father
D1011.1. Magic animal horn: is crushed by Eagle but restored by Chinook Salmon
D1011.1.1. Magic (mountain sheep) horn--cannot be split

F. Marvels

F11.3.1. Young salmon, sleeps, travels to otherworld without dying
F610. Remarkably strong man

G. Ogres

G11.16.1. Victorious army of birds and animals devour fallen foe, Salmon; cf. G20. Ghouls: persons eat corpses

H. Tests

H326.5. Suitor test: able to split mountain sheep horn
H331.8.1. Chinook Salmon wins suitor contest: able to crush and to make whole again animal horn
H921.2. Task set by king (father) --to split mountain sheep horn
H1228.1. Quest undertaken by son to avenge father's death
H1365. Quest for spirit-power to obtain supra-human strength
H1562.15. Test of Strength: splitting (breaking) mountain sheep horn; cf. H331.8. Suitor Contest: splitting antlers

K. Deceptions

K70. Contest in strength won by deception
K515.6.1. Salmon-egg escapes destruction by rolling into deep crevasse

L. Reversal of Fortune

L428. Young men of tribe fail suitor test: splitting the horn spoon

P. Society

P234.3. Rich chief and his beautiful daughter

Q. Rewards and Punishments

Q411.7.1. Four wolf brothers shot dead for bride theft [stealing father's wife] by Young Salmon

T. Sex

T68.6. Girl given as prize [wife] to Chinook Salmon

T92.7. Rival lovers do battle for girl

T92.10. Rival in love killed; cf. T72.2.1. Rejected [loser] suitor's revenge; cf.

T75.2. Scorned lover kills successful one

T299.1.1. Young Salmon falls asleep with his head in the lap of his [dead] father's wife

Z. Miscellaneous Groups of Motifs

Z71.0.2. Two [2 heroes vie for Wasco maiden]

Z71.3. Five [5 times Eagle breaks horn] [5 times Chinook Salmon restores it] [5 wolf brothers]

33. THE *AT!AT!A'LIA* WHO WAS DECEIVED BY HER TWO SONS

B. Animals

B360.1. Two boys grateful for rescue from peril of death by Ogre

B435.7. Helpful Coyote

D. Magic

D113.2.1. Wife transformed to grizzly bear; cf. G211.2.1. Witch in form of bear

D291.2. Ogre transformed into large rock on north side of Columbia River where now she leans against a bluff

D395.1. Transformation; frogs to people, dancing or gambling [four times]

D431.3.1. Transformation: leaves to men playing at ball

D431.5.1. Transformation: grass and reeds of swamp into dancing people

D772.1.1. Ogre-woman sees village and dancing people disenchanted when her two sons have safely fled [5 times]

D1132.3. Village produced by magic [4 times]

D1351.5. Magic village with dancers distracts ogress--she joins in dancing

D1840.3. Magic invulnerability of ogres; cf. G630. Characteristics of ogres

D1891. Transformation to old man to escape recognition; cf. D52.1.2. Transformation: man becomes hideous; cf. D56.1. Transformation to older person

F. Marvels

F713. Extraordinary lake surrounded by parched mud resembling Indian bread

F829.4. Extraordinary rattle made of broken mussel shells

G. Ogres

G10.1. Cannibalism: 3 youths eaten by woman-ogre; cf. S110. Murders

G10.2. All villagers, except her husband, eaten by ogress; cf. S110. Murders

G11.6.4.1. Woman is a child-stealing and devouring monster; cf. G11.3. Cannibal witch; cf. G262.0.1. Lamia: witch who eats children

G11.6.5. Ogre-woman pursues her sons to devour them [5 times]

G32. Brothers-in-law flee from Woman-become-a-bear, who would devour them

G552.1. Rescue from ogress by helpful Coyote; cf. R100. Escapes

H. Tests

H981.1. Younger brothers aid older brother in spying on errant wife

J. The Wise and the Foolish

J1056. Villagers hear warnings, but fail to kill ogress

J1919.10. Ogress begs Coyote to break her leg that she might have "elegant rattles"--he obliges

K. Deceptions

K815. Ogress induced by kind words to believe she too can have beautiful rattles--if her leg is broken

K1813.3. Husband's brother(s) spies on gluttonous wife

N. Chance and Fate

N478.2. Secret eating of ducks betrayed by meat and feathers in mouth

N483. Secret meat and feather eating disclosed by sleeping with mouth open-- teeth are full of meat and feathers

P. Society

P193. A Wasco man

P193.2. Man and his four brothers

P194. A Celilo woman

P235. Two sons; cf. P251.5. Two brothers

P236.8. Woman travels five times to her parents with game; cf. K2214.1. Treacherous daughter

P253.11. Brother warns villagers against ogress

P262.2. Kindly mother-in-law offers excess game for wife's people

P262.4. Mother-in-law given temporary care of children

P414.2. Hunters--kill many ducks

P672.5. Insult: shouted jibes at wife's gluttony

T. Sex

T135.16. Marriage by woman following man to his home

W. Traits of Character

W116.9. Singing and dancing and rattling by Coyote attracts Ogress

W125.2.2. Gluttonous wife eats all of game she is carrying for her people; cf. F632. Mighty eater

W151.11. Greedy daughter eats all of the game--gives her father and mother dried mud to eat as bread

Z. Miscellaneous Groups of Motifs

Z71.0.2. Two [2 sons] [calls insults twice]

Z71.2.1. Direction: northward

Z71.2.2. Four [4 brothers] [4 villages created] [4 transformations: frogs]

Z71.3. Five [man and 4 brothers] [5 trips] [5 disenchantments] [5 pursuits after Ogress' children]

34. THE HUNTER WHO HAD AN ELK
FOR A GUARDIAN SPIRIT

B. Animals

B500.1. Magic power from Elk; cf. D1720. Acquisition of magic power

C. Tabu

C947. Magic power lost by breaking tabu (by killing excess of game)

D. Magic

D782.3. When youth touches Elk, both sink to bottom of lake

D1009.4. Magic voice speaks five times--orders youth to be cast out of otherworld

D1746. Loss of Guardian Spirit power brings death

D1749.1. Guardian Spirit power lost when Great Elk leaves [shuns] youth

D2126.2. Magic underwater journey of youth--to "land of the animals"; cf. F153. Other-world reached by diving into water of lake

F. Marvels

F93.2.2. Lake entrance to Otherworld

F133.6. Otherworld at bottom of lake; cf. F153. Otherworld reached by diving into water of lake

F167.1.1.2. Animals in other world, including those killed as game, are all persons

F628.1.2.4. Youth kills many elk, five herds

F679.5.5. Skillful hunter knows where every game animal is--kills only what he needs; cf. D1923. Power to hit whatever one aims at

F1041.1.3.11. Death from sorrow and chagrin at father's lying

K. Deceptions

K2319.4. Father lies (twice) to son that scar on forehead was acquired while catching young elk bare-handed

M. Ordaining the Future

M411.3.2. Dying youth's curse on father

N. Chance and Fate

N397.1. Man cuts self on forehead while carrying wood

N773.3. Youth follows Elk to otherworld--ordered to stand beside Great Elk to be questioned

Q. Rewards and Punishments

Q304.2. Scolding punished--youth dies for loss of Guardian Spirit power

S. Unnatural Cruelty

S11.7. Cruel father's lies (3) to son exposed

W. Traits of Character

W230.3. An Indian hunter, his wife and son

Z. Miscellaneous Groups of Motifs

Z71.3. Five [5 herds of elk] [5 days and nights abed] [5 elkskins]

35. COYOTE AND EAGLE
A. Mythological Motifs

A1611.1. Origin of American Indian tribes

B. Animals

B299.2.2. Coyote becomes angry at brother
B435.3.1. Helpful Coyote--keeps up house
B810.3.3. Coyote
B810.9.1. Eagle [as younger brother]

F. Marvels

F679.5. Skillful hunter--Eagle kills, brings home 2-3 deer

H. Tests

H1305.3. Brothers seek best way to cook meat: boil venison vs. roast mice in ashes

J. The Wise and the Foolish

J1759.2.1. Hunter mistakes mice for game; cf. K1968. Sham prowess in hunting; cf. X584. Jokes about hunters

K. Deceptions

K1817. Coyote wanders forth after killing his brother; cf. Q502.3.1. Coyote's wandering as punishment

L. Reversal of Fortune

L31. Youngest brother helps elder

P. Society

P251.6. Two brothers
P251.9. Older brother slays younger brother
P487. Hunter(s)

S. Unnatural Cruelty

S73.1. Fratricide
S110. Murder (of younger brother)

Z. Miscellaneous Groups of Motifs

Z71.0. Two [two brothers]

36. A DESERTED BOY IS PROTECTED BY
ITC!i'XYAN'S DAUGHTER
B. Animals

B531.5.2. Magpies are trapped--three every day

B810.8.3. Magpies

D. Magic

D1009.4.1. Voices of boys are left behind to answer in their stead

D1030.1. Youth becomes chief, and feeds people with food brought out of the river by his wife; cf. D1652.1. Inexhaustible food; cf. D2105. Provisions magically furnished

D1765. Magic results produced by command (food is obtained)

D1810.1.1. Indian youths still sent out at night on river to obtain spirit [Guardian Spirit?] of the Water-spirit; cf. D1810.89. Magic knowledge from dream

D2061.1.6. Youth causes a storm to drown chief as he is crossing the river

D2141. Storm produced by magic; cf. D905. Magic storm; cf. D2091.5. Storms magically drawn down on foe

F. Marvels

F403.2.1. Spirit from river helps boy

F420.1.2. Water-spirit as woman

F420.1.7. Water-spirits give gifts to mortals

F420.5.1.7.5.1. Water-spirit gives boy much food

F420.6.1. Marriage or liaison of mortals and water-spirits

F771.2.8. Remarkable large house furnished with skins and carving made by water-spirit

F851.1. Extraordinary food, of meat and roots and salmon, in bundle from out of river

N. Chance and Fate

N500. Treasure trove. Survival articles for bad boy include fire, bone for fish-hooks, some food

N511.1.14. Survival articles buried in ashes of fire

N747. Chief sends his people back to live in village

N815.0.2. Helpful Water-spirit

S. Unnatural Cruelty

S301.1. Bad boy abandoned; cf. S144. Abandonment in desert

W. Traits of Character

W230.1.1. A chief

W230.2.1. Two grandmothers, provide for youth

W231.1.1. A bad boy

W231.1.2. Some boys

Z. Miscellaneous Groups of Motifs
Z71.1.1. Three [3 magpies]
Z71.2. Four [magpies trapped for 4 days]
Z71.3. Five [boy fishes 5 days][boy catches 5 fish] [the 5th day]

37. AN *AT!AT!A'LIA* HAS HER ARM PULLED OFF
B. Animals
B435.1.1. Helpful Coyote
B566. Coyote advises how to trap and to slay the 5 ogres
B810.4.4. Ground squirrel
B810.6.1. Bat
B810.4.5. Gray squirrel

G. Ogres
G11.6.5. Ogre-woman reaches into lodge after child--has arm torn off; cf.
      G512.6.1. Giant's arm pulled off by defender of house
G369.5. Ogre's long arm thrust down smokehole of lodge

K. Deceptions
K662. Two little ogres go home
K730.2.1. Coyote persuades Ogre sisters to dance into House as snare
K811. Victim(s) lured into house and killed; cf. K812.4. Owner burns intruder
K818. Dupe(s) lured to supposed dance and killed
K925.1. Coyote entices enemies [ogres] into building and sets fire to it
K955. Murder by burning; cf. S112. Burning to death

W. Traits of Character
W230.4. People of a lodge
W231.1.2. A boy who cries incessantly

Z. Miscellaneous Groups of Motifs
Z71.0. Two [2 little ogres]
Z71.1. Three [2 or 3 days later]
Z71.3. Five [5 ogre sisters]

38. A JACK RABBIT BOY TRICKS AN *AT!AT!A'LIA*
B. Animals
B302. Useful Woodtick(s) distract Ogre that boy can escape
B489.2. Helpful Woodtick
B810.4.3. Jack rabbit (boy)

D. Magic

D478.15. Lake made to freeze over

D478.16. Thick ice transformed into thin ice which breaks when Ogre stands on it

D676. Lake turns to ice to permit flight of youth

D1011.1. Magic animal horn (boy hides in it); cf.F988.4. Extraordinary horn of Mountain Sheep

D1349.4. Mountain sheep horn allows youth to hide inside

D2144.5.1.1. Ice over lake produced by magic

G. Ogres

G11.6.5. Ogre-Woman, painted in stripes: eats people

G312.8. Ogress tries to catch youth, pursues him to his village

G512.11.1. Ogress falls through ice, drowns

K. Deceptions

K500. Escape from death and danger by deception; cf. K515. Escape by hiding

K622.2. Escape by debasing appearance, making captor laugh to distraction

K634.2. Youth steals Ogress's dress, runs off

K839.2.1. Ogress lured onto lake--that she might retrieve her dress

K839.2.1.1. Stones break which are thrown onto lake to prove strength of the ice for Ogress [in other versions the "stones" are dung and so the ice doesn't break]

L. Reversal of Fortune

L311. Small hero overcomes large ogre(ss); cf. G510. Ogre(ss) killed or captured

Q. Rewards and Punishments

Q428.4. Thin ice breaks causing Ogress to drown; cf. S131. Murder by drowning

R. Captives and Fugitives

R211.10. Escape from animal horn by stealing captor's dress, running off

R219.2. Escape by causing captor to laugh, to be distracted; cf. K611. Escape by puting captor off guard

Z. Miscellaneous Groups of Motifs

Z71.0. Two [2 stones]

Z71.1.Three [Ogress 3 times larger than men]

Z71.3. Five [5 days played]

39. THE FIVE *AT!AT!A'LIA* SISTERS
STEAL A BOY

B. Animals

B463.3. Helpful Sandhill Crane

C. Tabu

C319.3. Tabu: to look toward Crane

C601. Youth not to step on knee of "crane-bridge"--lest he slip and fall off

C614.1.1. Forbidden direction: north; cf. C614.1.0.2.1. Tabu: hunting in northerly direction

D. Magic

D451.3.5. Transformation: chokecherries to blood

D672.1. Magic objects as decoys for pursuer

D673. Reversed obstacle flight: magic obstacles raised in front of fugitive--hot sun, dried-up streams, steep-walled canyons

D915.7.1. Five creeks produced by magic

D964. Fruited chokecherry bushes magically produced by youth

D1154.6. Youth's "babyboard" and blanket to be located and carried along

D2091.15.1. Deep ravines produced by magic

D2144.3. Heat produced by magic

D2151.0.2. Waters made to dry up

F. Marvels

F679.5. Skillful hunter: youth gets much small game

F932.13. Crane sighted across creek when tabu is broken

G. Ogres

G11.6. Man-eating woman: Ogress intends to eat Crane

G11.6.1.1. Four Ogress sisters wish to eat child (3 instances)

G11.6.5. Ogre-Women [5] steal and eat people

G519.6. Ogress sisters lured away across creeks to pick ripe berries

H. Tests

H599.7. Ogress ordered to step on Crane's knee [which is slippery]

K. Deceptions

K550.2. Youth escapes--tells sisters [falsely] that he has found a creek and many berries

K1810. Deception by disguise [Ogresses as sisters-in-law]; cf. F402.1.4. Demons assume human forms in order to deceive

L. Reversal of Fortune

L54.2. Compassionate youngest sister rears and protects youth

L73. Youngest Ogress sister survives

N. Chance and Fate

N469. Crane informs youth of his birth--youth came from far away

P. Society

P231.3.1. Mother love: mother mourns at long absence of son

P319.9. Ogress sisters call abducted youth their "son"

Q. Rewards and Punishments

Q411. Death as punishment for four Ogress sisters

Q428.4. Ogress slips on Crane's knee, falls from "Crane-bridge"--is drowned

R. Captives and Fugitives

R11.1. Youth abducted by five Ogress sisters

R49.4. Ogresses hold youth captive at their home

R135.2. Trail of child plus Ogress sisters

R157.2. Youngest sister keeps and rears youth

R246. Crane-bridge. Fugitive(s) are helped across a stream by a crane who
lets them cross on his leg

S. Unnatural Cruelty

S183.2. Ogresses and their children eat frogs and snakes [Youth is occasionally
fed snakes]

T. Sex

T29.2. Youngest Ogress falls in love with youth

W. Traits of Character

W230.2.1.2. Woman and child

W230.4. Five Ogre sisters

W230.4. Five sisters-in-law

Z. Miscellaneous Groups of Motifs

Z71.1. Three [Ogress draws back 3 times before crossing "Crane-bridge"]

Z71.2. Four [Ogresses ask 4 times to eat youth] [4 malevolent Ogress sisters]
[4 Ogress sisters die]

Z71.3. Five [5 sisters-in-law] [5 Ogress sisters] [5 creeks]

Z71.8. Twelve [youth is 12 years of age]

40. TWO CHILDREN ESCAPE FROM
AN *AT!AT!A'LIA*
B. Animals

B211.5. Speaking fish

B474.1. Fish set to eat Ogress

B491.5. Turtles set to eat Ogress

B495.3. Crawfish set to eat Ogress

D. Magic

D915.1.1. Five rivers produced by magic

F. Marvels

F639.13. Mighty inhaler--as hero is drawn near, exhalations repel him/them
again

F809.5.1. Large rock rolls on Ogress; cf. R261. Pursuit by rolling object; cf.
D1430. Magic object pursues

F809.10. A sharp flint
F809.11. Flint carried off by youth
F841.2.7.1. Paddles; cf. D1124.1. Magic paddle

G. Ogres

G11.6.5. *At!At!a'lia*, child-stealing and child eating Ogress
G11.6.5.1. Frightful, stupid Ogress, with huge and stripped body, steals and devours children; cf. G442. Child-stealing demon
G332.2. Ogress breathes in, draws victims to her jaws [but then exhales and repels them]
G441. Ogress carries victim(s) in bag (basket)
G519.6. Ogress, defeated by fishlife in river, retreats
G552. Rescue from Ogress by helpful animals

K. Deceptions

K439.1.1. Ogress discovers not two humans to eat, but only rocks and dirt in her basket
K526. Captor's bag filled with animals or objects [stones and dirt] while captives escape
K547.5.1. Ferocious animal (Ogress) misunderstands victim's remark: runs off to look to her children; cf. G572. Ogress overawed by trick
K2320.1. Deception by frightening: Ogress made to believe her children are in danger

P. Society

P253.6. Sister warns brother
P253.11. Sister forced to sit upon brother's foot--injures it

R. Captives and Fugitives

R11. Abduction by monster (Ogress); cf. G334. Ogre keeps human prisoners
R219.3. Brother and sister escape from Ogress

U. The Nature of Life

U43. Task: Children sent to gather flint

W. Traits of Character

W230.4. A brother and sister

Z. Miscellaneous Groups of Motifs

Z71.0. Two [2 fish children]
Z71.2. Four [girl calls out 4 times]
Z71.3. Five [5 good paddles] [5 rivers] [5 jumps] [jumps over 5 rivers 5 times]
Z71.4. Six [6th paddle full of holes]

41. OLD MAN GRIZZLY BEAR
DECEIVES THE FIVE BROTHERS

B. Animals

B268.5.1. Army of birds aids brothers in combat

B579.8. Bluejay as deliverer of haunch of meat to the Bear brothers

B584.2. Rattlesnakes give their teeth (fangs) to be made into arrowpoints

B768.4. Bear feigns death to maul the hunter

B810.3.5. Bear

B810.8.1. Meadowlark

B810.8.4. Bluejay

B810.19.1.1. Razorsnake, as ally of youth

B810.19.2. Rattlesnakes

B810.20.1. Frog, as ally of youth

D. Magic

D313.3.1. Transformation: bear to old man

D451.8.3. Leaves transformed into "arrowheads" (ferns; then wild grape (2); willow-leaves, yellow; then cottonwood leaves)

D822.1. Magic arrowpoints received from old man (several instances)

D959. Magical stump decked out with feathers--youth to stand on it; cf. D1157.1. Magic shooting platform

D995.2. Magic leg of Meadowlark. When broken and then mended, bird prophecies

D1092.2. Magic arrowpoints--always fail against bear

D1092.3. Magical arrowheads--power to kill exceeds magical power of grizzly bear

F. Marvels

F1051.3. False weeping by Grizzly transformed to old man

G. Ogres

G477.1. Bear-monster kills youth(s) [swallows four older brothers]

G512.0.1.1. Ogre shot and killed by youngest brother

G519.6. Ogre swallows fish with sharp fins behind the head--it cuts through bear's stomach; cf. F910. Extraordinary swallowings

H. Tests

H901.1.2. Hunting task imposed by "old man"

H1161.7. Task: killing ferocious animal [bear(s)]

H1219.9. Quest assigned to aid young hero win fight

H1242. Youngest brother alone succeeds on quest

H1345.1. Quest for magic arrowheads with real points--to his grandfather on mountains to southward

K. Deceptions

K952. Animal (monster) killed from within

L. Reversal of Fortune

L0. Youngest brother; cf. Z251. Boy hero

L177. People celebrate death of Grizzly bear

L311. Weak (small) hero overcomes large fighter; cf. G510. Ogre killed or captured

L396.1. Bear's skin and claws taken by youth

L396.2. People take meat home

L396.3. Meat given as gift token

M. Ordaining the Future

M301.21. Meadowlark as prophet

M302.8. When her broken leg is splinted, Meadowlark foretells the future [this is the usual form of this motif--but absent in this tale is the usual, prerequisite splinting of the leg]

M312.1. Prophecy of future greatness for youth--upon completing quest he will defeat the spirit-bear

P. Society

P251.6.2.1. (Five) Brothers

P251.9. Oldest brother

V. Religion

V96.2. Ritual sweat bathing at death of relative [at deaths of each brother]

W. Traits of Character

W230.1. Eldest brother--garbed for battle

W230.1.1. An old man

W231.1.1. Five brothers; five bear brothers

Z. Miscellaneous Groups of Motifs

Z71.0.1. One [one evening, near dark]

Z71.1.1. Three [3 brothers] [3d day]

Z71.2. Four [4 brothers]

Z71.2.2. Southward

Z71.3. Five [5 brothers] [5 days and nights--three instances] [5th night--two instances] [5 gifts of false arrowheads] [5 whoops]

Z210. (Five) Brothers as heroes

Z358. *La'daxat*, site of tale--specific location on Columbia River

42. EAGLE, A KLAMATH MAN, GOES TO THE COLUMBIA RIVER TO GAMBLE

A. Mythological Motifs

A2584.3. Why grizzly bears are scattered over the mountains

B. Animals

B298.2. Eagle gambles

B500. Magic power from animals [25 grizzly bears]

B810.8.3. Crow, as gambling partner

B810.8.3.2. Raven, as gambling partner
B810.9.1. Eagle [a Klamath man--from distant area]
B810.9.2. Hawk, as gambling partner
B810.18.2. Crab, as gambling partner

D. Magic

D1402.4. Magic fires [10] kill; cf. D1271. Magic fire
D1700. Magic powers from elder brother
D1701. Magic powers sought after
D1810.8.2.3. Magic knowledge gained by sons, of whereabouts of their father
D1812.0.2.1. Foreknowledge of unwished for guests
D1812.5.0.1. Omens from sneezing
D1816.4.2. Trail [tracks] of long-dead father located

E. The Dead

E13. Resuscitation by stepping over [5 times]
E35.2. Resuscitation by assembling together pieces of corpse and stepping
over it

F. Marvels

F600. Chief has extraordinary powers
F683.2. Magic power from fires burns faces of messengers from Chief

N. Chance and Fate

N1. Gamblers
N1.4. Two sons gamble and win back pieces of their dead father
N2.3.1. Head wagered in game--lost
N2.3.3. Eyes wagered in game--lost
N2.3.6. Both arms wagered in game--lost
N2.3.7. Both legs wagered in game--lost
N2.3.8. Both ears wagered in game--lost
N2.3.9. Both sides of body wagered in game--lost
N2.8. Items of attire wagered in game--all lost
N134.2. Persons [Crab] effects change of luck [good to bad luck]
N251.2.2. Lucky at first, gambler's luck turns--he loses all

P. Society

P322.4. Sons seeking to avenge father's death wish hospitality of Chief
P552.6. Two brothers war against people of village
P553.2. Magical fires [10] poised on one side against village
P553.3. Magical grizzly bears poised on one side against village
P555.4. All villagers are killed and burned to ashes
P716. Particular Place: Columbia River area at/near Wasco [The Dalles] site
of gambling

Q. Rewards and Punishments

Q421.1. Heads on stakes. Punishment by beheading and placing the heads on
stakes

S. Unnatural Cruelty

S139.2.2.1.1. Heads of losing gamblers impaled upon stakes; cf. S139.22.1.6.
Heads brandished to intimidate foe; Cf. H901.1. Heads placed on
stakes for failure in performance of tasks

W. Traits of Character

W230.1. A Chief
W230.2.3. Two old women
W230.4. People
W231.1.1. Brothers

Z. Miscellaneous Groups of Motifs

Z71.3. Five [5 years pass] [5 messengers] [5 times step over]
Z78.1. Formulistic ending of story: "they lived happily and well."

COMPARATIVE NOTES TO OTHER PLATEAU INDIAN TALES

The comparative notes hereafter cite similar narratives related by tribes residing over the Plateau Region. The tribes and the authors and titles of printed collections of traditional narratives cited hereafter follow.

YAKIMA

Beavert, Virginia 1974. *The Way It Was (Anaku Iwacha) (Yakima Legends)*, The Consortium of Johnson O'Malley Committees of Region IV, State of Washington. Yakima, Washington.

Hines, Donald M. 1992. *Ghost voices: Yakima Indian Myths, Legends, Humor and Hunting Stories.* Issaquah, WA: Great Eagle Publishing, Inc.

KLICKITAT

Jacobs, Melville 1929. *Northwest Sahaptin Texts, I*, UWPA 2, No. 5. Seattle, WA: University of Washington Press.

Jacobs, Melville 1969. *Northwest Sahaptin Texts*, CUCA 19, Part I. New York: AMS Press.

WASCO

Hines, Donald M. 1996. *Celilo Tales: Wasco Myths, Legends, Tales of Conflicts And Adventures.* Issaquah, WA: Great Eagle Publishing, Inc.

WISHRAM

Sapir, Edward 1909. *Wishram Texts Together with Wasco Tales and Myths.* . . . PAES II. Leyden: E. J. Brill.

NEZ PERCE

Farrand, Livingston (ed. Theresa Meyer) 1917. "Folk-tales of Sahaptin Tribes," in *Folk-tales of Salishan and Sahaptin tribes*, MAFS 11. New York: American Folk-Lore Society.

Hines, Donald M. 1984. *Tales of the Nez Perce*. Fairfield, WA: Ye Galleon Press.

Slickpoo Sr., Allen P. 1977. *Nu Mee Poom Tit Wah Tit (Nez Perce legends)*. NP: Nez Perce Tribe of Idaho.

Spinden, Herbert J. 1917. "Nez Perce Tales, in *Folk-Tales of Salishan and Sahaptin tribes*, MAFS ll. New York: American Folk-Lore Society.

COEUR d'ALENE

Reichard, Gladys A. 1947. *An Analysis of Coeur d'Alene Indian myths*. MAFS 41. New York, American Folklore Society.

Teit, James A. 1917. "Coeur d'Alene Tales," in *Folk-Tales of Salishan and Sahaptin tribes*, MAFS 11. New York: American Folk-Lore Society.

KUTENAI

Boas, Franz 1918. *Kutenai Tales*, BAE 59. Washington, D.C.: U.S. Government Printing Office.

LILLOOET

Hill-Tout, Charles 1978. *The Squamish and the Lillooet II, The Salish People*. Vancouver, BC: Talonbooks.

OKANAGON

Gould, Marian K. 1917. "Okanagon Tales," in *Folk-Tales of Salishan and Sahaptin Tribes*, MAFS 11. New York: American Folk-Lore Society.

Hill-Tout, Charles 1978. *The Thompson and the Okanagan I, The Salish People*. Vancouver, BC: Talonbooks.

Hines, Donald M. 1976. *Tales of the Okanogans*. Fairfield, Wa.: Ye Galleon Press.

Teit, James A. 1917. "Okanogan Tales," in *Folk-Tales of Salishan and Sahaptin Tribes*, MAFS 11. New York: American Folk-Lore Society.

THOMPSON

Hill-Tout, Charles 1978. *The Thompson and the Okanagan I, The Salish People*. Vancouver, BC: Talonbooks.

Teit, James A. 1898. *Traditions of the Thompson River Indians of British Columbia*, MAFS 6. New York: American Folk-Lore Society.

Teit, James A. 1917. "Thompson Tales," in *Folk-tales of Salishan and Sahaptin tribes*, MAFS 11. New York: American Folk-Lore Society.

PEND d'OREILLE
Teit, James A. 1917. "Pend d'Oreille Tales," in *Folk-tales of Salishan and Sahaptin tribes* MAFS 11. New York: American Folklore Society.

PART TWO. THE TRADITIONAL TALES OF THE WASCOS

I. TALES OF THE ORIGINS OF MAN, ANIMALS AND PLANTS, PHENOMENA

1. COYOTE IS SWALLOWED BY *ITC!I'XYAN*

In his *Tales of the North American Indians* (Bloomington: Indiana University Press, 1966), Stith Thompson includes invaluable comparative notes of representative motifs in Indian tales from across the United States on pp. 269-370. And see his bibliography of Indian tales in print, pp. 371-386.

YAKIMA Beavert 1974:28-31; Hines 1992:19-22; **KLICKITAT** Jacobs 1969:64-66; **WISHRAM** Sapir 1909:40-42; also 42-46; **NEZ PERCE** Farrand 1917:148-151 [Also second version]; Hines 1984:43-46; Slickpoo 1977:201-205; Spinden 1917:200-201; **COEUR d'ALENE** Reichard 1947:68-72; Teit 1917:121-122, 122; **OKANOGAN** Hines 1976:116-117; **PEND d'ORIELLE** Teit 1917: 115-116, 117.

2A. THE ASCENT TO THE SKY AND RETURN TO EARTH

Sapir 1909:164-173 contains many similar motifs describing the upper world. See also Boas, Franz 1901. *Kathlamet Texts*, BAE 26:11-19, where, according to Sapir on p. 276-279, the first part of the Kathlamet-Wishram myth is given by Curtin as a separate myth. And a comparable version of this narrative appears hereafter as 2B "Sky-Rope."

YAKIMA Hines 1992:141-146; **KUTENAI** Boas 1918:246-247 **THOMPSON** Teit 1898:7; Teit 1917:43.

2B. SKY ROPE

YAKIMA Beavert 1974:188-193; Hines 1992:141-146; **NEZ PERCE** Hines 1984:61-67, esp. 62; **KUTENAI** Boas 1918:246-247; **THOMPSON** Teit 1917:7.

3. TWO BROTHERS BECOME SUN AND MOON

According to Sapir, this tale may belong to a group of narratives which account for the animals or people who become substitutes for the sun which does not behave properly. See, for instance, Franz Boas, 1891. *Einige Sagen der Kootenay*, Verh. Berliner Ges. fur Anthro., p. 164; also Franz

Boas, 1908. "Eine Sonnensage der Tsimschian," *Zeitschrift für Ethnologie*, XL:776.

YAKIMA Beavert 1974:56-58; **THOMPSON** Teit 1898:54-55.

4. THE SUN-LODGE
NONE

5. LEGEND OF THE GREAT DIPPER
COEUR d'ALENE Teit 1917:125; **THOMPSON** Teit 1898:91-92.

6. BRIDGE OF THE GODS
This narrative includes subject matter usually found in two separate texts: conflicts of *Enum-klah*, Thunderbird, and mankind; origination of the Bridge of the Gods. The following comparable narratives from among the Plateau Indian tribes are noteworthy.

YAKIMA Hines 1992 #19:65-68, also #20:69-80. Magical tales recounting the defeat of Thunderbird include #58:192-193.

7. THE STAR ROCK OF THE TUMWATER
NONE

8A COYOTE'S BIG MISTAKE
YAKIMA Hines 1992:190-191; **KLICKITAT** Jacobs 1929:227-231; Jacobs 1969: 55-57, also 190-191; **WASCO** Hines 1996:#8B hereafter; **WISHRAM** Sapir 1909:106-113; **NEZ PERCE** Farrand 1917:178-179; Hines 1984:82-85, also 85-88; Slickpoo 1977:65-69; Spinden 1917:190-191; **COEUR d'ALENE** Teit 1917:125; **KUTENAi** Boas 1918:213; **LILLOOET** Hill-Tout 1978:146-147; **OKANOGAN** Gould 1917:106; **THOMPSON** Teit 1898:68-69; Teit 1917:27, also p. 45.

8B. ORIGIN OF DEATH
YAKIMA Hines 1992:190-191; **KLICKITAT** Jacobs 1929:227-231; Jacobs 1969:55-57, also 191-191; **WASCO** Hines 1996:#8A above; **WISHRAM** Sapir 1909:106-113; **NEZ PERCE** Farrand 1917:178-179; Hines 1984:82-85, also 85-88; Slickpoo 1977:65-69; Spinden 1917:190-191; **COEUR d'ALENE** Teit 1917:125; **KUTENAI** Boas 1918:213; **LILLOOET** Hill-Tout 1978:146-147; **OKANOGAN** Gould 1917:106; **THOMPSON** Teit 1898:68-69; Teit 1917:27, also p. 45.

9A. COYOTE AND THE TWO SISTERS
OF THE *N-CHE-WANA*
See especially *Tales of the Nez Perce*, "Coyote Causes His Son to be Lost, esp. pp. 64-65, which includes the episode of Coyote's transformation to an infant floating on a cradleboard, his subsequent rescue by the Swallow sisters who kept the dam which barred migration of the salmon somewhere on

the lower Columbia River. Coyote manages not only to break the dam, and to enable salmon to commence migrating upstream, but also impregnates each of the sisters. And see above here "The Star Rock of the Tumwater," which also mentions fish plus buffalo confined in a great teepee at the sundown from which they are released.

This narrative is frequently told to include segments often related separately: a) distribution of salmon into streams which pass fishing sites; b) origination of means of taking salmon; c) meat stolen from sleeper.

YAKIMA Beavert 1974:34-37, 42-44; Hines 1992:45, 121-126, 126-131, 131-139; **KLICKITAT** Jacobs 1969:74-76, 79-91, 91-93; **WASCO** Hines 1996:-#9B below; **WISHRAM** Sapir 1909:1-7; 7-9; 9-11; **NEZ PERCE** Farrand 1917:135-139, 139-144 [3 versions]; Slickpoo 1977:17, 99-101, 125-129; **COEUR d'ALENE** Reichard 1947:98-109; Teit 1917:121. **KUTENAI** Boas 1918:171-179 [esp. versions c - g]; **OKANOGAN** Hill-Tout 1978:87-100; Gould 1917:101-103; Hines 1976:23-28; Teit 1917:67-72; **THOMPSON** Teit 1898:21-29.

9B. COYOTE DECEIVES EAGLE, AND STOCKS THE COLUMBIA WITH FISH

YAKIMA Beavert 1974:42-44; Hines 1992:45, 121-126, 126-131; **KLICKITAT** Jacobs 1969:74-76, 79-91, 91-93; **WASCO** Hines 1996:#9A above; **WISHRAM** Sapir 1909:1-7, 7-9, 9-11; **NEZ PERCE** Farrand 1917:135-139, 139-144 [3 versions]; Hines 1984:see esp. p. 148, 64-65; Slickpoo 1977:17, 99-101, 125-129; **COEUR d'ALENE** Reichard 1947:98-109; Teit 1917:121; **KUTENAI** Boas 1918:171-179 [see esp. versions c-g]; **OKANOGAN** Gould 1917:101-103; Hill-Tout 1978: 87-100; Hines 1976:23-28; Teit 1917:67-72; **THOMPSON** Teit 1898:21-29.

10. CHIPMUNK'S STRIPES

YAKIMA Beavert 1974:130-136. But see also the origination of stripes borne by Raccoon, *"Kalaasya"* (Raccoon):116-120; Hines 1984:173-178; **WASCO** Hines 1996: See #11 hereafter; **WISHRAM** Sapir 1909:153-165, 152-153; **NEZ PERCE** Hines 1984:105-107; Slickpoo 1977:147-150; Spinden 1917:196-197.

11. RACCOON

YAKIMA Beavert 1974:116-120, but see also the origination of stripes borne by Chipmunk: "The Chipmunk and Witch:"130-136; Hines 1992:173-178; **WASCO** Hines 1996: see #10 above; **WISHRAM** Sapir 1909:152-153, 153-165; **NEZ PERCE** Hines 1984:105-107; Slickpoo 1977: 147-155; Spinden 1917:196-197.

II. TALES OF THE LEGENDARY

12. PANTHER AND WILDCAT FIGHT
WITH THE GRIZZLIES
KATHLAMET See Boas, Franz 1901. *Kathlamet Texts*, BAE 20. Washington, D.C.:90-97; **KLICKITAT** Jacobs 1929:192-194, 219-223; **WISHRAM** Sapir 1909:75-93.

13. THE DEAD CANOEMAN OF
THE *N-CHE-WANA*
WISHRAM Sapir 1909:29-31.

14. WASCO
NONE

15A. BATTLE OF THE *AT-TE-YI-YI*
AND THE *TO-QEE-NUT*
This narrative details the magical struggle between forces wishing long and extremely cold winters, and others who wished for short and mild winters in the vicinity of the Wasco and other tribes. A warm southerly wind during winter is often called a "Chinook" over the Pacific Northwest.

YAKIMA Beavert 1974:10-24; **KLICKITAT** Jacobs 1969:30-32, 32-33 [two versions]; **WASCO** Hines 1996: see 15B below; **WISHRAM** Sapir 1909:49-65, 103-105, 121-131, also 49-65; **NEZ PERCE** Farrand 1917:144-148, esp. 147-148; Hines 1984:120-127, esp. 124-127; Slickpoo 1977:3-6, 10-16; **COEUR d'ALENE** Reichard 1947:189-190; Teit 1917:124 [two versions]; **KUTENAI** Boas 1918:178-183; **LILLOOET** Hill-Tout 1978:154-155; **OKANOGAN** Gould 1917:104-105; Hines 1976:42-47; Teit 1917:74; **THOMPSON** Teit 1898:55-56; Teit 1917:21.

15B. BATTLE OF COLD-WIND
AND CHINOOK-WIND
A comparable narrative to Wasco narrative 15A above, this narrative details the magical struggle between forces wishing long and extremely cold winters, and others who wished for short and mild winters in the vicinity of the Wasco and other tribes.

YAKIMA Beavert 1974:10-24; **KLICKITAT** Jacobs 1969:30-32, 32-33 [two versions]; **WASCO** Hines 1996: see 15A above; **WISHRAM** Sapir 1909:103-105, 121-131, also 49-65; **NEZ PERCE** Farrand 1917:144-148, esp. 147-148; Hines 1984:120-127, esp. 124-127; Slickpoo 1977:3-6,10-16; **COEUR d'ALENE** Reichard 1947:189-190; Teit 1917:124, 124 [two versions]; **KU-TENAI** Boas 1918:178-183; **LILLOOET** Hill-Tout 1978:154-155; **OKANO-GAN** Gould 1917:104-105; Hines 1976:42-47; Teit 1917:74; **THOMPSON** Teit 1898:55-56; Teit 1917:21.

16. FOOD SMELLERS
YAKIMA Hines 1992:69-80; **WASCO** Hines 1996: see text 9A, "Coyote and the Two Sisters of the *n-Che-wana*", contains an episode concerning people without mouths; **WISHRAM** Sapir 1909:19-25.

17. *AN-TON-O-KAH* OF *SHE-KO-UN*,
A WASCO LEGEND OF MOUNT HOOD
NONE

18. *NIHS-LAH*,
A WASCO LEGEND OF MULTNOMAH FALLS
NONE

19. STORIES OF THE *GY-U-BOO-KUM*
YAKIMA Hines 1992:80-81, 82-83, 83-84; **WASCO** Hines 1996: see #20 below; **WISHRAM** Sapir 1909:117-121; **NEZ PERCE** F a r r a n d 1917:178-182; Slickpoo 1977:178-182; Spinden 1917:100-201.

20. THE *GY-U-BOO-KUM*
YAKIMA Hines 1992:80-81; 82-83, 83-84; **WASCO** Hines 1996: see #19 above; **WISHRAM** Sapir 1909:117-121; **NEZ PERCE** Farrand 1917:178-182; Slickpoo 1977:178-182; Spinden 1917:200-201.

III. TALES OF MAGIC
AND THE MARVELOUS

21. FIVE STARS VISIT THE EARTH
A very familiar Indian narrative, the "Star Husband Tale is discussed particularly in Gladys A. Reichard 1923. "Literary Types and Dissemination of Myths," *Journal of American Folklore* 34:269. And Stith Thompson's "The Star Husband Tale" appears in *The Study of Folklore*, ed. Alan Dundes. Englewood Cliffs, N.J: Prentice-Hall, Inc., 1965:414-474. See also Riggs, Stephen R. 1893. *Dakota Grammar, Texts and Ethnography* CNAE 9. Washington, D.C.:90

YAKIMA Beavert 1974:188-193; Hines 1992:141-146; **KUTENAI** Boas 1918:246-247; **THOMPSON** Teit 1917:7.

22A. COYOTE IMITATES FISH HAWK
AND MOUNTAIN SHEEP AND MEETS
WITH VARIOUS ADVENTURES
YAKIMA Hines 1992:109-110, 111-112; **WASCO** Hines 1996: see #22B below; **WISHRAM** Sapir 1909:145-147; **NEZ PERCE** Farrand 1917:164-168 [two versions]; Hines 1984:95-97; Slickpoo 1977:113-115; Spinden 1917:181-184; **KUTENAI** Boas 1918:8-11; **THOMPSON** Teit 1917:6.

22B. EAGLE DEFEATS FISH HAWK, AND PITIES SKUNK

YAKIMA Hines 1992:109-110, 111-112; **WASCO** Hines 1996: see #22A above; **WISHRAM** Sapir 1909:145-147; **NEZ PERCE** Farrand 1917:164-168 [two versions]; Hines 1984:95-97; Slickpoo 1977:113-115; Spinden 1917:181-184; **KUTENAI** Boas 1918:8-11; **THOMPSON** Teit 1917:6.

23. A SINGING AND DANCING FESTIVAL

YAKIMA Hines 118-120; **KLICKITAT** Jacobs 1969:57-59, 59-62; **WISHRAM** Sapir 1909:95-99, 121-131.

24. EAGLE HAS TOBACCO MAN AND WILLOW WRESTLE WITH *ABU'MAT*

WISHRAM Cf. Sapir 1909:117-121; **NEZ PERCE** Hines 1984:117-120, esp. 117-118;

25. A HARD WINTER NEAR THE DALLES
NONE

26. A HARD WINTER NEAR THE DALLES
NONE

27. AN ARROW POINT MAKER BECOMES A CANNIBAL
NONE

IV. TALES OF CONFLICTS AND ADVENTURES

28. A WASCO WOMAN DECEIVES HER HUSBAND

Other comparable Wasco texts of disharmonious married life include herein: 29 "A Woman Marries a Person Who is a Dog in the Day and a Man at Night;" 30 "The Discontented Woman and the Rattlesnake.

Accounts of discontented spouses, particularly women, are of considerable interest here. Narratives usually portray the maltreated or sexually frustrated spouse as taking up with another mortal, or with an animal, even a serpent.

YAKIMA Hines 1992:131-139, 189-180; **WASCO** Hines 1996: #29,#30; **NEZ PERCE** Hines 1984:109-115; **OKANOGAN** Hill-Tout 1978:156-159; Teit 1917:90-92; **THOMPSON** Teit 1898:64-66, 83-84; Teit 1917:30-32; 46-47.

29. A WOMAN MARRIES A PERSON
WHO IS A DOG IN THE DAY
AND A MAN AT NIGHT

Accounts of discontented spouses, particularly women, are of considerable interest here. Narratives usually portray the maltreated or sexually frustrated spouse as taking up with another mortal, or with an animal, even a serpent.

YAKIMA Hines 1992: 131-139, 178-180; **WASCO** Hines 1996:#28, #30; **NEZ PERCE** Hines 1984:109-115; **OKANOGAN** Hill-Tout 1978:156-159; Teit 1917:90-92; **THOMPSON** Teit 1898:30-32, 46-47; Teit 1917:64-66.

30. THE DISCONTENTED WOMAN AND
THE *WAHK-PUC* [RATTLESNAKE]

Accounts of discontented spouses, particularly women, are of considerable interest here. Narratives usually portray the maltreated or sexually frustrated spouse as taking up with another mortal, or with an animal, even a serpent.

YAKIMA Hines 1992:131-139, 178-180; **WASCO** Hines 1996:#28, #29; **NEZ PERCE** Hines 1984:109-115; **OKANOGAN** Hill-Tout 1978:156-159; Teit 1917:90-92; **THOMPSON** Teit 1898:64-66, 83-84; Teit 1917:30-32, 46-47.

31. *DIABEXWA'SXWAS*,
THE BIG-FOOTED MAN

This traditional narrative of an Oedipal character who wars upon his father with the aid of his mother, versions of which are widely told worldwide, Aarne-Thompson Type 931, was discussed in my article: "Of Big Foot, The Oedipal Tale Told Along the Columbia River." *Fabula* 36:1995, pp. 98-104.

KUTENAI Boas 1918:28-33; Other versions were found from among the Coast Salish, also the Cowlitz.

32. BATTLE BETWEEN EAGLE AND
CHINOOK: ORIGIN OF THE HORN SPOON

WASCO Hines 1996: See #15A, #15B; **NEZ PERCE** Hines 1984:146-151, 173-175; Slickpoo 1977:77-82; **COEUR d'ALENE** Reichard 1947:119-122; **KUTENAI** Boas 1918:72-83; **OKANOGAN** Teit 1917:85; **THOMPSON** 1898:77.

33. THE *AT!AT!A'LIA* WHO WAS
DECEIVED BY HER TWO SONS

YAKIMA Beavert:1974:78-82; Hines 1992:63-65, 188-189, 196-206; **WASCO** Hines 1996:#37, #38, #39, #40; **WISHRAM** Sapir 1909:35-39, 165-173; **OKANOGAN** Hines 1976:98-103; **THOMPSON** Teit 1898:26-30.

34. THE HUNTER WHO HAD AN ELK
FOR A GUARDIAN SPIRIT
NONE

35. COYOTE AND EAGLE
YAKIMA Hines 1992:126-131.

36. A DESERTED BOY IS PROTECTED
BY *ITC!I'XYAN'S* DAUGHTER
CHINOOK Boas 1895:221; **YAKIMA** Beavert 1974:53-58;
WISHRAM Sapir 1909:138-145; **NEZ PERCE** Hines 1984:100-103; **LILLO-
OET** Hill-Tout 1978:150-153; **OKANOGAN** Hill-Tout 1978:150-152;
THOMPSON Teit 1898:52-52; Teit 1917:34-35.

37. AN *AT!AT!A'LIA* HAS HER ARM
PULLED OFF
YAKIMA Beavert 1974:78-82; Hines 1992:63-65, 188-189, 196-
206; **WASCO** Hines 1996:#38, #39, #40; **WISHRAM** Sapir 1909:34-39, 164-
173; **NEZ PERCE** Farrand 1917:176-177; Spinden 1917:192-194; **KUTENAI**
Boas 1918:42-45, 44-47, 112-113, 272-279 [two versions] **OKANOGAN** Hines
1976:98-103; **THOMPSON** Teit 1898:63-64; Teit 1917:38-39, 98-103.

38. A JACK RABBIT BOY TRICKS
AN *AT!AT!A'LIA*
YAKIMA Beavert 1974:78-82; Hines 1992:63-65, 188-189, 196-
206; **WASCO** Hines 1996:#37, #39, #40; **WISHRAM** Sapir 1909:34-39, 164-
173; **NEZ PERCE** Farrand 1917:176-177; Spinden 1917:192-194; **KUTENAI**
Boas 1918:42-45, 44-47, 112-113, 272-279; **THOMPSON** Teit 1898:63-64;
Teit 1917:26-30.

39. THE FIVE *AT!AT!A'LIA* SISTERS
STEAL A BOY
YAKIMA Beavert 1974:78-82; Hines 1992:63-65, 188-189, 196-
206; **WASCO** Hines 1996: #37, #38, #40; **WISHRAM** Sapir 1909:34-39,
164-173; **NEZ PERCE** Farrand 1917:176-177; Spinden 1917:192-194;
KUTENAI Boas 1918:42-45, 44-47, 112-113, 272-279 [two versions];
OKANOGAN Hines 1976:98-103; **THOMPSON** Teit 1898:63-64; Teit
1917:26-30.

40. TWO CHILDREN ESCAPE
FROM AN *AT!AT!A'LIA*
A comparable version of this narrative includes especially "The
Beaver Brothers and the Modest Maiden," *Tales of the Nez Perce*, pp. 140-143.
Here two children are taken up not by an ogress, but a bear. They are put in
her basket even though they transform themselves into worms. Similarly as
in the tale above, she is frightened at the thought that her children (bear cubs)
have burned to death in their lodge, and flees there after hanging the basket
to a limb. Upon her return, she discovers that the children/worms have

escaped and that her basket is dented. As she attempts to pursue and to capture the children, she is beguiled into tying rocks to herself and is then tipped out of a canoe and into the river by Longlegs, or Crane, wherein she drowns.

YAKIMA Beavert 1974:78-82; Hines 1992:63-65, 188-189, 196-206; **WASCO** Hines 1996:#37, #38, #39; **WISHRAM** Sapir 1909:34-39, 164-173; **NEZ PERCE** Farrand 1917:176-177; Spinden 1917:192-194; **KUTENAI** Boas 1918:42-45, 44-47, 112-113, 272-279 [two versions]; **OKANOGAN** Hines 1976:98-103; **THOMPSON** Teit 1898:63-64; Teit 1917:26-30.

41. OLD MAN GRIZZLY BEAR
DECEIVES THE FIVE BROTHERS
See Boas, Franz 1901. *Kathlamet Texts*, BAE 26. Washington, D.C.:58-66, where the monster is disguised as an elk, not the grizzly bear of the Wasco text.

OKANOGAN Hill-Tout, 1978:147-149; Hines 1976:105-109; Teit, 1917:79-80.

42. EAGLE, A KLAMATH MAN, GOES
TO THE COLUMBIA RIVER TO GAMBLE
YAKIMA Beavert 1974:145-147; Hines 1992:49; **KLICKITAT** Jacobs 1969:10-11; **WISHRAM** Sapir 1909:74-93; **NEZ PERCE** Slickpoo 1977:26; **COEUR d'ALENE** Reichard 1947:128-129; **KUTENAI** Boas 1918:150-153; **LILLOOET** Hill-Tout 1978:147-149.

LIST OF INFORMANTS

Listed below are the three collectors of the oral traditional narratives of the Wascos found in this volume. Following each collector are the names, if known, of their informants and the dates when the Wasco narratives were obtained.

I. Jeremiah Curtin (Sapir)

Original narrator(s) and Date(s) Unknown: See Tales 1, 2A, 3, 9B, 12, 21, 22A, 22B, 23, 24, 25, 26, 27, 28, 29, 31, 33, 34, 36, 37, 38, 39, 40, 41, 42.

(Franz Boas collected Tale 35, date and informant unknown)

II. Leslie Spier

Frank Gunyer was a middle-aged Wasco who acted as an interpreter. During 1924-1925 he narrated the following: See Tales 2B, 8B, 10, 11, 16.

III. Lucullus V. McWhorter

1. Narrator and/or Date Unknown: See Tales 4(October 1921); 5(October 1921), 7(July 1918), 8A, 15A(July 4,1918).

2. *An-a-whoa* (Black Bear), elderly and nearly blind, was also known as Mrs. Mary Pilkins. [See again note 49.] Her daughter *Yes-to-lah-lemy*, Mrs. Caesar Williams, served frequently as interpreter for her mother. And in our *Magic in the Mountains, The Yakima Shaman: Power and Practice* see especially 50 "Presentiment of Death," pp. 184-185, the death vision/-presentiment seen by *An-a-whoa*; also see 60 "Vision of *Quas-qui Ta'chens*, pp. 203-206; *Quas-qui Ta'chens* was husband to *An-a-whoa*. Pictures of mother and daughter appear in the same volume between pp. 127/129: See Tales 6(September 1914), 15B(1917), 18(heard during a steamboat trip from Portland to The Dalles, September 12, 1911).

3. *I-keep-swah* (Sitting Rock), his Christian name was Jim Peter, was born at *Win-quat* "moving sands" or "washing sands," the Wasco name for what is now The Dalles, Oregon, about 1828. His father was half-Klickitat and half-Wasco. His mother, *Goos-hpah*, was half-Wasco and half-Wishom;. Both these tribes were warlike, speaking much the same language. *I-keep-swah* was baptized in youth by the Roman Catholics and christened Jim Peter. "Peter" was the Christian name of his father. Both were warriors in their day. *I-keep-swah* is also known as Wasco Jim. Of this name, when questioned, he said, "That is only fun-making name, whiskey name. Used to I drink lots whiskey. Injuns give me that name, shame name." [In our *Magic in the Mountains. . .*, see 53 "Vision of *I-keeps-swah*" his death vision experienced following a grave injury. See Tales 9A(July 1918), 13(July 1912), 14(1918), 17(July 1918), 20(1918), 32(October 1921).

4. *Et-wa-mish*: Tale 19.

5. *Yes-to-lah-lemy* (Mrs. Caesar Williams). [See *An-a-whoa*, above]. With her husband, her photograph, taken c. 1907-1908, appears following p. 234 of our *Ghost Voices*. . .. See Tale: 30.

SELECTED LIST OF READINGS ABOUT THE WASCO INDIAN NATION

A. GENERAL STUDIES

Alvord, B. 1857. "Report Concerning the Indians in the Territories of Oregon and Washington." *H.R. Exec. Doc.* 75 (Serial No. 906). 34th Congress, 3d Session, I:10-22.

Alvord, B. 1855. "Concerning the Manners and Customs, the Superstitions, . . . of the Indians of Oregon," *Information Respecting the History, Condition, and Prospects of the Indian Tribes of the United State s*. Henry Rowe Schoolcraft, ed. V:651-657. Philadelphia.

Attwell, Jim 1974. *Columbia River Gorge History*. Skamania WA: Tahlkie Books.

Cox, Ross 1832. *Adventures on the Columbia River*, 2d ed. New York, NY:335 pp.

Cobb, John N. 1921. *Pacific Salmon Fisheries* [Report of U.S. Commissioner of Fisheries for 1921, Appendix 1]--Bureau of Fisheries, Doc. 902. Washington D.C..

Curtis, Edward S. 1911. *The North American Indian.* See esp. vol. 8:86-154, 172-181, 185-191, 198-205. Norwood, Mass.: Plimpton Press. [Reprinted, New York: Johnson, 1970].

Eells, M. 1892. "Aboriginal Geographic Names in the State of Washington," *American Anthropologist* 5:27-35.

Franchere, Gabriel 1904. *Narrative of a Voyage to the Northwest Coast of America in the Years 1811, 1812, 1813, and 1814. . .*, VI in *Early Western Travels, 1748-1846*, ed. Reuben G. Thwaites. Cleveland OH.

Kane, Paul 1925. *Wanderings of an Artist Among the Indians of North America, from Canada to Vancouver's Island and Oregon...* Toronto: The Radisson Society of Canada Ltd., 329 pp.

Lee, Daniel and J.H. Frost 1844. *Ten Years in Oregon.* New York: J. Collord:344 pp.

Lockley, Fred 1928. *History of the Columbia River Valley from the Dalles to the Sea*. Chicago: S.J. Clarke:3 vols.

McArthur, Lewis L. 1974. *Oregon Geographic Names*, 4th ed. Portland: Oregon Historical Society:835 pp.

McWhorter, Lucullus V. 1913. *The Crime Against the Yakimas*. N. Yakima, WA.

_____; ed. Donald M. Hines 1995. *Tragedy of the Wahk-Shum: The Death of Andrew J. Bolon, Yakima Indian Agent As Told by Su-el-lil, Eye-witness; Also, The Suicide of General George A. Custer, as Told by Owl Child, Eyewitness*. Issaquah: Great Eagle Publishing Inc.

Meany, E.S. 1923. *Origin of Washington Geographic Names*. Seattle WA:357pp.

Meinig, D.W. 1968. *The Great Columbia Plain: A Historical Geography, 1805-1910*. Seattle: University of Washington Press.

Moorhouse, Lee 1906. *Souvenir Album of Noted Indian Photographs*. Pendleton OR: East Oregonian Print:25 pp.

Quaife, Milo M. 1916. *The Journals of Captain Meriwether Lewis and . . . Sergeant John Ordway Kept on the Expedition of Western Exploration, 1803-1806*, Collections 22. Madison: State Historical Society of Wisconsin.

Roe, Frank G. 1955. *The Indian and the Horse*. Norman OK: University of Oklahoma Press.

Schafer, Joseph ed. 1940. *Memoirs of Jeremiah Curtin*. Madison WI: 1940.

Stewart, Edgar I. and Jane R. Stewart, eds. 1957. *The Columbia River*. Norman OK: University of Oklahoma Press. [For original edition of Ross Cox, see above].

Strong, Thomas N. 1906. *Cathlamet on the Columbia*. Portland OR.

Thwaites, Reuben G. ed. 1904-1905. *Original Journals of the Lewis and Clark Expedition*, New York NY:7 vols.

Vaughn, Thomas ed. 1971. *Paul Kane, The Columbia Wanderer, 1846-47; Sketches and Paintings of the Indians and His Lecture, "The Chinooks."* Portland: Oregon Historical Society:154 pp.

Wallace, W.S. 1952. "The Intermontane Corridor," *SWL* 18:38-46.

Wyeth, Nathaniel J. 1899. "The Correspondence and Journals of Captain Nathaniel J. Wyeth, 1831-1836: A Record of Two Expeditions for the Occupation of the Oregon Country, with Maps, Introduction and Index. . . ," edited by F.G. Young, in *Sources of the History of Oregon*:1, parts 3-4. Eugene OR: University Press.

B. RELIGION, SHAMANISM, MAGIC, THE MISSIONARIES

Barnett, Homer G. 1957. *Indian Shakers; A Messianic Cult of the Pacific Northwest*. Carbondale: Southern Illinois University Press: 378 pp.

Boas, Franz 1893. "The Doctrine of Souls and of Disease Among the Chinook Indians," *Journal of American Folklore* 6:39-43.

Cominsky, Sheila 1964. *An Analysis of Wasco-Wishram Mythology*. Pullman, WSU, M.A. Thesis:108 pp.

Crowder, Stella I. 1913. "The Dreamers," *Overland Monthly* 62:607-609.

Dixon, Roland B. 1904. "Shamans of Northern California," *Journal of American Folklore* 17:23-27.

_____ 1908. "Some Aspects of the American Shaman," *Journal of American Folklore* 21:1-23.

DuBois, Cora 1938. *The Feather Cult of the Middle Columbia*, GAS 7. Menasha: George Banta:1-45.

Gatschet, A.S. 1893. "Medicine Arrows of the Oregon Indians," *Journal of American Folklore* 6:111-112.

Gunther, Erna 1928. *A Further Analysis of the First Salmon Ceremony*, UWPA 2(5). Seattle: University of Washington Press:129-173.

_____ 1926. "An Analysis of the First Salmon Ceremony," *American Anthropologist* 28:605-617.

Harmon, Ray 1971. "Indian Shaker Church: The Dalles," *Oregon Historical Quarterly* 72:148-158.

Hines, Donald M. 1993. *Magic in the Mountains, The Yakima Shaman: Power & Practice*. Issaquah: Great Eagle Publishing, Inc.

Huggins, E.L. 1891. "Smohalla, The Prophet of Priest Rapids," *Overland Monthly* 17:208-215.

The Last Salmon Feast of the Celilo Indians--Mid-Columbia, 1956 [Motion Picture]. Portland: Oregon Historical Society:18 min., sd., b&w, 16mm.

Larsell, Orloff 1947. "Medicine Among the Indians," in *The Doctor in Oregon, A Medical History*. Portland: Binfords & Mort (The Oregon Historical Society).

MacMurray, J.W. 1887. "The 'Dreamers' of the Columbia River Valley in Washington Territory," *Transactions of the Albany Institute* 11:241-248.

Mooney, James 1896. *The Ghost-Dance Religion and the Sioux Outbreak of 1890*, ARBAE 14(2). Washington DC:641-1110.

Murdock, George P. 1965. "Tenino Shamanism," *Ethnology* 4:165-171.

Park, W.Z. 1938. *Shamanism in Western North America*, NUSSS 2. Evanston IL:1-166.

Radin, Paul 1914. *Some Aspects of Puberty Fasting Among the Ojibwa*, BGSC 2(4). Ottawa, Canada.

Ray, Verne F. 1937. "The Bluejay Character in the Plateau Spirit Dance," *American Anthropologist* 39:593-601.

Ruby, Robert H. 1966. "A Healing Service in the Shaker Church," *Oregon Historical Quarterly* 67:347-355.

Smith, M.W. 1954. "Shamanism in the Shaker Religion of Northwest America," *Man* 54:119-122.

Spier, Leslie 1927. *The Ghost Dance of 1870 Among the Klamath of Oregon*, UWPA 2(2). Seattle WA.

_____, 1935. "The Prophet Dance of the Northwest and Its Derivatives . . . ," *General Series in Anthropology* 1. Menasha: George Banta Publishing Co.:1-74.

_____, 1921. *The Sun Dance of the Plains Indians: Its Development and Diffusion*, AP-AM 16(7). New York NY.

Strong, William D. 1945. "The Occurrence and Wider Implications of a 'Ghost Cult' on the Columbia River, Suggested by Carvings in Wood, Bone and Stone," *American Anthropologist* 47:244-261.

C. TRIBAL ECONOMIC STUDIES,
CONTEMPORARY ACCOUNTS

Griswold, Gillett G. 1970. "Aboriginal Patterns of Trade Between the Columbia Basin and the Northern Plains," *Archaeology in Montana* 11:1-96.

The Indian Dip Net Fishery at Celilo Falls on the Columbia River, 17. Salem: Oregon Fish Commission.

Michael, Elva Olson 1980. *Governmental Policies and the Preservation and Display of Native American Cultural Resources in the Middle Columbia Basin.* Corvallis: OSU M.A. Thesis:201 pp.

Toepel, Kathryn Ann, et al 1980. *Cultural Resource Overview of BLM Lands in North-Central Oregon: Archaeology, Ethnography, History,* UOAP 17. Eugene OR:215 pp.

D. INDIAN TRIBAL HISTORY,
WARS, REGIONAL RELATIONS

Brown, Joseph H. 1892. *Political History of Oregon. Provisional Government, Treaties, Conventions, and Diplomatic correspondence on the Boundary Question;. . . History of the Cayuse War. . .,* I. Portland: W.B. Allen:462 pp.

Browne, J. Ross 1857. "Indian War in Oregon and Washington Territories," *Special Report to the Secretary of War and the Secretary of the Interior* (Dated December 4, 1857). 35th Cong., 1st Sess., House Exec. Doc. No. 38, pp. 1-66 (Serial set 955). Also in Sen. Exec. Doc. No. 40, Serial set 929.

Clark, Robert C. 1935. "Military History of Oregon, 1849-1859," *Oregon Historical Quarterly* 36:14-59.

Curry, George C. 1855. "Expeditions Against the Indians," in *Correspondence and Official Proceedings, Governor of Oregon Territory, George C. Curry, to the Citizens.* Salem: Asahel Bush, Territorial Printer.

Deutsch, Herman J. 1956. "Indian and White in the Inland Empire: The Conquest for the Land, 1880-1912," *Pacific Northwest Quarterly* 47:44-51.

Doty, James 1855. "A True Copy of the Record of the Official Proceedings at the Council in the Walla Walla Valley, Held Jointly by Isaac L. Stevens Govn & Supt., W.T., and Joel Palmer, Supt. Indian Affairs, O.T. on the part of the United States with the Tribes of

Indians Named in the Treaties Made at That Council June 9th and 11th, 1855: National Archives, Record Group 75. Washington, D.C.: Records of the Bureau of Indian Affairs [See Microcopy T-494, roll 5, item 3].

Gunther, Erna 1950. "The Indian Background of Washington History," *Pacific Northwest Quarterly* 41:189-202.

Indian Hostilities in Oregon and Washington Territories. Message from the President of the United States, Transmitting the Correspondence on the Subject of Indian Hostilities in Oregon and Washington Territories. (U.S. 34th Congress. House 1st sess. Ex. Doc. No. 118). Washington DC 1856:58 pp.

Indian Hostilities in Oregon and Washington; Message from the President of the United States (U.S. 34th Congress, 1st sess., House Ex. Doc. No. 93). Washington DC 1856:144 pp.

Memorial of the Legislative Assembly of Oregon Territory, August 10, 1848 [repr. 1972] Fairfield, WA: Ye Galleon Press, 1972:26 pp.

Reese, J.W. 1965. "OMV's Fort Henrietta: On Winter Duty, 1855-56," *Oregon Historical Quarterly* 66:132-160.

Thompson, Flora Cushinway n.d.. "Interviews of Flora (Cushinway) Thompson, Wife of the late Tommy Thompson, Chief of the Celilo Indians." n.p., Oregon Historical Society:3 tapes/cassette.

Victor, Frances F. 1894. *The Early Indian Wars of Oregon.* Salem, Frank C. Baker.

E. FOLK ART, DECORATION, AND COSTUME

Boas, Franz 1927. *Primitive Art.* Oslo, Norway.

Cornhusk Bags of the Plateau Indians, 1974. Spokane: Cheney Cowles Memorial Museum, Eastern Washington State Historical Society:12 pp.

Gogol, J.M. 1979. "Columbia River Indian Basketry," *American Indian Basketry Magazine* 1:4-9.

_____, 1980. "Cornhusk Bags and Hats of the Columbia Plateau Indians," *American Indian Basketry Magazine* 1:4-11.

Haeberlin, H.K., James A. Teit and Helen H. Roberts 1928. *Coiled Basketry in British Columbia and Surrounding Region*, BAE 41. Washington DC:119-484.

Kuneki, Nettie, et al., 1882. *The Heritage of Klickitat Basketry; A History and Art Preserved*. Portland: Oregon Historical Society:54 pp. [Biblio. pp. 53-54].

Schlick, Mary D. 1980. "Art Treasures of the Columbia Plateau," *American Indian Basketry Magazine* 1:12-21.

_____, 1979. "A Columbia River Indian Basket Collected by Lewis and Clark in 1805," *American Indian Basketry Magazine* 1:10-13.

Spier, Leslie 1925. *An Analysis of Plains Indian Parfleche Decoration*, UWPA 1. Seattle: University of Washington Press:89-112.

_____ 1931. *Plains Indian Parfleche Designs*, UWPA 4. Seattle, University of Washington Press:293-322.

F. FOLKTALES, LEGENDS AND MYTHS

Boas, Franz 1894. *Chinook Texts*, BAE 20. Washington DC.

Clark, Ella 1952. "The Bridge of the Gods in Fact and Fancy," *Oregon Historical Quarterly* 53:29-38.

_____ 1955-56. "George Gibbs' Account of Indian Mythology in Oregon and Washington Territories," *Oregon Historical Quarterly* [Part I] 56:2-93-325; [Part II] 57:125-167.

_____ 1953. *Indian Legends of the Pacific Northwest*. Berkeley: University of California Press.

Cornelison, J.M. 1911. *Weyekin Stories: Titwatit Weyekishnim*. San Francisco: E.L. Mackey & Co.:30 pp.

Curtin, Jeremiah 1940. *Memoirs of Jeremiah Curtin*, WBS 11, ed. Joseph Schafer. Madison WI. [See especially Curtin's recounting of his collecting traditional texts among the Wascos at Warm Springs, Oregon, during the winter of 1885, pp. 351-361.]

Hines, Donald M. 1995. "Of Big Foot, The Oedipal Tale Told along the Columbia River," *Fabula, Journal of Folktale Studies* 36:98-104.

_____ 1991. *The Forgotten Tribes, Oral Tales of the Teninos and Adjacent Mid-Columbia River Indian Nations.* Issaquah: Great Eagle Publishing, Inc.

_____ 1992. *Ghost Voices: Yakima Indian Myths, Legends, Humor and Hunting Stories.* Issaquah: Great Eagle Publishing, Inc.

Hymes, Dell H. 1953. "Two Wasco Motifs," *Journal of American Folklore* 66:69-70.

Lowie, Robert H. 1924. "Shoshonean Tales," *Journal of American Folklore* 37:1-242.

Lyman, W.D. 1915. "Indian Myths of the Northwest," *PAAS* 25:375-395.

Randall, B.U. 1949. "The Cinderella Theme in Northwest Coast Folklore, *CUCA* 36:243-286.

Sapir, Edward J. 1909. *Wishram Texts by Edward Sapir Together with Wasco Tales and Myths, Collected by Jeremiah Curtin. . .,* PAES II. Leyden: E.J. Brill:314 pp. [See Wasco tales, pp. 239-311].

Thompson, Stith. *Tales of the North American Indians.* Bloomington IN: Indiana University Press. [See esp. "Sources," pp. 368 ff; also "Bibliography," pp. 373-386].

G. SOCIOLOGICAL, ANTHROPOLOGICAL, ARCHAEOLOGICAL STUDIES

Aikens, C. Melvin 1986. *Archaeology of Oregon,* 2d ed. Portland: U.S. Department of Interior, Bureau of Land Management, Oregon State Office:133 pp. [Biblio. pp. 129-133].

Barrett, S. A. 1910. *The Material Culture of the Klamath Lake and Modoc Indians of Northeastern California and Southern Oregon,* UCPAE 5(4). Berkeley CA.

Barry, J.N. 1927. "The Indians of Oregon," *Oregon Historical Quarterly* 28:49-61.

Berreman, J.V. 1937. *Tribal Distribution in Oregon,* MAAA 47. Menasha: American Anthropological Association:7-65.

Biddle, H.J. 1926. "Wishram," *Oregon Historical Quarterly* 27:113-130.

Boas, Franz 1911. "Chinook," BAE 40. Washington DC:638-645, 650-654.

_____ 1894. *Chinook Texts*, BAE 20. Washington DC.

_____ 1901. *Kathlamet Texts*, BAE 26. Washington DC.

_____ 1897. *The Social Organization and the Secret Societies of the Kwakiutl Indians*, Report: U.S. National Museum-1895. Washington DC:311-737.

Browman, David L. and David A. Munsell 1969. "Columbia Plateau Pre-History: Cultural Development and Impinging Influences," *American Antiquity* 34:249-264.

Brunton, Bill B. 1968. "Ceremonial Integration in the Plateau of Northwestern North America," *Northwest Anthropological Research Notes* 2:1-28.

Cook, Sherburne F. 1955. "The Epidemic of 1830-1833 in California and Oregon," *University of California Publications in American Archaeology and Ethnology* 43:303-326.

Cope, Leona 1919. *Calendar of the Indians North of Mexico*, in *University of California Publications in American Archaeology and Ethnology* 16(4). Berkeley CA:University of California Press:119-176 .

Cressman, Luther, et al. 1960. *Cultural Sequences at the Dalles Oregon; A Contribution to Pacific Northwest Prehistory*. Philadelphia: American Philosophical Society:108 pp.

_____ 1937. "Petroglyphs of Oregon," *UOSA* 2:1-78.

_____ 1981. *The Sandal and the Cave; the Indians of Oregon*. Corvallis: OSU Press:81 pp.

Daugherty, Richard D. 1956. *Early Man in the Columbia Intermontane Province*, University of Utah Anthropological Papers, No. 24. Salt Lake City: University of Utah Press.

Driver, Harold E. 1961. *Indians of North America*. Chicago: University of Chicago Press:667 pp. [Biblio. pp. 613-633.]

French, David 1961. "The Wishram-Wasco." in *Perspectives in American Indian Culture Change*, ed. Edward H. Spicer. Chicago: University of Chicago Press: 340-430.

French, Kathryn and David 1955. "The Warm Springs Indian Community," *AMI* 7:3-16.

Gatschet, Albert S. 1890. *The Klamath Indians of Southwestern Oregon*, CNAE 2, 2 Pts. Washington DC.

Gibbs, George 1967. *Indian Tribes of Washington Territory* [repr]. Fairfield WA: Ye Galleon Press:56 pp.

Goddard, Pliny Earl 1903. *Life and Culture of the Hupa*, UCPAE 1(1). Berkeley, CA

Gunther, Erna 1927. *Klallam Ethnography*, University of Washington Publications in Anthropology 1(5). Seattle, WA 1927).

_____1950. "The Westward Movement of some Plains Traits," *American Anthropologist* 52:174-180.

Hodge, Frederick Webb, ed. 1907. *Handbook of American Indians North of Mexico*, BAE 30 [repr. 1959]. New York: Pageant Books, Inc. See "Wasco:"917-918.

Jorgensen, Joseph G. 1980. *Western Indians; Comparative Environments, Languages and Cultures of 172 Western American Indian Tribes.* San Francisco CA: W.H. Freemason & Co.:673 pp.

Krieger, H.W. 1927. "Archeological Investigations in the Columbia River Valley," *Smithsonian Institution Miscellaneous Collections* 38:187-200.

_____ 1928 . "A Prehistoric Pit House Village Site on the Columbia River at Wahluke, Grant County, Washington," *Proceedings of the U.S. National Museum* 73:1-29.

Kroeber, A.L. 1925. *Handbook of the Indians of California*, BBAE 78. Washington D.C.

Lewis, Albert B. 1906. *Tribes of the Columbia Valley and the Coast of Washington and Oregon*, MAAA I:147-209.

Loring, J. Malcolm and Louise 1982-1983. *Pictographs and Petroglyphs of the Oregon Country.* Los Angeles: Institute of Archaeology, University of California:2 vols. [Biblio., Vol. 1:306-313; Vol. 2:334-341.]

Loud, Llewellyn L. and M.R. Harrington 1929. *Lovelock Cave*, UCPAE 25(1). Berkeley, CA.

Mason, Otis. T. 1894. *North American Bows, Arrows, and Quivers*, Report: Smithsonian Institution 1893. Washington DC:631-679.

_____1896. *Primitive Travel and Transportation* Report: U.S. National Museum-1894. Washington DC:235-593.

Minto, John 1900. "The Number and Condition of the Native Race in Oregon.
. . ," *Oregon Historical Quarterly* 1:296-315.

Mooney, James 1928. *The Aboriginal Population of America North of Mexico,* Smithsonian Misc. Coll. 80, no. 7 [Publ. 2955]. Washington
DC.

Olson, Ronald L. 1927. *Adze, Canoe, and House Types of the Northwest
Coast,* UWPA 2(1). Seattle WA.

Ray, Verne F. 1939. *Cultural Relations in the Plateau of Northwestern America,* Publications of the Frederick Webb Hodge Anniversary Publication Fund, No. 3. Los Angeles: Southwest Museum:154 pp.

_____ 1941. "Historic Backgrounds of the Conjuring Complex in the Pla
teau and the Plains," in *Language, Culture, Personality, Essays in
Memory of Edward Sapir.* Menasha WI:204-216.

_____ 1936. "The Kolaskin Cult," *American Anthropologist* 38:67-75.

_____1936. "Native Villages and Groupings of the Columbia Basin,"
Pacific Northwest Quarterly 27:99-152.

_____1938. "Tribal Distribution in Eastern Oregon and Adjacent Regions,"
American Anthropologist 40:384-415.

Sapir, Edward 1907. "Notes on the Takelma Indians of Southwestern Oregon,"
American Anthropologist 9:251-275.

Smith, A.H. 1953. *The Indians of Washington,* RSSCW 21:85-113.

Spier, Leslie 1928. *Havasupai Ethnography,* PaAM 29(3). New York NY.

_____1936. *Tribal Distribution in Washington,* General Series in
Anthropology 3. Menasha WI: George Banta: 1-43

_____ & Edward Sapir 1930. *Wishram Ethnography,* UWPA 3. Seattle,
University of Washington Press:151-300.

Spinden, Herbert J. 1908. *The Nez Perce Indians,* MAAA 2, pt. 3. Lancaster
PA: The New Era Publ. Co.

Steward, Julian H. 1928. "A Peculiar Type of Stone Implement," *American
Anthropologist* 30:314-316.

Strong, Emory 1959. *Stone Age on the Columbia River.* Portland OR:
Binsfords and Mort

Strong, W.D., W.E. Schenck and J.H. Steward 1930. *Archaeology of the Dalles-Deschutes Region, UCP* 39:1-154.

Strong, W.D. and W. E. Schenck 1925. "Petroglyphs Near the Dalles of the Columbia River, *American Anthropologist* 27:76-90.

Sturtevant, William C. ed. 1978. *Handbook of North American Indians.* Washington DC: Smithsonian Institution. See esp. Vol. 7.

Suphan, Robert J. 1974. *Oregon Indians II: Ethnological Report on the Wasco and Tenino Indians; Ethnological Report on the Umatilla, Walla Walla, and Cayuse Indians: Commission Findings,* American Indian Ethnohistory Series: Indians of the Northwest. New York: Garland Publishing Co.:534 pp.

Swanson, Earl H. Jr. 1962. *The Emergence of Plateau Culture,* Occasional Papers 8. Pocatello: Idaho State University Museum.

_____1970. "Sources for Plateau Prehistory," *American Antiquity* 35: 495-496.

_____ C. Melvin Aikens, David G. Rice, and Donald H. Mitchell 1970. "Cultural Relations Between the Plateau and Great Basin," *Northwest Anthropological Research Notes* 4:65-125.

Swanton, John R. 1952. *The Indian Tribes of North America,* BAE 145. Washington DC 1952:762 pp. [Biblio. pp. 643-682. See "Wasco," p. 475; also "Wishram," pp. 449-450.]

_____ 1968. *Indian Tribes of Washington, Oregon and Idaho.* Fairfield WA: Ye Galleon Press:80 pp.

Teit, James H. 1928. *The Middle Columbia Salish,* UWPA 2(4). Seattle WA.

_____ 1900. *The Thompson Indians of British Columbia,* M-AMNH 2(4). New York NY.

Wight, E.L., Mary Mitchell and Marie Schmidt, comps. 1960. *Indian Reservations of the Northwest; the People, Their Land, Their Life.* Portland: U.S. Bureau of Indian Affairs (Portland Area Office):97 pp.

Wissler, Clark 1910. *Material Culture of the Blackfoot Indians,* PaAM 5(1). New York NY.

Zucker, Jeff, et al. 1983. *Oregon Indians: Culture, History, and Current Affairs, An Atlas and Introduction.* Portland, OR: Western Imprints,

Press of the Oregon Historical Society:229 pp. [Biblio. pp. 193-221].

H. FOLK SPEECH, LANGUAGE

Boas, Franz 1904. "The Vocabulary of the Chinook Language," *American Anthropologist* 6:118-147.

Gatschet, A.S. 1877. "Indian Languages of the Pacific States and Territories," *MAH* 1:145-171.

Dyk, W. and Dell H. Hymes 1956. "Stress Accent in Wishram Chinook," *International Journal of Anthropological Linguistics* 22:238-241.

Jacobs, Melville 1937. "Historic Perspectives in Indian Languages of Oregon and Washington," *Pacific Northwest Quarterly* 28:55-74.

Sapir, Edward 1926. "A Chinookan Phonetic Law," *International Journal of Anthropological Linguistics* 4: 105-110.

_____ 1907. "Preliminary Report on the Language and Mythology of the Upper Chinook," *American Anthropologist* 9:533-544.

_____1916. "Terms of Relationship and the Levirate," *American Anthropologist* 18:327-337.

_____1909. *Wishram Texts, Together with Wasco Tales and Myths*, PAES II. Leyden: E.J. Brill. [Sapir's Wishram language versions of tales appear here alongside English translations.]

Swanton, John R. 1900. "Morphology of the Chinook Verb," *American Anthropologist* 2:199-232.

I. GAMES

Butler, B.R. 1958. The Prehistory of the Dice Game in the Southern Plateau," *TEBIWA* 2:65-71.

K. BIBLIOGRAPHIES

Ault, Nelson A. 1959. *The Papers of Lucullus Virgil McWhorter*. Pullman WA: Friends of the Library, State College of Washington [WSU-]:144 pp.

Bjoring, Bob and Susan Cunningham 1982. *Explorers' and Travellers' Journals Documenting Early Contacts with Native Americans in the Pacific Northwest, 1741-1900*, Bibliographic Series, UW Libraries 3. Seattle WA:15 pp.

Bonnerjea, Biren, comp. 1963. *Index to Bulletins 1-100 of the Bureau of American Ethnology; With Index to Contributions to North American Ethnology, Introductions, and Miscellaneous Publications* BAE 178. Washington DC: U.S. Gov't Printing Office:726 pp.

Butler, Ruth Lapham comp. 1937. *A Check List of Manuscripts in the Edward E. Ayer Collection, The Newberry Library*. Chicago: The Newberry Library:295 pp.

Carriker, Robert C. and Eleanor R. 1987. *Guide to the Microfilm Edition of the Pacific Northwest Tribes Missions Collection of the Oregon Province Archives of the Society of Jesus*. Wilmington DE: Scholarly Resources:97 pp.

Field, Thomas W. repr. 1951. *An Essay Towards an Indian Bibliography. Being a Catalogue of Books, Relating to the History, Antiquities, Languages, Customs, Religion, Wars, Literature, and Origin of the American Indians, in the Library of Thomas W. Field*. [New York: Scribner, Armstrong & Co. 1873]. Columbus: Long's College Book Co.:430 pp.

Freeman, John F. comp. 1966. *A Guide to Manuscripts Relating to the American Indian in the Library of the American Philosophical Society*, MAPS 65. Philadelphia PA: American Philosophical Society:491 pp. {But see "Kendall" below}.

Hewlett, Leroy, comp. 1969. *Indians of Oregon; A Bibliography of Materials in the Oregon State Library*. Salem OR:125 pp.

Index to Literature on the American Indian, 1970. [Published for the American Indian Historical Society] San Francisco CA: Indian Historian Press.

Kendall, Daythal comp. 1982. *A Guide to Manuscripts Relating to the American Indian in the Library of the American Philosophical Society*, MAPS 65s [supplemental]. Philadelphia PA: American Philosophical Society:168 pp. {See "Freeman" above}.

Larner, John W. comp. 1987. *Guide to the Scholarly Resources, Microfilm Edition, of the Papers of the Society of American Indians* Wilmington DE: Scholarly Resources:74 pp.

Murdock, George P. and Timothy J. O'Leary 1975. *Ethnographic Bibliography of North America*, 4th ed. New Haven CT: Human Relations Area Files Press:5 vols.

Schuster, Helen H. 1982. *The Yakimas, A Critical Bibliography*. Bloomington IN: Indiana University Press:158 pp.

Seaburg, William R. 1982. *Guide to Pacific Northwest Native American Materials in the Melville Jacobs Collection and in Other Archival Collections in the University of Washington Libraries*, Communications in Librarianship 2. Seattle WA: University of Washington Libraries: 113 pp.

Young, Frederick G. ed. 1897-1899. *Sources of the History of Oregon*. Eugene OR: University Press.

ACKNOWLEDGEMENTS

This manuscript was prepared in WordPerfect 4.2/5.1 under OS/2 Warp. Printing of the manuscript was done by Thomson - Shore Inc., Dexter, Michigan.

For the cover design and preparation for press I am grateful to Mrs. Kathleen S. McAffrey of Starr Design, 7123 W Weaver Pl., Littleton CO 80123.

I am indebted to the following individuals for publication permissions. First, Prof. John Guido, Head, Manuscripts, Archives and Special Collections, Holland Library, at Washington State University, gave permissions to publish materials from the Lucullus McWhorter Papers. Second, I am especially grateful to Mrs. Judy McWhorter Goodwin for allowing me to publish from the papers originally compiled by her grandfather, Lucullus V. McWhorter. And I am also grateful to the Wisconsin Historical Society for permission to republish excerpts from Joseph Schafer's *Memoirs of Jeremiah Curtin*, excerpts in which Jeremiah Curtin and his wife recalled their wintry stay on the Warm Springs Reservation during January to April 1885. For providing photographs I am grateful to the Special Collections and Preservation Division, the University of Washington, especially Librarian for Photographs Prof. Richard H. Engeman. Also, to the Oregon Historical Society, Portland, Oregon, also the American Museum of Natural History, New York, NY.

For sharp-eyed proofreading I am grateful to Alan Hines. All remaining errors are mine alone.

ORDER FORM

GREAT EAGLE PUBLISHING, INC.
3020 Issaq.Pine Lk. Rd SE   STE 481
Issaquah WA 98029
FAX 206 391 7812

Please Send:

_____ copies of **CELILO TALES: WASCO MYTHS, LEG-ENDS, TALES OF MAGIC AND THE MARVELOUS** at $21.95 per copy.

_____ copies of **TRAGEDY OF THE WAHK-SHUM: THE DEATH OF ANDREW J. BOLON, AS TOLD BY SU-EL-LIL, EYEWIT-NESS; ALSO, THE SUICIDE OF GENERAL GEORGE A. CUSTER, AS TOLD BY OWL CHILD, EYEWITNESS** at $10.95 per copy.

_____ copies of **MAGIC IN THE MOUNTAINS, THE YAK-IMA SHAMAN: POWER & PRACTICE** at $17.95 per copy.

_____ copies of **GHOST VOICES, YAKIMA INDIAN MYTHS, LEGENDS, HUMOR AND HUNTING STORIES** at $23.95 per copy.

_____ copies of **THE FORGOTTEN TRIBES, ORAL TALES OF THE TENNOS AND ADJACENT MID-COLUMBIA RIVER INDIAN NATIONS** at $10.95 per copy.

I understand that I may return any book for a full refund--for any reason, no questions asked.

Name_____

Address_____

City_____ State_____ Zip_____

Phone (   )_____

Sales Tax
Please add 8.2% for books shipped
to WAshington State Addresses
Shipping
Book rate: $2.00 for the first book
and $0.75 for each additional book
(Surface shipping may take 3 or 4 weeks)

Please photocopy this order form.